TRENDS AND ISSUES IN CONTEMPORARY ARAB THOUGHT

SUNY Series in Middle Eastern Studies
Shahrough Akhavi, editor

Trends and Issues in Contemporary Arab Thought

Issa J. Boullata

State University of New York Press

Published by
State University of New York Press, Albany

Printed in the United States of America

For information, address State University of New York Press, State University Plaza, Albany, N.Y., 12246

Library of Congress Cataloging-in-Publication Data

Boullata, Issa J., 1929–
Trends and issues in contemporary Arab thought / Issa J. Boullata
p. cm. — (SUNY series in Middle Eastern studies)
Bibliography: p. 195
Includes index.
ISBN 0-7914-0194-4. — ISBN 0-7914-0195-2 (pbk.)
1. Arab countries—Intellectual life. I. Title. II. Series.
DS36.88.B68 1990
909.′.0974927—dc19 89-31277
CIP

10 9 8 7 6 5 4 3 2 1

For André and Thérèse,
with all my heart.

Contents

Preface

Various aspects of the contemporary Arab world have been studied in a plethora of books recently published in the West, concentrating mostly on current political developments and economic matters relating to Western interests in the area. Those of them that show how the Arabs themselves feel and what they think about their own contemporary life have been fewer, and most of these emphasize the recent dramatic resurgence of Islam in the political arena. The false impression often left by these books is that the Arab world is seething with religious Islamic fervor and xenophobia.

While Islam is truly an important component of Arab culture, and while radical Islamic groups are surely to be found in a number of Arab countries, it is not true that these radical groups represent all Muslims or all Arabs; nor is their significance as big as it is sometimes made out to be. They should be studied, of course, but only in proportion to their relative importance and not at the expense of other trends and issues in the Arab world. Particularly insufficient in Western studies are publications on Arab intellectuals who are grappling with the idea of modernity, with the Arab desire for societal change to bring about social justice and freedom, and higher standards of living and education, and those wrestling with the problem of accommodating Arab culture to modern times, and with the need for full and positive Arab participation in building and sustaining a peaceful and prosperous international community that includes them.

In this book an attempt is made to study some of these almost neglected trends and issues in contemporary Arab thought. Against the background of an old Arab-Islamic culture currently undergoing change and even political resurgence, and from the viewpoint of a Third World society suffering from underdevelomment and economic dependency on the West, a number of Arab intellectuals are presented to show how they struggle to understand themselves, their culture and their contemporary world; how they hope to change themselves and certain elements in their society and culture in order to become modern; and what they believe to be the means to reach their goals, and the deterrents that prevent them.

The period on which this book focuses is limited to the last two decades or so, especially since the 1967 Arab defeat by Israel, a defeat which occasioned a great amount of Arab self-examination and self-criticism, and encouraged the development of new ideas on understanding the Arab past and envisioning the Arab future. Intellectuals from various parts of the Arab world are analyzed for their thoughts on the Arab-Islamic heritage and its modern relevance to a changing society. The connections which they see between economic dependency and the lack of genuine political and cultural freedom in their society are explored. The contributions of Arab women to the call for change are studied. In all these efforts, Arab thought is seen to be in crisis, not so much because of differences among Arab intellectuals as because of a perverse system of societal control in the Arab world insidiously tied to a global system of hegemony which perpetuates present conditions. The very legitimacy of the Arab political regimes is in question, and some intellectuals believe nothing but drastic and revolutionary change can bring about a resolution of the crisis.

* * * * *

The initial research for this book was begun in the academic year 1984–85 with a grant from the Social Sciences and Humanities Research Council of Canada, in conjunction with a sabbatic leave granted me by McGill University. I am grateful to both institutions for their generous support. I am also grateful to the staff of the Islamic Studies Library at McGill University for their constant help, particularly Salwa Ferahian, who invariably expedited my requests for inter-library loans, and Emile Wahba, who unfailingly ordered the books I needed and permitted me to borrow a few from his private collection when the same titles were held up in the library's cataloguing backlog. My thanks go to Dr. George N. Atiyeh, Head of the Near East Section of the Library of Congress, for his courteous and prompt assistance. My thanks also go to Dr. David Partington, Head of the Middle East Department of the Widener Library at Harvard University, and to his colleague Dr. Fawzi Abdulrazak for their unstinting help. I owe a special sense of obligation to my colleagues and graduate students at McGill University, with whom much of what constitutes this book was the object of stimulating discussions.

Chapter One

Introduction: The Dilemmas of Arab Intellectuals

Heirs to an old and great civilization, twentieth-century Arabs have—for several decades now—been modernizing many aspects of their society. The process of change towards modernity has not been uniform or simultaneous in all parts of the Arab world. Deeper and more pervasive in some parts than in others, modernization has forged its way into several Arab societal structures and has begun to make inroads into well-established institutions and to affect traditional values, patterns of behavior and attitudes.

Forces of change have been mainly inspired by models of modern Western culture, especially during colonial hegemony. Even after political independence, Arab countries continued to modernize by emulating Western paradigms. All this change towards modernity has not been without opposition which, sometimes mild and sometimes violent, kept steadily growing but rarely produced a full stop to the process.

Recently, after several years of military modernization, political reorganization, economic development and social change and following coups d'état or revolutions against what was perceived as corrupt rule, the Arab defeat by Israel in the six-day war of June 1967 was a shock that gave Arabs food for thought. Not that the Arabs were fully satisfied with their newer modernizing regimes that had gained ascendancy about mid-century or thereafter, but those newer regimes were popularly considered to be, by and large, better oriented and better equipped to effect progress in Arab life than earlier ones. The 1967 defeat was the acid test of Arab modernization.

Even when external factors were taken into consideration, such as the total commitment of the U.S.A. and some Western countries to the victory and survival of Israel at all costs, the general trend of Arab reaction to the 1967 defeat, after initial shock, was an inward call to account and responsibility. Arab intellectuals voiced and articulated the frustration of the Arab masses against Arab regimes and the prevalent culture of Arab society. Their writings were characterized by deep social insight, self-analysis and a great measure of self-criticism. Similar writings continue to be produced to the present day and their popularity is a healthy sign that an Arab national debate is needed. The illiteracy of large segments of the Arab population and the various restrictions on the freedom of speech and communication may hamper a full-scale national debate. Yet despite this, a vast literature has grown to deal with the issue. The Arab intellectuals' debate has even developed into a wider discourse that has gone beyond the immediate factors governing the 1967 Arab defeat. The October war of 1973 in which the Egyptians could not sustain an initial victory over Israel and the 1982 Israeli invasion of Lebanon, which Arab states watched in shameless impotence and inaction, rendered this discourse even more relevant as it widened and began to deal with Arab culture as a whole, its impact on the relation between tradition and modernity, and the results of all that on the effectiveness of the Arabs in the world community.

Although some writings of a similar, though more limited, nature were produced earlier in the twentieth century and even in the nineteenth century, those published in the 1960s, 1970s, and 1980s are more urgent and more poignant. They have an anguished tone about them and they exhibit a profound desire to grapple with the problem of modernity. They are exuberantly dedicated to a process of change, even if they are often too abstract or too idealistic. Not all these writings are by specialists but some of them are being written by young Arab sociologists, political scientists, educators, historians and philosophy professors. Creative writers have dealt with the issue in their poems, novels and plays, but some have also contributed to the discourse in several essays and studies of great sensitivity. Conservative thinkers have entered the fray by countering the process of change towards modernity and by supporting the preservation of tradition. Some of them belong to established religious institutions or newly mushrooming politico-religious groups, and many of them are professional graduates of secular universities who have been converted to traditionalism and religious conservatism because they perceived modernization as a process bent on destroying the fabric of Arab society and its age-old, venerated values.

In this current discourse, there may be disagreement in identifying the problem and in suggesting a solution, but there is hardly a lack of sincerity. Whether progressive or traditional, Arab intellectuals engaged in the discourse are serious in their belief that airing their ideas will help Arab society to proceed wisely in its quest for better life. The plethora of books and articles, the multiplicity of symposia and conferences, the frequent talks on radio and television programs, the intergovernmental discussions—all point to the urgency of the issue at hand. Yet there may be a lot of heat and very little light, a great deal of rhetoric and very little action—a fact which further adds to the pent-up frustrations and often results in mounting disillusionment. The question is asked: Why has Japan been able to modernize, preserve its culture and become one of the leading industrialized countries of the world while the Arabs, engaged in similar processes since a much earlier time, have failed?

The painful introspection of Arab intellectuals during the last twenty years or so, which will be the subject of this book, has various trends. Though these trends do not form specific schools of thought, the more pronounced among them may be the following three. First, there is the group of Arab intellectuals who see nothing useful short of a cultural revolution. They are not all equally radical but generally tend to be leftists whose aim is to transform Arab society and inculcate new ideas and new values in it. Arab culture in their view should be so changed that it will be fully remade. What they consider to be its basically religious outlook on life and the universe should be discarded and replaced by a secular outlook, rooted in rationalism, science and technology, and grounded in a socialist economy. Second, there is a larger group of Arab intellectuals who consider traditional Arab culture to be viable in modern times if only it is interpreted and understood better, and if certain of its elements are developed in the light of modern needs and the experience of modern nations. Their major thrust is towards renewal rather than radical change. They want to reform, not transform, Arab society. Though they want to discard some traditional values of Arab culture, they continue to believe in many others which they like to reinterpret and supplement with new elements that, according to them, would make Arabs function better in modern times. They would separate religion from politics, and emphasize science and technology. Some of them may endorse a socialist economy but most would only want some improvement of the present economic system in the Arab world to ensure a reasonable distribution of wealth. Third, there is a vocal group of Arab intellectuals who are committed to the religious aspect of Arab culture. They view the Islamic elements of Arab culture as the principal, if not the only, ones that must predominate. They advocate the elimination from Arab society of all external cultural influences, mainly Western ones, and they call for a return to the original, pristine essence of Islam as they perceive it to have been in the early centuries, particularly during the Prophet's lifetime. They do not want to transform or reform Arab culture; they rather want it to conform to what they consider to be its authentic Islamic origins. They too call for change, but it is a change that will revive old values, institutions and traditions. They do not negate science and rationalism but consider them to be modern products of the earlier efforts of Muslims during the heyday of Islamic civilization, and they teach that those products must be re-acquired. They want the economic system and, in fact, the totality of life to conform to the rules and ideals of Islam which they consider to be as sufficient for human well-being in modern times as they were in old times.

These three general trends do not have definite boundaries, for there are intellectuals belonging to one trend as far as some issues are concerned who may fit better in another regarding other issues. Like colors of the rainbow, they interpenetrate at the transition from one to another in a subtle and imperceptible way. Some intellectuals have even consciously and visibly moved from one trend to another at certain junctures of their personal lives or of social and political developments in the Arab world. This state of flux reflects in many ways the transitional conditions of Arab society in which there is social and geographic mobility at the demographic and economic levels. Consider the large population growth, the migration from villages to cities, the increase in the size and influence of urban centers, the oil wealth that has percolated to some degree to lower strata of society and to poorer Arab regions, the dissemination of education, the rising expectations of larger numbers of younger people, the expansion of the lower middle class and lumpen proletariat, the relative improvement of means of transport and communication: all these are factors that have helped to shape Arab thought which, in turn, has attempted to influence the ever-growing and changing masses, even as it voiced and articulated their needs. The nature of the political institutions has also been influenced by these changes, even as Arab regimes were trying to control and orient them.

The story is one of trial and error, successes and failures. There may be an advance in one area at one time, only to be followed by retreat at another. There may be certain areas that have not seen any success whatsoever but rather experienced relative deterioration. Other areas may have improved absolutely, only to become, by comparison, factors of discord and conflict in the context of general conditions in the Arab world or within one of its countries. Development in the economic, political and social aspects of Arab life continues to be uneven, and Arab thought is trying to come to grips with this reality as it ponders the ways of introducing change into Arab society so that Arabs may regain their erstwhile flourishing life in the world and retain their identity as a people with a specific national culture.

The issues discussed by Arab intellectuals are many. Though they all touch on the problematic issue of change, some of them have generated more interest than others and have been the focus of a greater debate. For example, the position of Arab women in society has generally occasioned more discussion than the system of Arab education. The place of Islam in Arab culture has been of greater concern to many intellectuals than the human and civil rights of the individual. Political issues, especially those pertaining to foreign policy, have most often taken precedence over economic issues. The ideas of nationalism and socialism in the Arab world have attracted more study than those of freedom and democracy. Western imperialism and Zionism as deterrents or deflectors of Arab progress and of peaceful development have been more deeply analyzed than the Arab class system. And so on, and so forth. Of course, all these important issues are interrelated, but some of them have acquired priority over others in the eyes of Arab intellectuals and their Arab readers or audiences. To study them all is beyond the scope of one book and the efforts of one author, not only because of the large geographical extent to be covered but also because of the complexity of the many specialized topics to be treated.

A useful approach seems to be one in which the dynamics of change in the Arab world are studied from one selected angle. If this angle is a vantage point, more issues than otherwise possible may be dealt with and they may be seen in their relatedness, and not as isolated phenomena. The angle that has suggested itself to us as being best for our purpose is that of the struggle between modernity and tradition in the Third World. Being part of the Third World, the Arab countries are seen from this angle as societies undergoing change with the ostensible aim of improving the lot of their people and they are also seen as going through a struggle between modernity and tradition. The forces of modernity, using mostly external ideas and models for change, are oriented towards the future, which they see as opening new horizons for the Arabs. Opposing them, the forces of tradition, using mostly internal ideas and models for change, are oriented towards the past, which they see as an ideal to be repeated because they perceive it as having the promise of certainty and the surety of proven success. The intellectuals of interest to us in this struggle are those individuals who are not happy with the prevailing conditions and who therefore formulate ideas which they believe will help to change them. Policy-makers and decision-makers are concerned with the nature of change and the actual course it will take. They may be intellectuals themselves but, more often than not, they are rulers and bureaucrats who may or may not be affected by the intellectuals and their ideas. Whether rulers and bureaucrats are affected or not, the intellectuals keep producing ideas of change in one direction or the other with the hope that enough people will adopt their ideas to influence those in power over them. If the latter are not influenced, the legitimacy of their power is called into question as an increasing number of people become convinced of the ideas and necessity of change.

This is why intellectual activity in Third World countries is ultimately and inevitably political. This is also why political regimes in Third World countries are often wary of intellectuals. These regimes try to co-opt intellectuals by employing them in the state system in order to obligate them to state loyalty. Intellectuals in many Arab countries have often occupied prominent positions in the ministries of culture or information, in the ministries of education or youth, in state universities and colleges, in the media of mass communication under government control such as television, radio, newspapers or periodicals, and in the state-subsidized theater and cinema. Several Arab countries have also made great efforts to help artists, poets, writers; to institute state competitions and prizes for them; to sponsor exhibitions, and public occasions for recitals and lectures; and sometimes to hold regional or international conferences for them. By the same token, intellectuals in many Arab countries have often found themselves under house-arrest or in prison; they have often suffered from job insecurity; they have been subjugated to government censorship, to book or magazine seizure and to other publication harassment; and in certain instances they have preferred to live in exile either in Arab countries other than their own or in non-Arab lands. But the struggle between modernity and tradition still goes on, as does the struggle for freedom of expression and other human and civil rights.

What complicates the Arab struggle is the fact that Arab economies are becoming increasingly tied to the dominant global economies of Westesrn countries and especially American capitalism and its multi-national corporations. Arab imports of Western manufactured products, among them an inordinate amount of consumer goods, are paid for by the export of Arab raw materials, some agricultural goods and Arab services. The Arab need for arms to bolster national independence, keep the restive population under control and additionally to offset the Israeli threat and other external threats weakens the Arab capacity for development. Arab countries are increasingly in need of foreign aid and investment as well as foreign consultation. A state of Arab dependency on the West (especially the U.S.A.) is becoming increasingly a fact of economic reality for many Arab countries. Politically, most Arab regimes are leaning in the same direction as their economies, in spite of occasional flirting with the Soviet Union and Eastern Bloc countries. The non-alignment tendencies of earlier decades following the 1955 Bandung Conference have all but vanished, though some Arab countries still retain shrill vociferation but have little effect in stemming the forces leading to Arab dependency. In this state of affairs, the Arabs are not alone but are in the company of most countries of the Third World.

Given these general conditions in international relations and national economies, Arab intellectuals like other Third World intellectuals have resorted to the inner reserves of their culture in order to reinforce elements that accentuate national identity in the face of foreign cultural influence that has accompanied dependency. Notwithstanding this almost expected and natural reaction to Western cultural influence, many Arab intellectuals have not altogether discounted Western culture as such in their efforts at reconstructing their own culture for modern times. They have continued to keep open minds towards the West. Even the most traditional among them have acquiesced in the necessity of acquiring certain elements of Western culture, though, in many cases, this has been made to appear as if Arabs are merely borrowing back what Western culture has earlier learnt from the Arabs of the past. The more progressive among Arab intellectuals have tried to analyze the relationship of contemporary Arabs and the modern West. They have been genuinely interested in learning the secrets of the West's progress and power, especially its science, technology and societal organization, but also its literature and thought. They have come to realize that Western culture is not a uniform whole though it may have a core of common elements. From the extreme right where American capitalism and free enterprise are predominant to the extreme left where Soviet socialism and state control are supreme, Western culture has been correctly seen by modernizing Arab intellectuals as a multi-faceted civilization. A century earlier, Arab intellectuals had mostly France or England in mind when they spoke of the modern West. Their models of emulation were therefore limited, however complex. Today Arab intellectuals have a larger variety of models to speak of and their complexity is even greater. Meanwhile, Arab intellectuals feel they have to remain faithful to their own culture even while they are interested in that of the West. There are those among them who view Arab culture as if it were a monolithic entity, but there are others who have come to believe that Arab culture is not a uniform whole and that it has not been static either. This author believes that culture is a growing system of relations, beliefs, attitudes and values rooted in institutions that keep developing and changing in accordance with the historical experiences and needs of the human group. The modernizing Arab intellectuals see that some Arab institutions have become too rigid for a healthy growth of their society and are therefore advocating change. The traditional Arab intellectuals believe that change has gone too far in the direction of modernity which they equate with Westernization, and they fear that their identity as a people is endangered if their institutions are not preserved or, indeed, if they are not changed to conform to what they perceive as the authentic models of the past.

The conflict among Arab intellectuals is alive and is bound to continue for many years to come. Arab policy-makers and decision-makers are alert to its directions and often try to foresee and control its outcome. There is no synthesis yet and Arab regimes are trying hard to preserve the status quo until the scene on the national and international theater becomes clear. The Arab cultural crisis will therefore continue but its dimensions will become so strongly polarized that by the turn of the twenty-first century something will have to happen or will have to be done to bring about a synthesis.

This book, concerned with the present-day Arab culture and its crisis, will attempt to present a number of important themes that have engaged Arab intellectuals. It cannot hope to be anything but selective in this regard. Intellectuals discussed in it will be those who represent a trend and whose thought is influential; but there may arguably be others of the same trend and of equal influence who are not discussed. The point to be made is that individual authors are not studied here for themselves but for the contribution they make to the general picture of Arab culture today. It is hoped that by the end of the book the reader will come to sense the climate in which all Arab intellectuals live, and will therefore have a better idea where Arab culture is heading. This may give him or her an idea also where the Arab world itself is heading.

One caveat, however, seems to be necessary at the outset. This author does not believe that thought alone can change society, yet he believes strongly in the power of thought to contribute to any social change. Being itself a product of the social conditions of any group, thought has a dialectical relation to society. It is affected by the conditions of society but it is also capable of affecting them in turn. The material conditions of life, the environment, the production and distribution of wealth, as well as the legal and political and moral systems that sustain them, the institutions that preserve them and the class system that upholds them: all are factors that shape thought. But they are all dialectically related to thought in that, faced by new challenges and needs in these very material conditions of life, man develops ideas that help to create the will to change them. Arab thought is therefore not seen in the writings of these contemporary Arab intellectuals as if it were independent of the material conditions of Arab society. It is rather intimately linked to them as has been explained in this introduction. As such, it will also contribute to change under certain circumstances, as the conclusion of this book will try to show.

Chapter Two

The Arab Heritage in Contemporary Arab Discourse

> "The culture of the past is not only the memory of mankind, but our own buried life, and study of it leads to a recognition scene, a discovery in which we see, not our past lives, but the total cultural form of our present life."
>
> Northrop Frye, *Anatomy of Criticism* (Princeton: Princeton University Press, 1957), Paperback edition, 3rd printing 1973, page 346.

Every living human group has a cultural heritage which is a function of its societal structure and which it keeps modifying in accordance with its needs and its own established principles. The latter may vary from group to group but they normally comprise principles of inclusion and exclusion which help the group to determine what cultural elements to include in its heritage and which to exclude in the light of the group's historical experience and felt needs. The aim of modifying the heritage is to enhance the group's viability and ensure its continuity as an identifiable group. As the group moves in time and space it meets with new circumstances that necessitate new institutions, values, attitudes and behavior. Change becomes required but the group does not usually rush into it. For the sake of self-preservation and identity, the group's cultural heritage, entrenched in its institutions, changes only with guarded care and considerable prudence in which intricate systems of checks and balances operate. There may be occasions when quick, radical action may be necessary to preserve the group. Checks are, therefore, relaxed on these occasions to the degree that is optimal, as the benefits accruing to the group from such action are balanced against the harms that may ensue otherwise. In revolutionary change, the checks are so relaxed or removed by forceful means that many new cultural elements of a radically novel nature are permitted to be included in the heritage in a short period of time, and they eventually become part and parcel of the heritage or, at least, as many of them do as serve the purposes of self-preservation and continuity. Evolutionary change, on the other hand, permits the accretion of new cultural elements and the deletion of old ones in a complex process that takes a much longer time but may achieve results similar to those of revolutionary change, though at a different cost to the group. There may be times when members of the group do not agree among themselves on the necessity or the degree or the modality of change. If disagreement is allowed to continue, the group is in the throes of crisis which must be resolved or else the group's internal conflict will lead to violent change that may affect not only its cultural heritage but also its nature, its unity, its very existence—depending on the situation.

These dynamics of change have acted in Arab society in all periods of history, as they have in other societies. In the contemporary Arab world, the situation has perhaps reached the dimensions of unresolved crisis in that there is prolonged disagreement of wide proportions between the forces of change, some of which tend towards modernity and others towards tradition. Arab society has earlier faced and resolved various other crises in its long history. The present-day one is of long standing since it can be dated from the beginnings of the nineteenth century when traditional Arab culture first encountered modern European culture on a large and—later—increasing scale, particularly in the context of Western colonial hegemony accompanied by gradual cultural penetration. The current crisis manifestations entangled with Arab underdevelopment, domination by Western imperialism and defeat by Zionism have prompted several Arab intellectuals to devote much of their effort to discussions on their cultural heritage with regard to its content, function and value; and some have come up with hypotheses to explain present stagnation and to chart desirable future development.

It is not surprising that, not long after the June war of 1967 and the initial shock of Arab defeat by Israel, the Arab League Educational, Cultural and Scientific Organization (ALECSO), established in 1970, called for a "Conference on Authenticity and Renewal in Contemporary Arab Culture" which was held in Cairo between October 4 and 11, 1971. Apparently prepared in haste and with little imagination by the Arab League's bureaucrats, it featured eight papers only,[1] and not many of the leading Arab intellectuals were invited.[2] Some of the papers, however, presented acute analysis and deep insight.

In his paper, Zakī Najīb Maḥmūd went to what he considered to be the heart of the matter by saying:

> The essence of Arab culture, old and modern alike, is that it distinguishes decisively between God and His creatures, between the absolute idea and the universe of change and transience, between eternal truth and events of history, between the immutability of the Everlasting Being and the dynamism of the everchanging being. The former is substance that does not change, the latter is accident that appears then vanishes. The distincton, however, does not place the two modes of existence at one level: it rather makes the world of events a symbol pointing to the world of eternity. . . .[3]

Maḥmūd then analyzed various aspects of the old Arab heritage to show how it dealt with foreign cultural influences throughout history by subjecting them to the characteristic essence he claimed for Arab culture. In a similar fashion, he treated some aspects of modern Arab life and thought, and he showed that they too had to adapt foreign influences to the basic essence of Arab culture in order to be acceptable. He concluded that, in order to be faithful to its authentic and historical roots, Arab culture in modern times had to forego many aspects of modernity because it insisted on clinging to the absolute values of its past. In particular, it rejected the modern concept of man as part of nature and subject to its laws as uncovered by science. Though contemporary Arabs have accepted the results of modern science, especially technology and its products, they have declined to subject all natural phenomena (including man) to the empirical method of science because of the latter's relativity.

In other words, Maḥmūd tried to identify the principles of inclusion and exclusion that operated in the Arab cultural heritage and that gave identity and continuity to Arab culture and the Arab way of life. He seems to believe that very important elements of modernity are excluded, and those of its elements that are included are cut off from the logical principles that produced them, thus leaving them in a precarious position within the Arab consciousness.

On the other hand, Muḥammad al-Mazālī argued in another paper that modernity did not negate Arab authenticity.[4] He analyzed the powerful influence of Western culture and science on Arab thinking but, instead of Arab withdrawal in self-defense or Arab fusion in foreign culture with total loss of identity, he called for a better understanding of the Arab self by a dynamic study of the Arab past and its cultural heritage that would identify the positive characteristics it continued to have. He also called for freedom to shape Arab life within a vital scale of renewed human values, derived from being open to the heritage as well as to the contemporary circumstances and conditions.[5] He affirmed:

> Authenticity is openness or else it is non-existent. For it is an intelligent, sensitive listening to the spirit of the age, an awareness of its given data, a constantly renewed assimilation of its various cultural currents and scientific trends, and a capability for giving, borrowing, reacting, and digesting without [inferiority or superiority] complex or submission.[6]

As Shukrī ᶜAyyād showed in his paper at the same conference, the term authenticity (*aṣāla*) seldom appeared in the Arabic critical literature of the 1920s and 1930s. He surmised that it began to be widely used after the middle 1950s to mean, among other things, individuality, invention and liberation from tradition.[7] In this sense it meant opposition to imitation, be that imitation of Arab or foreign cultural elements. Yet ᶜAyyād mentioned another usage of the term authenticity which went beyond the first, though it was sometimes associated with it, and it meant the continuous preservation of original ancestral elements in one's culture. This latter meaning contradicted the former but ᶜAyyād argued that the contradiction was only apparent, since the latter related to national characteristics while the former related to individual talent. What united both meanings was the concept of personality: the personality of the nation depicted in its literature as a whole, and the personality of the individual writer seen in his literary product when compared to that of his peers and contemporaries in the same culture.

The encounter between these two personalities, ᶜAyyād maintained, was the problem of Arab culture in our age.[8] The Arab writer had to reconcile both personalities so that authenticity could unify the group's values and those of the individual. The writers who succeeded did so by critically selecting only those elements of the old culture that were worthy of survival and by discarding those that were not; the successful writers also adopted new elements from modern Western culture and adapted them to the Arab-Islamic culture. This process, ᶜAyyād affirmed, became in time insufficiently acceptable as new literary forms departed further from those of the heritage. Authentication necessitated a deeper dialectical relationship between the imported forms and the Arab ones so that, in effect, authenticity appeared as a relative and ever-developing process wherein one could look for constant qualities and changing ones, provided constancy was not understood to mean immobility but rather continuity.[9]

Although ᶜAyyād spoke mostly of Arabic literature, his analysis can be extended to all aspects of the Arab cultural heritage because, as he himself suggested, they are all interconnected. The achievement of acceptable, genuine authenticity in a fluid, continuously changing process in which old and new elements are in constant dialectical relationship is indeed the crux of Arab intellectual endeavors aiming at solving the civilizational crisis of the contemporary Arab world. New elements alone are not acceptable or possible, nor are old ones alone; but the particular circumstances of Arab culture made the call for renewal more vocal in the first quarter of the twentieth century, as ᶜAyyād says, and that for authenticity more so in the third quarter, both calls being demonstrably complementary.[10]

The debate over the heritage and authenticity in the ever-changing scene in the contemporary Arab world led eventually to a more widely organized conference of Arab intellectuals held in Kuwait between April 7 and 12, 1974 and hosted by Kuwait University and its Alumni Association. This was only six months after the October 1973 war in which Egypt scored a limited victory of sorts over Israel, and the Arab oil-producing countries imposed a somewhat effective oil embargo on certain Western nations. The focus of the conference, as its theme announced, was "The Crisis of Civilizational Development in the Arab Homeland."[11] There were twenty-two papers presented by notable Arab thinkers and commented on by their peers, then these were followed by animated discussions and further by evaluation panels. A final declaration contained statements in fourteen areas of interest to the Arab intellectuals present.[12] But the central issue of the conference remained the relation of the past to the present and the future of the Arabs. In the fourth statement, "On the Heritage," the conference's Final Declaration said:

> The problem which the symposium continually encountered in more than one of its study-papers and in different ways was the role of the Arab past in orienting the [Arab] future. Whether we call this problem that of authenticity and renovation, or the heritage and modernization, or atavism and westernization, or anything else, it has taken this role of multiple facets and influence in Arab civilizational development only because our look at it has been ahistorical.
>
> This heritage is part of us and part of our civilizational formation. But it ought not to make our future possessed by our past. The attempt to project the past onto the future, besides being doomed to failure, leads to a rupture between the Arab and his present, and between him and his future. The fusion of the idea of authenticity with that of the heritage is a dangerous pitfall. Authenticity does not consist in literal clinging to the heritage but rather in setting out from it to what follows, and from its values to a new phase in which there is enrichment for it and development of its values. Real revivification of the heritage is possible only through a creative, historical, and critical comprehension of it; through transcending it in a new process of creation; through letting the past remain past so that it may not compete with the present and the future; and through a new assimilation of it from the perspectives of the present and the future.[13]

The conference declaration recognized the fact of intellectual backwardness in the Arab world and its strong relation to other kinds of historically-caused societal backwardness. The school of thought which attempted to revive the old Arab culture without renewing it, and that which rejected Arab culture altogether and moved towards the modern culture of the present age were both declared to be wrong.[14] Support was given to the school of thought, considered as not yet deeply rooted in the Arab world, which would create authentic and—at the same time—modern Arab thought by adopting a transcending and renewing attitude to the Arab heritage, and not a static and retrieving one. In particular, the conference declaration called for a deepening of scientific thinking and rational method and for a linking of Arab thought to the foundations of modern civilization based on science, technology, organization and planning.[15]

More than any other participant, Zakī Najīb Maḥmūd called for rationality in his address to the conference.[16] He said that resort to reason was the one single criterion common to all civilizations, be it that of Pericles's Athens, al-Ma'mūn's Baghdad, the Medicis' Florence, or Voltaire's Paris. He claimed that contemporary Arabs paid only lip service to rationality but did not follow it through by changing their lifestyles, customs and values accordingly. They accepted modern technological products like cars, airplanes and appliances of heating and cooling, but not the necessary rational underpinnings of the modern age based on science, technology and utilitarian ethics. According to him, the Arabs had either to live the life of the modern age with all its ethical and rational requirements or else "wring its neck" so that it might see the world through Arab eyes. He claimed that contemporary Arabs did neither, but were content to live simultaneously in two contradictory cultures, thus permitting themselves to fall into a civilizational crisis. The way out for the Arabs, in his view, was to adopt the model of modern life prevalent today in parts of Europe and America, the Arab cultural distinctiveness being in the retention of certain aspects of religious doctrine, art and social conventions not conflicting with the scientific movement in any of its branches.

In their comment, Suhayl Idrīs and ᶜAbd Allāh ᶜAbd al-Dā'im agreed with Maḥmūd on the necessity of rationality, but they both disagreed with him on his understanding of civilization. They argued that civilization had other components besides reason and they pointed to the importance of affective elements like religious or ideological faith, will power, innovation and aesthetic creativity in literature and the arts. Furthermore, Idrīs averred America was not such an ideal model: where freedom had contradictory meanings depending on whether one was white or black, where Zionism and Israel were lavishly funded to exterminate Palestinians and where Arabs were generally scorned and considered to be second-class human beings.[17]

Shākir Muṣṭafā's contribution to the conference started from the anguished conscience of the committed Arab who asked why the efforts of the Arabs to become modern failed tragically even though they had spent more years being involved in modern civilization than had contemporary China, Russia and Japan, and yet the latter nations had all reached modernity but not the Arabs.[18] His answer was that the relations of the Arabs to what they called their past, their history, their heritage or their ancestors, unlike that of any other nation, had a particularly strong influence on them. Thus in their modern search for identity, their concern with authenticity (*aṣāla*) was often almost overwhelmed by ideas of history and the heritage which outweighed other meanings of authenticity related to innovation and creativity.[19] In recent years which witnessed revolutions, development projects, educational expansion and socialist trends in the Arab world, there was a parallel recourse to the Arab heritage and a felt need to define the Arab attitude to it. Muṣṭafā regretted that the Arab view of history continued to be a static, reactionary one. He said:

> We [Arabs] do not look at [history] as points of departure but as end boundaries; we do not look at it as mere sap but as ready branches to hang on and swing. We do not see it as a history that bore a thousand possibilities but rather as a one-dimensional history that has the one form it actually took.[20]

He explained that that was why the heritage continued to be the central problem of debate that divided the Arabs into rightists and leftists, reactionaries and progressives, traditionalists and modernists.[21]

Muṣṭafā then analyzed the prevailing Arab value system and institutions in the light of the historical influence of the heritage with particular reference to the modes of economic production, the system of political authority, the nature of social relations, and the intellectual activity of the Arabs. In spite of the admitted existence of many positive values and ideals in the Arab cultural heritage, Muṣṭafā noted the predominance in practice of negative ones, both in the past and in the present. He observed that obedience to authority pervaded all societal structures and intellectual constructs. Whether in the Arab patriarchal family, the Arab government, the Arab educational system or the Arab religious establishment—conformity, coercion and repression were the rule. Emphasis was on the forbidden and on the necessity of preserving the order of things. As a result there was, in Muṣṭafā's view, a general atmosphere of apathy and submission in Arab society, and also a great measure of dissimulation and hypocrisy. Social solidarity functioned only at the primary levels of social structure where the crushed individual could find some security, as in the family, the tribe, the ethnic group or the religious sect. Even there he or she was followed, as everywhere else, by taboos on sex relations and emphasis on duties and obligations. Otherworldly values and concepts loomed large in the life of the individual as havens of hope and consolation, but the ultimate tendency was one of submissiveness and surrender to a coercive reality. In spite of recent economic development, the basic mode of production, in Muṣṭafā's view, remained the traditional one because only a few benefited from the change introduced, and they were largely the same who had been elite before any change occurred. The intellectual basis of contemporary Arab culture, Muṣṭafā affirmed, was mainly the great past contributions of the second and the third centuries of the Islamic era which had witnessed immense creativity, later followed by mere repetition and rumination, but hardly any development.[22]

The present age is generally characterized by a static condition in all aspects of Arab life, according to Muṣṭafā. The heritage places the Arabs in a problematic situation: on the one hand they are alienated from it because of long contentment with its static elements alone, and on the other they are alienated from the modern age because of their ignorance of its basic intellectual principles. The challenge to the Arabs today,

Muṣṭafā believes, is to adapt the inner structures of their age-old heritage to the modern age, and to do that at a speed that will make the Arab bloc of vast masses catch up with the ever-racing modern civilization. This should be done, not by getting out of history (which is impossible), but indeed by historical thinking, using the instrumentality of history itself and its logic to direct Arab vision, thought, language and action from the past to the future, not in a sense of continuity, but in a dialectical sense that is committed to the past, the present and the future.[23]

The heritage came up again at the conference as a discussion topic in the paper presented by Fu'ād Zakariyyā who condemned its Arab critics as well as its Arab supporters because both groups, in his view, had an ahistorical vision of the heritage: the former when they considered it as the cause of present Arab backwardness because of its negative elements, and the latter when they considered it as the only way for future Arab progress because of its eternally useful and rich content.[24] For him the correct historical view of the heritage was one that placed it in its actual context of the past and looked at it from a relative perspective as a phase that had come to an end and vanished in later phases which it gradually transcended until it brought the Arabs to the present.[25] According to this view, Zakariyyā said, the past was not a rival force to the present, for the present bore the seeds of the past, and the past gave rise to the present, by gradually transcending itself. All functional elements of the past heritage were thus continuously borne and developed in the historical process and have eventually come down to the present. Those not functional were abandoned, causing a cultural or civilizational rupture with the past. There is no need, in Zakariyyā's view, to revivify the heritage because its life has continued to the present. Those who would revivify dead and, therefore, useless elements of the past heritage to solve modern problems were rather seeking functions that the heritage could not perform.[26] Progress would depend on a new Arab beginning. The real problem, according to Zakariyyā, was not that the heritage had—among other things—irrational, otherworldly or superstitious elements (undesirable as they might be) but that it competed with the present meaninglessly and divided thinkers uselessly, and was a main cause of intellectual backwardness.[27]

Qusṭanṭīn Zurayq, in his comment, agreed that this view of the heritage that Zakariyyā criticized was ahistorical, but he added that it was more an aspect and a result of Arab backwardness than a main cause of it.[28] He also agreed that there was a rupture in Arab civilization, but he rejected Zakariyyā's attitude of merely accepting that as a fact without going into its causes, for here lay the factors leading to present Arab intellectual backwardness.[29] He did not consider this rupture unique to the Arabs, as Zakariyyā had done, and he explained that what was ruptured was civilizational creativity and progress, and not the heritage as such.[30]

Anwar ᶜAbd al-Malik's paper on Arab specificity and authenticity used Egypt's historical example as a society dependent for civilized continuity on a long-standing national heritage of political centralization and military control because of its geographical features and location. Egyptian specificity thus lay in these permanent factors which, in his view, ought to be taken into consideration by anyone who would bring modernity and progress to the country.[31]

Maḥmūd Amīn al-ᶜĀlim in his comment refused to accept the generalization and abstraction of ᶜAbd al-Malik's view, and insisted that each historical period had its own specificity within a general concept of historical continuity, and that there was a need to transcend such specificity by consciously controlling it and changing it by mass struggle that would lead to progress.[32] The heritage, to him, was to be critically and historically comprehended in its totality, not in a utilitarian manner nor by blind imitation, sanctification or partial selection, but by deepening the historical sense of Arab reality and firmly rooting the Arab self in it so that the heritage could be creatively invoked,[33] the real repository of national specificity being always the Arab masses.[34]

There were other discussions of the heritage at the conference, notably that of Adonis (ᶜAlī Aḥmad Saᶜīd) who, taking al-Ghazālī as a model of thought that pervaded the Arab-Islamic cultural heritage, concluded that the prevailing contemporary Arab thought was conformist, not only confirming the tradition, but also rejecting and condemning innovation. He therefore called for Arab liberation from all atavism. He advocated the elimination of all sanctity attributed to the past, and asked that it be considered as an experience or knowledge absolutely not binding. He called upon Arabs to believe that "the essence of man is not in being a conforming inheritor but rather in being a transforming creator."[35]

One other notable discussion of the heritage at the conference was that of Muḥammad al-Nuwayhī[36] who opined that the greatest Arab problem lay, not in the purely intellectual encounter between Islam and modern civilization, but rather in the practical and social needs of contemporary Arab society. The cause of this problem is, in al-Nuwayhī's view, the prevalent belief that the Islamic Sharīᶜa is an immutable and comprehensive system of law which is sufficient for all human needs and is good for all times and places without amendment or addition.[37] He said that this belief arose only gradually after the Sharīᶜa had witnessed continuous development in the first five centuries of the Islamic era. Neither in the Prophet's lifetime nor later in the period of his Companions and their Followers was there a belief that God alone was the sole legislator. It was only in the sixth century A.H. that this belief began to grow and only in the eighth century and onwards that it became petrified.[38] Al-Nuwayhī gives a brief account of how Islamic law, in its dynamic and formative period, developed to accommodate changing circumstances of society from the time of Prophet Muḥammad himself onwards until its development slowed down in the sixth and the seventh centuries A.H., then entered its dark ages of rigidity following the eighth century A.H.[39] He agrees with Muḥammad ᶜAbduh and his *al-Manār* disciples that Islam has fundamentals (*uṣūl*) and branches (*furūᶜ*): the former relating to doctrine, worship rituals and ethics that cannot be changed; the latter relating to all rules governing social transactions and relations that may be changed in accordance with the needs of changing conditions.[40] He therefore openly calls for an organized, continuous and brave campaign against the traditional view of Islam to convince people that the role of religion is to purify worship, cleanse the soul and guide creatures to the Creator and that, in dealing with worldly matters, it only gives general principles and ideals and, in legislating for urgent needs, it does not give rules for all future times nor mean to perpetuate certain patterns of life. Al-Nuwayhī clarifies his ideas more frankly when he says:

> The aim of the required intellectual campaign is to convince people of the necessity of adopting a purely secular view in all matters relating to their living conditions and their world. [The campaign] will not succeed unless it convinces them that—apart from matters of doctrine—Islam, the religion of the majority [of Arabs], does not conflict with the secular view. Rather, it is not an exaggeration for us to affirm that its stance regarding matters of our world is a purely secular one.[41]

In his comment, Muḥammad Abū Rīdah disagreed with al-Nuwayhī's call for secularism. He asserted that Islam cannot really have a secular view of human life in this world. On the contrary, Islam considers man's life to be a part of the comprehensive divine plan for everything, and thus related to high wise aims in which man is held responsible for his deeds on earth.[42] But Abū Rīdah agreed that there was need for development in Islamic law and doctrine to build on the dispersed efforts of individuals or small groups, and he called for the convening of two international conferences, one on Islamic law and another on Islamic doctrine, to study ways of developing both so that they may be appropriately fit for the Arab renaissance and modern civilization.[43]

There was no discussion at the conference regarding Arab women in the process of change in the Arab world. There were references to the inferior position of the female in the Arab autocratic family in Hishām Sharābī's paper on "The Family and Civilizational Development in Arab Society."[44] The thrust of his paper was an analysis of the stunting conditions of child-rearing in the Arab family. In fact all the speakers at the conference were men,[45] and problems related to Arab women were all but ignored.

For Mahdī ᶜĀmil, what was really absent from the Kuwait conference was Marxist-Leninist thought (except for Maḥmūd Amīn al-ᶜĀlim's comment on Anwar ᶜAbd al-Malik's paper).[46] ᶜĀmil's book, appearing three months after the conference, is a scathing criticism of all the presentations (except al-ᶜĀlim's comment), declaring them to be confused expressions of the crisis of the Arab bourgeoisies that dominate the Arab world. Thus, according to him, the crisis is not that of civilizational development in the Arab homeland, nor is it inherent in the Arab mind or the Arab heritage that is considered to be unable to adapt itself to changing conditions of modernity and is therefore deficient. The crisis is rather in the intrinsic structural inability of the locally dominant Arab bourgeoisies to transcend themselves because, as colonial bourgeoisies, they are dependent on the Western imperialist bourgeoisies and they lack the will to shake themselves loose lest they lose their local dominance in the Arab world. Their only recourse is to the illusion of being like the Other, i.e., like the Western imperialist bourgeoisies. According to ᶜĀmil, the dependence of the colonial Arab bourgeoisies on the Western imperialist bourgeoisies is a structural alliance which necessarily dictates difference between them, not likeness; hence the impossibility, for the Arab bourgeoisies, of attaining the perfect model they see in this Other, particularly because their pre-capitalist origins are in a dominant aristocratic or feudal class that never really broke away from its past thought but rather adapted itself internally to colonial bourgeois needs, and thus adapted bourgeois thought accordingly.[47]

For Mahdī ᶜĀmil, Arab thought can be liberated from the dominance of bourgeois ideology only by the theoretical tools of the Marxist-Leninist concepts which alone produce the scientific knowledge able to possess full cognition of the social historical reality. This liberation should necessarily start from the working class position whose ideology is the contradiction of dominant bourgeois thought. The movement to socialism is, therefore, the production of Arab thought that recognizes the universality of Marxism-Leninism with regard to class struggle in the Arab world as a movement of national liberation, i.e., a revolutionary transformation of the prevailing structure of the relations of production in the Arab world and the formation of a new structure.[48]

As for the present-day Arab debate on the heritage (at least the intellectual heritage), it is nothing but an expression of contemporary Arab bourgeois thought that reproduces itself ideologically, since it is absolutely impossible for it, or for anybody else, to see the past or look at it except from the present, which is itself ideologically determined by class position. On the other hand, the proletarian view of the heritage, according to Mahdī ᶜĀmil, is the scientific view, i.e., the Marxist-Leninist view, that takes the Arab heritage as a subject of knowledge to be possessed as history, now wrongly seen through bourgeois interpretation only. Scientific knowledge of Arab history is none other than the movement of the Arab working class to possess its own social reality by producing the historical knowledge that liberates it through revolution.[49] Thus, Mahdī ᶜĀmil rejects the notion hatched at the Kuwait conference that the crisis of the Arab world lies in its backwardness caused by the continuity of the past in the present without change. He also rejects the idea that its resolution lies in the movement of Arab society to the present technological age under the Arab bourgeoisies leadership. The only solution for him is the movement of the Arab world, not from its own past to the present of the Other, but from its present colonial reality to socialism.[50]

There is no doubt that the Kuwait conference was one of the most important cultural events to occur in the Arab world in recent years, if only for its attempt to raise questions and address them freely. It cannot be said that there was agreement in it among Arab intellectuals. In fact there was not only disagreement (despite the Final Declaration), but also lack of common ground in the understanding of basic terms like heritage, culture and authenticity, and in the viewpoints from which culture could be said to be related to society and history. Nevertheless, the conference proceedings stimulated further thought which, directly or indirectly, engendered the publication of more books and articles, and the holding of more conferences and symposia. The Arab world was entering a period that was highlighted by the Kuwait conference and characterized by a climate of intense discourse focusing on identity and self-analysis. Arab intellectuals of all ideological leanings participated in this discourse to the exhilaration of growing numbers of avid listeners or readers among the Arab public. The issue of the heritage (*turāth*) was the hub of much intellectual activity. The word 'crisis' (*azma*) began to be commonplace.

ᶜAbd Allāh al-ᶜArwī's book, *The Crisis of the Arab Intellectual: Traditionalism or Historicism?* had already appeared in a different Arabic version as *al-ᶜArab wa-l-Fikr al-Tārīkhī* (The Arabs and Historical Thinking)[52] and had condemned the ahistorical thinking of both the traditionalists and all the other Arab intellectuals dubbed "eclectics" because they adopt selected elements from Western culture. Al-ᶜArwī's position is that their thought leads nowhere but to continued dependence on the West on all levels. The traditionalists reliving medieval Islamic thought and perpetuating it, and the "eclectics" borrowing what is not theirs and impossibly trying to graft it to their Arab heritage—remove themselves from reality, both remaining subordinate to others. The only way to liberate Arab thinking, according to al-ᶜArwī consists in strict submission to the discipline of historical thought and acceptance of all its assumptions. He agrees that the Arabs can find the best school of historical thought in Marxism, which can explain contemporary Arab alienation and help make long-term plans of action toward liberation.[53]

He believes that the Arab intellectual, whether traditionalist or "eclectic," has not been able to help his society to liberate itself because he is always separated from the real environment he lives in by intellectually inhabiting another world, the world of the past or the world of the Other, which he turns into absolute reality. Thus, both traditionalist and "eclectic" live in an unrealistic perpetual present and are consequently ineffective in their society, which, as a result, is controlled by those calling for sheer continuity. The only weapon against this ineffectiveness, according to al-ᶜArwī, is the acquisition of historical thinking. The latter cannot be learnt from the study of history as such, but rather requires conviction of a theory of history; and this, it is claimed, does not exist today anywhere in a comprehensive and persuasive manner but in Marxism. Al-ᶜArwī recognizes that historicist Marxism is not the whole truth of Marxism, but he believes that this is what the Arab world needs in the present conditions in order to create an intellectual elite able to modernize it intellectually, politically and economically. After the establishment of the economic base, he believes, modern Arab thought will become stronger and will develop further.[54]

The necessity for a comprehensive review of the Arab-Islamic past in order to determine what the heritage was and what its relation to the present should be was increasingly becoming an imperative for many Arab intellectuals. It is not that previous generations of modern Arab intellectuals had not gone through a similar exercise, for there were writers like Aḥmad Amīn,[55] Ṭāhā Ḥusayn,[56] ᶜAbbās Maḥmūd al-ᶜAqqād,[57] Muḥammad Ḥusayn Haykal,[58] to mention only a few of the immediately previous generation, who had left voluminous works on the subject. But there was now an urgent new need to reassess the past in the light of pressing new issues and events. Several attempts were undertaken in this regard, but I will give a brief survey of the most relevant to the issue at hand and will limit myself here to some of the writings of Adonis (ᶜAlī Aḥmad Saᶜīd), al-Ṭayyib Tīzīnī, Ḥusayn Muruwwa, Ḥasan Ḥanafī and Muḥammad ᶜĀbid al-Jābirī. All of these are anguished writers concerned for the Arab future: they study the past in order to rehabilitate the present and suggest ways of achieving a better tomorrow.

Adonis, a Syrian-Lebanese poet of extreme versatility and fecund creativity, had compiled in the 1960s a three-volume anthology featuring the best of the poetic heritage of the Arabs from pre-Islamic times to the First World War.[59] His observation that Arab poetic taste was governed by a strict conformist aesthetic led him to embark on a systematic investigation of Arab culture as a whole, particularly in its formative first three centuries following the rise of Islam, in order to discover its ethos and the extent to which the latter might still exercise power over the Arabs of today. His findings have been published in a three-volume work entitled *al-Thābit wa-l-Mutaḥawwil: Baḥth fī-l-Ittibāᶜ wa-l-Ibdāᶜ ᶜInd al-ᶜArab* (Continuity and Change: A Study of Conformity and Creativity among the Arabs).[60] His interpretation in it of the prevailing Arab culture as rooted in the dominant Arab-Islamic heritage is one of the sharpest and most daring indictments of Arab culture in modern times.

Adonis argues that the mentality (*dhihniyya*) which has dominated and oriented Arab life, being that of those historically in power, had four characteristics.

First, on the ontological level is its theologism (*lāhūtāniyya*), by which he means an excessive tendency to separate God from man and to consider the religious conception of God as the origin, the axis, and the end of everything. Thus for Adonis, the Arab mind is the mind of abstract oneness and absolute metaphysics. In socio-political life this reflects itself in the reification of the nation, the community or the state which is nothing but a theologistic projection and, therefore, a metaphysical abstraction. Man does not exist by himself, but by God, and hence, in the world, he only exists by religion, by the community, by the state and by the family. He cannot, therefore, practice his human essence as an individual man, for he does not have the freedom of creativity and innovation. He exists secondarily by others and primarily by God, the totally Other.

Second, on the psychological-existential level, is the Arab mind's preteritism (*māḍawiyya*), by which Adonis means its clinging to what is already known and its rejection, even fear, of what is unknown. The Arab feels that his existence depends on the continuity of past symbols and structures, and he is often violent to anyone who threatens them. He uses what is known, his heritage, to understand everything. If that does not illumine the unknown, the latter is not worth validation.

Third, on the level of expression and language is the Arab mind's separation between ideas and speech. Ideas are considered as existing before speech, the latter being only a form or an embellished image of ideas. There cannot, therefore, be any innovation in ideas but only in the form they may take. Hence, Arabic literature is essentially conformist.

Fourth, on the level of civilizational development, is the Arab contradiction with modernity because, for an Arab, what is old and known is the source of all his private and public values and of all that regulates his relations with the world. The Arab personality, like Arab culture, revolves around the past. Real modernity lies in creativity and innovation, which the Arab rejects because he rejects doubt, experimentation, the absolute freedom of search and the adventure of exploring the unknown and of accepting it.[61]

These four characteristics of the mentality of the historically dominant groups in Arab society represent, for Adonis, the forces of continuity that have imposed conformity since the rise of Islam, because change would threaten their existence. The Arab-Islamic groups that have been taken by the idea of creating a new world are those that have created new concepts regarding the relation of God and man, and that of man and man, and have given religion, politics and life new dimensions. The Sufi experience, for example, was a negation of the abstract idea of divine transcendence in traditional Islamic theology. The rationalist tendencies of the Muᶜtazila and Muslim scientists, the socialistic tendencies of the Qarāmiṭa, the atheistic tendencies negating the need for prophets and religion, and those that opposed chauvinistic Arabism and wanted to replace it by brotherly Islamism, as well as those that introduced ideas of a new hermeneutic giving priority to reason over tradition, and those that supported *ḥaqīqa* (truth) over *sharīᶜa* (law), and all movements to revolutionize the Arabic poetic language—all these have historically been forces of change and creativity in the Arab heritage, according to Adonis, though they have all been subdued by the dominant forces of continuity and conformity.[62]

Adonis suggests, therefore, that Arab culture in its prevalent inherited form has a religious structure and is thus conformist and past-oriented. It does not only confirm the tradition, it rejects innovation and condemns it. This culture in its present form obstructs any real progress. Arab life, for Adonis, cannot prosper and the Arab person cannot create unless the traditional structure of the Arab mind is destroyed so that the manner of viewing and understanding things can be changed. This should start from the idea that the basis of Arab culture is multiple, not unitary, and that it does not have the vitality of transcending itself unless it gets rid of the religious structure so that religion may become a purely personal experience.[65]

This deconstruction of the old traditional structure of Arab culture should not, according to Adonis, be done by any other instrumentality than that of the Arab heritage itself, and emphasis must be made in it on the fact that truth is not to be found in the mind but rather in experience. True living experience changes the world. Yet the primary elements of change are within the Arab heritage itself. They are, however, without value insofar as they are past: their value is in the power they have to become part of the future when used innovatively. Arabs should therefore consciously resort to these vital elements of potential change in their own heritage and thereby transcend their past creatively, radically, comprehensively and irrevocably,[64] or else there will be no change at all, but rather repetition and imitation of the past.

Essentially Adonis's study calls for:

> . . . the necessity of liberating the Arab from every kind of atavism (*salafiyya*), and the necessity of eliminating sanctity from the past and of considering it part of an experience or knowledge that is absolutely not binding. Consequently, man must be viewed as one whose true human essence is in being a transforming creator more than a conforming inheritor.[65]

Modernity for Adonis is not merely the quality characteristic of a contemporary or a recent period of history. It is rather a mode of thought, an attitude to the world, a conception of time and a philosophy of man totally different from those of the received wisdom of tradition. Thus, for example, in discussing atheism in the context of the rationalist thought of Ibn al-Rāwandī (died probably A.D. 910 or 912) and al-Rāzī (died probably A.D. 925 or 932), Adonis says approvingly that atheism "is the first form of modernity, because the criticism of Revelation in a society built on Revelation is not only the first condition for all criticism but also the first condition for all progress."[66] Further to the criticism of Revelation, it is necessary to eliminate religion from society and establish reason. This elimination should not be limited to the state or to public religion, but private religion should also be eliminated, i.e., the religion of the individual himself.[67] Modernity is thus equated with absolute secularism and rationalism, which alone can bring about social justice, equality, and progress. Man, not God, must be the center of the universe and he himself should, by his freedom and his will, make history and build society and the state in accordance with the dictates of his reason. Only man's experience and effectiveness in the outside world can lead to the knowledge of truth, not any speculation, contemplation or religious *a priori* presumption.[68]

It is obvious how this flies in the face of traditional Islamic views of man, the world and God. Adonis has been severely criticized and even accused of being anti-Arab. His dependence on historically-marginal personalities and views in Arab culture as elements of change was raised to show his misunderstanding of the thrust of the mainstream of the culture. His interpretations of both the mainstream and the marginal elements were further criticized as totally out of context, particularly in the way he was thought to have misread and distorted the original intentions of the texts he studied. He was said to have been influenced by Orientalists hostile to Islam and, as a poet with an emotive sensibility, to have lacked the very things that he called for, namely, rationalism and objectivism.[69]

This, however, did not deter Adonis, for he pursued this line of thinking dauntlessly in his subsequent writings. In his book *Fātiḥa li-Nihāyāt al-Qarn: Bayānāt min Ajl Thaqāfa ᶜArabiyya Jadīda* (Overture to the Endings of the Century: Declarations for a New Arab Culture),[70] he brazenly says:

> Different culture can begin only by a criticism of the heritage in a radical and comprehensive way, for we cannot build a new culture if we do not critically shake the structures of the old culture. Without that, the new culture will [merely] be a layer that accumulates on the layers of the old culture so that these latter will [eventually] absorb it, and it will have no effectiveness.[71]

This radical position of Adonis's is matched by another Syrian's, this time a full-fledged Marxist one, namely, that of Ṭayyib Tīzīnī, who has planned a twelve-volume study of the intellectual Arab-Islamic heritage, two tomes of which have already been published.[72] Tīzīnī acknowledges at the start that the heritage has two aspects, the cognitive and the utilitarian, which are in a dialectical relationship to each other. He believes that the utilitarian aspect has often been wrongly seen as the only truth about the heritage, and thus the dialectical unity of its two aspects has been bracketed off and its cognitive aspect sacrificed. This happens, he says, whenever the heritage is vulgarly made to serve certain pragmatic interests and needs of a segment (usually the dominant class) of society, thus in fact revealing an ideological stand. Tīzīnī emphasizes the necessity of a scientific and progressive methodology that takes into serious consideration the inner historical movement of the heritage in its true contextual circumstances, far from any ideological imposition or forced interpretive intrusion. He says, "In heritage research, as in scientific research generally, truth is such (i.e. truth), not because it is utilitarian but rather, on the contrary, it is utilitarian because it is true."[73]

Basing his views on Marxism, Tīzīnī develops a theory of studying the intellectual Arab-Islamic heritage as a constructive alternative to what he considers to be the ahistorical, aheritagial (*lā-tārīkhī lā-turāthī*) approaches of the reactionary traditionalists, the liberal eclectics, the ultra-modernists, the pseudo-objectivists and the Eurocentric Orientalists, all of whom he criticizes.[74]

Tīzīnī believes in the dialectical relationship between the socio-economic and political conditions in society, on the one hand, and the corresponding intellectual structure on the other. The relationship between these two poles is not one-dimensional in matters of influencing or being influenced, nor is it one in which either has an exclusive power to determine it. He maintains that the former pole has a decisive edge because it has an indirect, mediating characteristic that defines the horizons of progress or backwardness in society in any of its historical periods, and therefore it has an advantage in defining the general path of intellectual life in it.[75] Nevertheless, Tīzīnī believes thought retains a measure of relative autonomy from socio-economic and political conditions and he argues that their relationship is not a mechanical, but rather a complex, one. Socio-economic and political relations indirectly and mediately set the possibility for the rise and development of thought over long periods, but it is the inner structure and logic of human thought itself that transforms this possibility into a necessity. Thought continually attempts to free itself from social reality, but this freedom remains relative because, however far-reaching, it cannot release itself from social reality in an absolute manner.[76]

In this framework, Tīzīnī sees history (*tārīkh*) and heritage (*turāth*) as an objective reality in that both emphasize the past, be it an event or an artifact or a human product of any sort. But whereas history cannot be said to constitute an element of the present moment, inasmuch as it continues to be past and retains its previous characteristics, the heritage extends into the present, forming some of its dimensions as they both (past and present) interpenetrate and interlock. Thus the heritage is history, i.e. the past, continuing into the present.[77]

Tīzīnī says that this continuation into the present is not only what occurs spontaneously but also what is humanly assimilated and stored up from the past by way of conscious selection from the heritage. Such selection is a continuous process in human existence: it happened in the past and continues to happen in the present. Every moment in human history was a present at one time and, as such, it was the focal point at which socio-economic, political and intellectual forces of continuity met with similar forces of discontinuity. The historian should disentangle the factors that make up these forces and, to do so successfully, he should have a rigorous, scientific methodology as well as a progressive, ideologically-conscious approach. Both are necessary for valid research in authenticating original sources and in interpreting them and discerning their past historical import within the comprehensive, civilizational social framework in which they were formed.[78] Tīzīnī admits there is here a preconceived manner in the method, but he insists it is not, nor should it be, arbitrary and artificial in its application, but rather it should be developed and refined to the point of accuracy in the very act of its application and in the light of its results.[79] The point is that no research can be done without preconceived notions of the problems of scientific research. Awareness of this fact should help the preconception to continuously perfect itself scientifically. Ignoring it makes the researcher liable to methodological superficiality and arbitrariness without even knowing it.

Tīzīnī calls his theory "historical heritagial dialectics" (*al-jadaliyya al-tārīkhiyya al-turāthiyya*) and he avers it is an embodiment, enrichment and development of historical dialectical materialism.[80] Two concepts are essential for its application: the first is the concept of "the contemporary national phase," the second is that of "heritagial selectivity." The first concept is equivalent to what Marx and Engels called "the socio-economic formation," later developed further by Lenin, and it refers to the totality of exigences, requirements and horizons of the prevailing social structure of a society in a particular phase of its development as a societal unit with a class system.[81] It is essential for the theory because it requires the inclusion of socio-economic factors in the understanding of the history and the heritage of the society studied and it requires this understanding to be from the viewpoint of the national aspirations and needs of that society in the period studied. The concept of "heritagial selectivity" is also essential because it allows for conscious choice from among the elements of the national heritage, the choice being of those elements that had relative value in the past as well as those that continue to have absolute value for the present and the future, the criterion being the requirements of the contemporary national phase. Tīzīnī says there are two aims here: the first is scientific and academic, and it lies in highlighting progress achieved in the past within the social class struggle of the period studied; and the second is scientific and academic but also practical and applied, and it lies in carrying forward this progress into the present and the future. He admits of the conscious and intentional politicization of heritage study but stresses the fact that it is not imposed on the scholarly study of it but is rather a necessary contemporary embodiment of it, impelled by the needs of the contemporary national phase.[82]

The purpose of the theory is to create a "heritagial revolution," meaning not only a revolution in the cognitive understanding of the heritage but also a revolution grounded in the progressive elements of the heritage continuously looking out to a future horizon in which scientific socialism becomes possible. This "heritagial revolution" is one aspect of the "cultural revolution" needed in the Arab world, its relation to it being that of the particular to the general. The cultural revolution does not happen in a vacuum but rather within the framework of specific social relations, hence the primal necessity of a "social revolution" which will deal with two realities in the Arab world: civilizational backwardness and national dismemberment.[83] According to Tīzīnī this two-pronged social revolution should be a socialist revolution because the Arab hybrid class of the bourgeois-feudalists which has continued to dominate the Arab world since the beginnings of the Arab *nahḍa* (renaissance) of the 19th century is economically incapable and socially unable and, in fact, ideologically unwilling to achieve a social revolution because of its dependent relations with capitalist imperialist forces. Only the working classes of the Arab homeland are qualified and able to achieve the three interdependent revolutions mentioned above, i.e., the heritagial, the cultural and the socialist revolutions; and only they can transcend the present-day socio-economic structure in the Arab world and bring about the socialist revolution and its necessary, though transitional, dialectical concomitant, pan-Arab national unity.[84]

There is no doubt that Tīzīnī has made diligent efforts to relate Marxism to Arab history and the Arab heritage, unlike some other leftists whom he criticizes and who have presented socialist ideas and doctrines in a way that has alienated them from the Arab masses and Arab intellectuals.[85] Yet one does not have to wait until all twelve volumes of his project are published to see how he applies his new theory to Arab history and the Arab heritage, because he has already given a foretaste of that in the first volume by several examples of application. He has been criticized by other Arab thinkers for too rigid a schematization in the application of Marxist analysis to Arab history[86] as well as for factual errors in historical data and lack of sufficient or appropriate documentation.[87] There is still need for greater scholarly efforts in order to unearth all the socio-economic and political data in Arab-Islamic history before a meaningful, let alone a Marxist, interpretation of Arab culture can be adequately made relating culture to societal conditions. Yet it must be conceded that Tīzīnī's efforts are pioneering and must be appreciated as such for their definite contributions and for all the discussions and further research they have occasioned.[88]

Ḥusayn Muruwwa (d. 1987) is another pioneer in the application of Marxist theory to Arab thought. In his impressive two-volume work, *al-Nazaᶜāt al-Māddiyya fī-l-Falsafa al-ᶜArabiyya al-Islāmiyya*[89] (Materialist Trends in Arab-Islamic Philosophy), he studies the intellectual activities of the Arabs and relates them to change in societal conditions on a grand scale from pre-Islamic times to the middle of the thirteenth century A.D. His long introduction[90] makes it quite clear that his work is not just another history book on Arab-Islamic philosophy but rather a serious attempt to deal with a modern Arab problem, namely, how contemporary Arab thought should view its past intellectual heritage in a new light that accords with the revolutionary orientations of the Arab national liberation movement of the present.

Muruwwa notes that although the heritage is a single heritage, there have been numerous interpretations of it. He explains that this is due to the ideological differences of the interpreters which are basically class differences, a facet which is true of any society.[91] The ideology he consciously adopts is that of the contemporary Arab social classes and groups suffering from material and spiritual misery under all kinds of national repression and despoilment by imperialism and Zionism. The scientific revolutionary thought of this ideology is, he says, the thought of scientific socialism with its two bases: dialectical materialism and historical materialism.[92] Through the latter, the heritage will be understood historically from the viewpoint of its relation to the past social structure which produced it and the historical conditions which engendered that specific social structure. This will bring about a new understanding of the heritage and hence it will lead to the liberation of present-day Arab thought from its state of dependency on Western imperialist thought and Arab bourgeois ideology which have pervaded it and the contemporary Arab social structure. According to Muruwwa, this new understanding will reveal the historical dimensions of the present Arab revolutionary movement and will show that Arab authenticity agrees with modernity and interacts with it, thus dispelling the incorrect notion of their being contradictory to each other, which Western imperialist thought and Arab bourgeois thought have propagated.[93] The Arab present will thus be seen as a movement of becoming, in which the achievements of the past and the possibilities of the future interact dynamically and move developmentally forward. The past heritage will no more be characterized by metaphysical, idealistic and fatalistic qualities in which Arab-Islamic society seems lacking human will and creativity, and thus merely reflecting the present-day ideology of the Arab bourgeoisies controlled by that of the imperialists. It will rather be a living heritage, throbbing with the movement of history, as thought will be shown to be related to the movement of Arab-Islamic society with all its contradictions and social-ideological conflicts in which human forces alone make history through human will and within specific societal conditions.[94]

Muruwwa proceeds along these lines to give an account of Arab thought, beginning in pre-Islamic Arabia and moving through the rise of Islam to the advent of the caliphates of the Rāshidūn, the Umayyads and the cAbbasids, discussing the intellectual content of the Arab-Islamic theological, philosophical and Sufi discourse of the various schools and sects as an embodiment of the changing societal conditions, but also always allowing thought a certain measure of relative autonomy with regard to political, social and economic factors.

To give an example of Muruwwa's treatment, I will refer to his Marxist analysis of the history and doctrines of the Muctazila.[95] To start with, he situates the beginnings of this rationalist theological movement in the thick of the political conflict of the Muslim community over the legitimacy of the caliphate of the Umayyads. He relates the movement to the earlier religio-political debate on whether or not one who commits a grave sin (*kabīra*) continues to be a believer. The Khārijīs maintained that such a person was an unbeliever, since they coupled faith with good deeds, while the Murji'īs argued that he continued to be a believer, since they considered faith to be an internal matter unrelated to deeds and accordingly the final decision was God's, and human opinion regarding this matter should be suspended. Ḥasan al-Baṣrī (d. 728) considered the grave sinner to be a hypocrite (*munāfiq*) because his faith was not perfect since he said or did something and secretly believed in something else, and thus deserved the punishment due an unbeliever. Wāṣil ibn cAṭā' (d. 748), on the other hand, considered such a person to be iniquitous (*fāsiq*), a believer doctrinally speaking but one who did not obey the Sharīca, his position being intermediate between that of a believer and an unbeliever (*al-manzila bayn al-manzilatayn*). The Muctazila adopted the latter doctrine of the intermediate position for political reasons, since at the bottom of the question was whether Mucāwiya, as avenger of cUthmān's murderers and as his successor, was a believer and hence a legitimate caliph, as opposed to cAlī, who succeeded cUthmān as caliph after the latter's murder. The relative autonomy of thought in these societal matters exhibited itself in the manner in which the Muctazila conceptualized the issue at hand and developed it into a general abstract doctrine about the grave sinner, rather than keeping it particularized in specific persons or times.

Muruwwa subjects the other four doctrines of the Muctazila to detailed content analysis in the light of societal conditions and relates them to the prevalent intellectual debate as well as to the socio-economic and political development of Muslim society. He accepts the influence of external factors on the Muᶜtazila, such as Greek, Persian or Indian thought and Christian theology, but he shows how the necessities of the internal factors shaped their doctrines by a process of innovative assimilation that responded to the perceived needs of their own Muslim society.

In all this intellectual development, Muruwwa observes that over long periods there is a quantitative accumulation of factors that leads eventually to a qualitative transformation in accordance with Marxist theory. He considers the successive events that followed Prophet Muḥammad's death as quantitative accumulations beginning with the conflict over who should be caliph, and going on to the conflict over the material gains of ᶜUthmān's supporters, then reaching a climax in the civil war between ᶜAlī and Muᶜāwiya. All these quantitative accumulations led to a qualitative transformation which initially expressed itself politically in the rise of the Umayyad state, supported by socio-economic transformation and eventually giving rise to an intellectual transformation. As time went on, the new order soon began to exhibit internal contradictions within the relations of production and the political hegemony of the Umayyad state, creating new quantitative accumulations that grew rife in Caliph ᶜAbd al-Malik's rule and eventually sought various qualitative transformations in the political, social and intellectual spheres, sometimes accompanied by armed revolts,[96] and culminating in the rise of the ᶜAbbasids.

Muruwwa opines that theological discourse (*ᶜilm al-kalām*) began with the question of predestination as an intellectual form of qualitative transformation resulting from the accumulation of social disaffection among groups of *mawālī* (non-Arab clients), land workers, small landowners and bands of slaves working on the land or in the public services, and numerous poor people in the cities including small wage earners and employees of crafts shops. While social disaffection expressed itself in occasional armed revolts with class struggle undertones, the intellectuals were expressing it theologically, protesting the absolute Umayyad political and economic hegemony and its deterministic ideology, and they were teaching that human will was free and man was not predestined. Other topics were eventually included in the discourse, such as the question of the grave sinner, be his sin political or otherwise, and the question of God's transcendence, unity and justice.[97] The Mu^{c}tazila were the intellectuals who built up a unified theological system reflecting all these concerns.

Muruwwa explains that although the early Mu^{c}tazila constituted theological opposition to the Umayyad caliphate, they were later in favor with the ^{c}Abbasid Caliph al-Ma'mūn and his two successors who supported them. He observes that the social forces that brought al-Ma'mūn to power in his struggle with his brother al-Amīn were those representing city economy and its mercantile society based on trade, banking, the crafts and the innovative thinking of liberal intellectuals. Although the social groups in the growing Iraqi cities were people of mixed ethnic origins and of various economic classes, their interests as a whole were opposed to the conservative rich owners of feudal lands in the countryside and their agricultural agents who supported al-Amīn. The Mu^{c}tazila, among whom were many men of non-Arab origin, were in the ascendancy with al-Ma'mūn and his successors until the socio-economic conditions changed, whereupon another theological school, the Ash^{c}arī school, formally rationalist but ideologically conservative, came eventually to the fore to express the view of another dominant political force.[98]

Muruwwa admits that his attempt is not more than laying the preparatory foundation to a full study of this matter in the light of the method of historical materialism, because he had nothing to guide him but a few socio-economic indicators and the general rules of social dialectic.[99] However, his efforts in generally relating Arab thought to societal conditions, as he understood them to be from the limited data, are commendable though not always precise and exact. He has been correctly criticized by Arab thinkers, some of whom are Marxists, for his inclination to abstraction and to ready schematization.[100] He has also been justly criticized for lack of correct or honest documentation and for his summary generalizations and categorical conclusions not fully justified.[101] But his work, by all accounts, is respected for its courage and its breadth of vision.[102]

Ḥasan Ḥanafī's work is another massive project of heritage study that is respected for a different kind of courage and broad treatment. His project entitled *al-Turāth wa-l-Tajdīd* (Heritage and Renewal) is still in its early stages, since only an introduction has been published,[103] to be followed by several planned volumes on three areas of relevant study: the first (in eight volumes) on the required attitude of the Arabs to their own heritage, the second (in five volumes) on their required attitude to the Western heritage and the third (in three volumes) on a new hermeneutical theory that reconstructs human culture on a global scale (mainly Judeo-Christian and Islamic) and rehabilitates a reconstructed Arab heritage within it as the foundation for mankind in a modern world existentially liberated from alienation and given a comprehensive program of positive action. Ḥanafī's earlier writings, even as he himself views them,[104] all contribute to his project, which he considers to be that of his lifetime. Hence it is possible to study his project before it is completed.

As in the case of many other Arab thinkers, Ḥasan Ḥanafī's point of departure is the Arab present and the necessity of solving its problems and putting an end to all that deters its development. The heritage in itself has no value to him except inasmuch as it is a means that can give the Arab nation a theory of action in the reconstruction of man and his relation with the world.[105] What is needed first and foremost, in his opinion, before any industrial, agricultural, or political revolution can succeed in the Arab world, is a human revolution that rebuilds the new man.

As Ḥanafī sees it, the Arab present is permeated with values of the past heritage. Its institutions and structures are an embodiment of that heritage. And since the heritage, in his view, is not merely manuscripts or books that have come down to contemporary Arabs, but all the interpretations that every past generation has given to them in response to its needs, he believes the heritage is not made up of eternal truths and immutable doctrines but of specific realizations of certain beliefs and attitudes under particular historical circumstances.[106] Being neither material stock stored up in libraries and museums, nor a conceptual theoretical entity independent of historical reality, the heritage to him is thus a psychological store of influences from the past pervading the Arab masses and forming part of Arab reality.[107]

It is this affective aspect of the heritage, i.e., its emotive power to influence conscience and behavior among the masses, that gives Ḥanafī the motivation to study the heritage—not in order to defend it, as he says, but in order to study the present through it and identify the negative elements of weakness and backwardness in it and eliminate them, and in order to emphasize the positive elements of strength and authenticity in it and make them the basis of a contemporary Arab *nahḍa* leading to change and progress.[108]

Ḥanafī's project proposes to rethink all the basic questions posed in the past, the answers to which have constituted the heritage of the contemporary Arabs, and then to select from all the valid, possible solutions those that respond to the requirements of the present age. He does not agree with the traditionalists who believe the heritage has given all the correct answers once and for all, nor with the modernizers who ignore the heritage and rush into programs of modernization in various fields, building the new beside the old or even on top of its decrepit structures. Nor does he agree with those who attempt to reconcile the heritage with modernity or those who attempt to reconcile modernity to the heritage, eclectically choosing elements from one or the other with a prepondering bias against one or the other, and without a view to the logical structure of the whole and its viability among people imbued with a psychological store of complex influences from the past.[109]

Ḥanafī considers the intellectual heritage of Islamic civilization to be essentially based on divine revelation recorded in one book, the Qur'ān. For him, Islamic civilization itself is nothing but an attempt at a methodical, intellectual presentation of this revelation to the world in a specific historical period and under specific socio-cultural circumstances. The revelation per se is not an issue in his opinion since the Qur'ān is an unquestionably authentic, historical document untouched by corruption or alteration of any kind and verifiably sincere and truthful, judging from its effect, in human experience, on initiating change and giving the world ideal structures leading to perfection. What is at issue in his view is the manner in which this revelation has been interpretively presented and the theoretical structures which have informed the presentation.[110] Not that this presentation and the structures are necessarily wrong, for Ḥanafī's claim is that they are only the result of specific historical circumstances in which Muslims chose particular solutions, among many others that were possible, in order to respond to the needs of their time. Thus, for example, if the old Islamic theory is studied today as part of the Arab heritage, the purpose for him is not merely to study raw texts or to declare certain wanting theologians of the past as unbelievers, but rather to illuminate the genesis and development of theological ideas arising from their first origins in revelation, and to note their response to the need of the time for a theorization of reality and for a conceptual foundation explicating the events of the day on the basis of an inherited source, pure reason, or the requirements of reality. This response may have been to conditions internal to the Islamic community and it may have been to attacks external to it. In all cases, Ḥanafī affirms, Islamic theology should be analyzed for its lopsided solutions, its important though conditional conclusions, and its intricate methods and arguments related to its historical times. But then the analysis should be continued and should reach the present day in order to encompass the few modern attempts at theological renewal and make Muslims aware of the necessity for a new and more comprehensive approach that will adequately answer today's questions which are necessarily different and require new methods of presentation, though the old subjects will remain valid.[111]

With the Qur'ān and the Prophet's Sunna at the center of Islamic civilization, Hanafī proposes to review all Islamic intellectual disciplines that make up the Arab cultural heritage. He says that there are Islamic disciplines only marginally related to the religious axis of the Arab heritage, such as mathematics and physics, as well as certain aspects of what is now called the humanities and social sciences like geography, history, linguistics, literature, psychology, sociology, ethics, politics, economics, logic and aesthetics. But he believes they have all contributed to form the Islamic world view and should, therefore, be shown to be grounded in the divine revelation, which should thus be rightly seen as the most comprehensive human science.[112] As for the religious sciences that arose to control the correctness of the text of revelation and to interpret it, some of them were temporary sciences which fulfilled their function and came to an end, such as certain Qur'anic and Ḥadīth sciences dealing with variant readings and the authentication of oral sources; some others among those sciences need to be developed further to explore any new significance they may have for the present age and its needs, and they include Qur'ān exegesis (*tafsīr*), law (*fiqh*) and the Prophet's biography (*Sīra*).[113]

But there are four intellectual Islamic disciplines to which Ḥanafī pays greater attention and they are: (1) theology (*ᶜilm al-kalām* or *uṣūl al-dīn*), (2) philosophy (*falsafa*), (3) jurisprudence (*uṣūl al-fiqh*) and (4)Sufism (*taṣawwuf*).[114] Ḥanafī maintains that all of them are inspired by the Qur'ān and the Sunna and he deals with them in some detail for a dual purpose:

(a) to establish their provenance as disciplines related to divine revelation on the one hand, and to specific conditions of their times on the other;

(b) to reconstruct them within a new and comprehensive cultural system that responds to the conditions and needs of the modern age.

Ḥanafī does not believe that any of these disciplines owes its existence, or at least its beginnings, to cultures outside Islamic civilization. For Islamic theology, in his opinion, was the first attempt by Muslims to find a purely rational theory for their religious text, its function being to consolidate the doctrine and, later, to defend its world view against internal sectarian dissension or other religions within Islamic territory. Islamic philosophy, in his view, was a wider and more comprehensive rational attempt by Muslims, its function being to transform the Muslim theological conceptions into general theories of the universe in order to deal with foreign, especially Greek, philosophical theories by using their linguistic tools and rational methods. Islamic jurisprudence was perhaps the earliest intellectual discipline the Muslims attempted, its earliest function being, according to Ḥanafī, the rationalization of the process of deriving new legal prescriptions for acts not prescribed in the Qur'ān or the Sunna, and its result was the establishment of an Islamic method of theorization of reality and community behavior.[115] Sufism, as he explains, arose out of the needs of certain Muslims who did not want to share positively in the political turmoil of the Islamic community and devoted themselves in seclusion to spiritual enhancement and, later, developed a distinctive orientation in interpreting the revealed text based for the most part on the heart and on feeling, and only to a limited degree on reason.

Ḥanafī argues that all these Islamic disciplines have been perverted through generations of ignorance so that, in modern times, Arabs lack the depth of intellectual insight and emotive experience which these disciplines reflect as evidence of their free encounter with the sacred text of revelation. In his view, most Arabs now live a superficial, superstitious religious life and lead an impoverished spiritual existence, close-minded to anything but their captivity to the literal understanding of the Qur'ān and the Ḥadīth. They are without any imaginative, comprehensive vision that experiences the whole universe and conceives of it as God's, and are internecinely divided into mutually exclusive views based on vulgar knowledge or material interests.

Ḥanafī's project aims at reconstructing, unifying and integrating all the Islamic civilizational sciences in the light of modern needs, making of them an ideology for modern man by which he lives a full and perfect life. Man and history, the two invisible dimensions of the old Arab heritage, absorbed as they have been in the divine, will be revealed as being at the center of modern consciousness in a reconstructed Islamic world view based on revelation which, in his opinion, is the logic of existence.[116]

In addition, Ḥanafī proposes to reconstruct the heritage of Western culture, which he characterizes as a purely historical culture in which divine revelation has ceased to be central except by inertia, his aim being to show its limitation and provincialism, and to refute its claim to universality and leadership, and thus to reduce Europe and its culture to what he terms its natural size within world culture.[117]

In all this, Ḥanafī sees himself as bearing the torch unto a new age of Enlightenment (*tanwīr*), using rationalism but at the same time not ignoring the fund of human feeling. Holding in great esteem Marxist analysis as used in Latin American liberation theology, he sees himself as a spearhead of a new Islamic Left[118] aiming at improving the life of the crushed Arab masses by making them regain their identity and shed their alienation and rid themselves of all that deters development, better standards of living and self-determination while developing a new Islamic theology of man. He sees himself as a philosopher with a new hermeneutic that combines an innovative understanding of Islam, Marxism and phenomenology and creates a revolutionary ideology that gives people everywhere a theory of action and behavior leading to change, progress and fulfillment based on revelation.

In spite of his great efforts, I believe Ḥanafī overestimates the ability of his encyclopedic endeavor to change the Arab world, let alone the Third World or the whole world and let alone how much real scholarship one single person can command. His project is inordinately cerebral and too theoretical to be practical in the real world. Although he repeatedly refers to the importance of social reality, his project dangerously skirts the material basis of this reality and is essentially predicated on the prior necessity of spiritual reconstruction, thus ignoring the dialectical relation between matter and spirit, between reality and thought. Besides, wishful thinking does not create reality. Ḥanafī's voice, however, should be taken into consideration as the rising Arab chorus builds up, calling for a new vision of the future.

If Ḥanafī's approach is admittedly ideological, Muḥammad ᶜĀbid al-Jābirī's is the most serious attempt in the Arab world to go beyond ideology to epistemology in order to analyze the workings of the Arab mind.

In his book *Naḥnu wa-l-Turāth: Qirā'āt Muᶜāṣira fī Turāthinā l-Falsafī* (We and the Heritage: Contemporary Readings in Our Philosophical Heritage),[119] al-Jābirī maintains a procedural distinction between the epistemological and the ideological content of Arab-Islamic philosophy. He deems this distinction particularly useful whenever the epistemological and the ideological elements of an intellectual structure do not form a single entity but rather belong to two different worlds. In the case of Arab-Islamic philosophy, al-Jābirī believes that its epistemological content (i.e., science and metaphysics) belongs to a different intellectual universe which is primarily the space of Greek thought, and that its ideological content belongs to the space of Arab-Islamic thought which is related to the sociopolitical conflicts in which it developed. The function of philosophy in Islamic civilization was, according to al-Jābirī, the employment of the Greek epistemological content to serve the ideological aims of one party or the other in the Arab-Islamic conflicts. Whether he was discussing the religious and political philosophy of al-Fārābī, or the oriental philosophy of Ibn Sīnā, or the theory of Ibn Rushd regarding the relation of religion and philosophy or aspects of the thought of Ibn Bājja or Ibn Khaldūn, al-Jābirī turned his attention mainly to their ideological content to show the partisan Arab and Islamic elements that colored their philosophy, and to highlight the Arab-Islamic societal conflicts reflected in it.

However, when studying Arab thought in the modern period, al-Jābirī concentrates on its logical structure and epistemological foundations because he does not want to explore its historical and intellectual relation to its social conditions as he did when studying Arab-Islamic philosophy, but rather to discover why, since the beginnings of the Arab *nahḍa* in the latter quarter of the nineteenth century, Arab thought to date has not seemed to be making any significant progress but has appeared to him to be going in circles. In his book *al-Khiṭāb al-ᶜArabī al-Muᶜāṣir: Dirāsa Taḥlīliyya Naqdiyya* (The Contemporary Arab Discourse: A Critical Analytical Study),[120] he approaches the major intellectual concerns of the Arab thinkers in the past hundred years with the purpose of discovering how they thought, not what they thought. He applies himself to the study of the general cultural discourse first and the Arab perception of modernity and tradition. He then moves to the modern political discourse in which Arab perceptions of religion and state, democracy and nationalism play a big role. After that, he studies the nationalist discourse and analyzes Arab perceptions of unity and socialism, and pays particular attention to the Arab perceptions of the liberation of Palestine and its role in the Arab intellectual discourse. Finally, he moves to the modern philosophical discourse and studies Arab perceptions of the achievements of past Arab philosophers and analyzes the formulations of present-day philosophers in the Arab world who want to present a contemporary Arab philosophy. In all these investigations covering intellectuals from Jamāl al-Dīn al-Afghānī, Muḥammad ᶜAbduh, ᶜAlī ᶜAbd al-Rāziq and Rashīd Riḍā to Ḥasan Ṣaᶜb, Anwar ᶜAbd al-Malik, ᶜAbd al-Raḥmān Badawī and Zakī Najīb Maḥmūd passing through Sayyid Quṭb,

Michel ᶜAflaq, ᶜAbd Allāh ᶜAbd al-Dā'im and Salāma Mūsā in addition to many others, al-Jābirī discerns an Arab mind that is still going in vicious circles, having achieved no significant progress in any of the issues it has dealt with in the past hundred years. He notes that there is a basic problematic structural character to the Arab mind which pervades all its intellectual endeavors, and that is its proneness to always give referential authority to a past-model (*namūdhaj-salaf*). He argues that the Arab mind does not depart from reality to build up a particular trend of thought, but rather works from a past-model which constantly deters it and keeps it from facing reality and consequently diverts its discourse into dealing with what is intellectually possible as if it were a real fact. Resort to a past-model makes memory, and hence the emotional and the irrational, take the place of reason. Al-Jābirī says:

> Modern and contemporary Arab discourse is in truth a discourse of memory, not a discourse of reason; it is a discourse which does not speak in the name of a conscious self that possesses independence and enjoys complete personality, but rather one which speaks in the name of a referential authority that employs memory and not reason. This is very serious, because intellectual concepts in this condition are not related to the reality of which the discourse speaks but rather to another reality which establishes the past-model in the consciousness as the directing, referential authority.[121]

In other words, al-Jābirī says that the intellectual concepts of modern and contemporary Arab discourse do not reflect actual Arab reality, and that they are, rather, borrowed. What complicates matters further is that those concepts are, in his view, either borrowed from medieval Arab-Islamic thought in which they had a specific real (or imagined) content, or else they are borrowed from European thought in which they designate a foreign reality that has been achieved in Europe (or is in the process of being achieved). In both cases, and whether the past-model is Arab-Islamic or European, the intellectual concepts of the Arab discourse are using a rather unclear and obscure, copied "reality" in order to give expression to an indefinite, hoped-for "reality." Thus, there is a break between Arab thought and its object. For example, if Arab thinkers use an intellectual concept such as *shūrā*, i.e., consultation, borrowed from medieval Arab-Islamic thought, or if they use an intellectual concept such as *proletariat*, borrowed from modern European thought, in both cases they are using indefinite borrowed concepts that cannot have the same meaning or content in their present-day Arab reality as they did in their original usage, because of objective contextual difference. Nonetheless, Arab thinkers use such concepts and many others in order to give expression to what they hope will be Arab reality and the result is confused thinking that is ridden by contradictions because it cannot be related to an objective, actual reality but rather to a memory which is easily colored by emotional and wishful thinking that makes the possible appear to be real.

Of course every ideology has an epistemological (objective) side to it and an ideological (subjective) side, the former expressing socio-political and cultural reality as a result of a more-or-less scientific analysis of it, the latter expressing biased interests, desires and aspirations. In contemporary Arab ideology, according to al-Jābirī, the two sides do not coincide because the epistemological does not express Arab reality, and does not even reflect it or enter into a direct or indirect relation with it. Its referential framework, vague as it may be, is a reality other than contemporary Arab reality. Its referential framework is medieval Arab or modern European reality. Its concepts function basically as a cover-up and compensation for the epistemological deficiency of contemporary Arab discourse, hence its dogmatic character which is not amenable in argument to logical reference to reality but to further ideological tenacity and make-believe.[122]

It follows from this that differences and disagreements among Arab thinkers are not reflections of varying interpretations of contemporary Arab reality, but reflections of the differing and disagreeing referential authorities of each, namely the past-model each adopts and interprets, be it medieval Arab or modern European. Obsessed by the necessity of a past-model external to present-day Arab reality, intellectual activity takes the shape of jurisprudential analogy which, when entrenched in the mechanism of thinking, limits the intellect to a search for a past-model to every new thing with the aim of reconciling the new to the past-model. Thus thought becomes increasingly farther from reality, a prisoner of discourse and not its master. As a result, it considers what is possible and what is real as equal, and it treats what is intellectually possible as if it were a given fact.[123]

These, then, in al-Jābirī's view, are the four basic characteristics of modern and contemporary Arab discourse: (1) the dominance of the past-model, (2) the entrenchment of the mechanism of jurisprudential analogy, (3) the treatment of what is intellectually possible as given facts and (4) the use of the ideological to cover up the deficiency of the epistemological in the knowledge of reality. These characteristics are structurally interrelated and, whether considered cause or effect, they are related to the lack in contempoary Arab personality of what Gramsci called "complete historical independence," or rather they are related to the Arab inability to achieve such independence.

Since having such independence is necessary for Arab liberation from any model and from any concomitant analogical thinking, al-Jābirī suggests that Arabs should achieve it by liberating themselves from the referential authority of both the Arab-Islamic model and the European model, i.e., the referential authority of the Arab-Islamic heritage and of Western culture and thought. He explains that this does not mean the heritage should be disposed of (which is impossible) but that it should be fully possessed by being critically studied then transcended: it must be reconstructed through a rearrangement of the relations of its components to one another on the one hand, and through a rearrangement of the relation of the Arabs to it on the other. This would restore to it its historicity and the relativity of its concepts and categories in the Arab mind so that the past in Arab consciousness should no longer be a focal element of its present problematic. Similarly, al-Jābirī explains that his approach does not mean that Western culture and thought should be emotionally ignored or wishfully declared to be declining and disintegrating or morally dismissed as evil,[124] but rather that Arabs should enter into a critical dialogue with Western culture by understanding its historicity and the relativity of its concepts and categories and by learning the foundations of the West's advancement based on science and critical rationality, which the Arabs must implant in their own culture and thought.[125] Furthermore, al-

Jābirī insists on the necessity of the conscious presence of Arab identity as a personality with distinctive history and uniqueness as well as with contradictions and a specific development. A necessary point of departure for the practice of self-criticism is the Arabs' awareness of themselves as a product of historical development, as al-Jābirī says in agreement with Gramsci. The image which the Arabs have forged of themselves, their past and their future, in the last hundred years since the *nahḍa*, is an image influenced partly by the challenge of Western culture and partly by the Arab reaction to this challenge, an image drawn by a passive, not an active, self. This image should now be corrected by a critique of the Arab mind, not merely since the faulty beginnings of the *nahḍa*, but since the formative beginnings of Arab culture as recorded in the early centuries of Islamic history.[126]

It is for this reason that al-Jābirī wrote his two-volume book *Naqd al-ᶜAql al-ᶜArabī* (Critique of the Arab Mind), the first volume of which appeared in 1984 under the title of *Takwīn al-ᶜAql al-ᶜArabī* (The Formation of the Arab Mind)[127] and concentrates on the early development of the epistemological structure of Arab learned culture, i.e., on the mechanism of the production of Arab thought. The second volume, which appeared in 1986 under the title of *Bunyat al-ᶜAql al-ᶜArabī: Dirāsa Taḥlīliyya Naqdiyya li-Nuẓum al-Maᶜrifa fī-l-Thaqāfa al-ᶜArabiyya* (Structure of the Arab Mind: A Critical Analytical Study of the Systems of Knowledge in Arab Culture),[128] continues al-Jābirī's discussion in a detailed study of the Arab epistemological systems that have been operative in Arab culture.

Al-Jābirī's aim in both volumes is to analyze the epistemological systems of Arab-Islamic culture as methods of perceiving reality. In this endeavor, he sees the various intellectual disciplines of this culture as interconnected rooms in a single palace and not as secluded independent tents in an open space, as the prevalent view may suggest. Following Michel Foucault, he recognizes the essentially political nature of culture (any culture) in which cultural hegemony is the primary, if not the only, aim of every social force—political, religious or otherwise; hence in Arab-Islamic culture, the organic conflictual relation between the ideological and the epistemological, which gives it its historicity. Al-Jābirī also recognizes the undercurrents of counter-culture as part of the whole, including the irrational and esoteric elements, since both culture and counter-culture developed and defined themselves in relation to each other.

For al-Jābirī, the most important period in the history of Arab-Islamic culture to date is the age of recording (*ᶜaṣr al-tadwīn*), when the knowledge prevalent in the middle of the second century of the Islamic era began to be systematically written down by Arab scholars.[129] Though there had been earlier individual recordings dating back to the Prophet's time and that of the early Caliphs, they were sporadic, unorganized, limited in scope and not given the formal support of the state and the community. The age of recording stretched under the ᶜAbbasids for over a century, during which much of the oral tradition of the Arabs and of Islam was collected, translations from non-Arab cultures made and the systems of Arab-Islamic thought established. Al-Jābirī argues that this recording inevitably had the unconscious stamp of its own age, particularly when it referred to pre-Islamic Arabia, early Islam, and most of the Umayyad period. In fact, it was a reconstruction of Arab-Islamic culture and has ever since been its foundation and its referential framework.

In studying the intellectual contributions of Arab-Islamic thinkers in the formative period such as al-Khalīl ibn Aḥmad,[130] al-Shāfiᶜī,[131] al-Ashᶜarī[132] and others who were essential in establishing the interconnected intellectual foundations in philology, legal theory and theology, al-Jābirī, while conceding their genius, attempts to show that they were establishing limits for reason by emphasizing the necessity, in their systems, of reference to past models and the analogical authority of past patterns and texts. In studying the intellectual contributions of the great Sufi and Shīᶜa thinkers and of esoteric thought generally in Arab-Islamic civilization,[133] al-Jābirī argues that reason in their systems resigned its duty, mostly under the influence of the Hermetic tradition and in opposition to the dominant established culture. In studying the intellectual contributions of the great Arab-Islamic philosophers al-Kindī, al-Fārābī,[134] Ibn Sīnā, al-Ghazālī[135] and others, al-Jābirī concludes that their rational approach was either governed by societal considerations (mainly political as in al-Kindī's case and al-Ghazālī's), or tainted with the esoteric gnostic influence of the resigned intellect (mainly Hermetic as in al-Fārābī's case, ibn Sīnā's and al-Ghazālī's). With al-Ghazālī, the Arab mind reached a crisis which was reflected in his personal life and withdrawal from politico-intellectual pursuits, and which continues to this day to be reflected in many contemporary Arab thinkers.[136]

Only in the Andalusian and Maghribi intellectual experience does al-Jābirī see a temporary exception to the workings elsewhere of the Arab mind under the influence of the resigned intellect or of the epistemology dependent on analogy and past models. In the thought of Ibn Ḥazm, Ibn Tūmart, Ibn Bājja and Ibn Rushd[137] he recognizes the insistence on reason and sense experience as sources for the production of knowledge not contradicting Revelation, and he sees an opposition to imitation (*taqlīd*) and analogical thinking (*qiyās*) in an attempt at a new cultural construction. He relates this exception to the political desire of the authorities in Andalus and the Maghrib for independence from the power structures in the Mashriq and the thought systems they supported. He excludes from this experience Ibn Masarra, Abū Midyan, Ibn ᶜArabī and other Sufis of the West who consecrated what al-Jābirī calls the resigned intellect (*al-ᶜaql al-mustaqīl*) already known in the East.

The general thesis of al-Jābirī is that Arab thought since the age of recording has been repeating itself, with little addition worth mentioning, because of its unconscious epistemological structure, which did not allow for movement from one intellectual stage to another, whereby the latter would transcend the former by negating and abolishing it, preserving only what was useful and renewable in it as a foundation for addition and development based on experience and need. Any apparent movement in Arab thought has been motion in the same place and in the same cultural time, motion of conflict and interpenetration between the three established epistemological systems which have been its basis. These systems in al-Jābirī's scheme, which are still operative today, are:

(1) The disciplines of explication (*ᶜulūm al-bayān*) based on an epistemological method which applies analogical thinking and produces knowledge analogically by subjecting the unknown to the known, the unseen to the seen, the new to a past-model. This method pervades

the earliest of all Arab-Islamic disciplines, which include grammar, rhetoric, prosody, philology, lexicography, Qur'ān exegesis, Ḥadīth sciences, Islamic law and legal theory, theology (*kalām*).

(2) The disciplines of gnosticism (*ᶜulūm al-ᶜirfān*), based on inner revelation and insight as an epistemological method, and including Sufism, Shīᶜī thought, Ismāᶜīlī philosophy, esoteric Qur'ān exegesis, oriental illumination philosophy, theosophy, alchemy, astrology, magic, numerology.

(3) Disciplines of inferential evidence (*ᶜulūm al-burhān*) based on an epistemological method of empirical observation and intellectual inference. They include logic, mathematics, physics (all branches of natural sciences) and even metaphysics.[138]

Al-Jābirī argues that the subject of the Arab-Islamic cultural discourse in the disciplines of explication was the text which, unlike nature—the subject of ancient Greek thought and modern European thought—had limitations which exhausted all possibilities of intellectual progress after a certain time in the age of recording, leaving only a closed circle of repetitious motion governed by rules limiting the intellect itself.[139] As for the disciplines of gnosis, al-Jābirī believes they lead to no intellectual and societal progress by the very nature of their concern. In the disciplines of inferential evidence, the Arab-Islamic cultural discourse was mostly dominated and vitiated by the political desire of defeating gnosticism and thus achieved limited progress, although in the field of strictly empirical practice it achieved real progress, as in algebra (al-Khawārizmī), optics (Ibn al-Haytham), astronomy (al-Baṭrūjī) and other natural sciences completely outside the political struggle in Arab culture.[140] These and similar empirical Arab achievements were continued by Europe after the Renaissance, as al-Jābirī asserts; but the modern European experience avoided the error of the ancient Greek experience and did not limit itself, as did the Greeks, to an intellectual dialectic which scorned experiment but rather built natural science on it and constructed technical instruments which were constantly improved with the advance of science and which affected this very advance itself positively, establishing an open-ended dialectical relationship between science and technology in the study of nature. European philosophy then broke with theology and entered a new phase related to science.[141]

What al-Jābirī advocates is a similar Arab advance, following a reconstruction of the Arab-Islamic culture. His argument calls for a scientific historicizing of the Arab-Islamic heritage and a rational relativizing of its value, not in order to know the facts only, as is the purpose of the Orientalist philological project but in order to liberate contemporary Arab discourse from the influence of those facts and establish a new intellectual discourse for the Arab future.

While not ignoring the achievements of modern science and thought, this discourse, in his view, should be founded on those viable intellectual achievements of the Arab-Islamic heritage which are characterized by rationalist critical qualities usable in the epistemological structures of modern civilization. For al-Jābirī, these viable intellectual achievements are basically in the disciplines of inferential evidence (*ᶜulūm al-burhān*), particularly as developed since the fifth century A.H./eleventh century A.D. in Andalus and the Maghrib by such great creative thinkers as Ibn Ḥazm, al-Shāṭibī, Ibn Rushd and Ibn Khaldūn, whose contributions in the direction of new epistemological structures and methodologies have not been adopted by the prevalent Arab-Islamic culture but have rather been all but ignored. The Arab mind has to renew and modernize itself if it is not to continue ruminating the old issues in an endless alienation from contemporary reality. A new "age of recording" should be inaugurated in order to replace the old foundations upon which traditional Arab-Islamic culture has been built.[142]

According to al-Jābirī, there is no final answer to the question of how Arabs should practice renovation and modernization from within their own heritage, because the answer is a continuously growing and renewed answer, gradually emerging from within that historical process of the practice itself, not before it, not above it and not outside it.[143]

Al-Jābirī's contribution to the contemporary Arab debate on the heritage is very clever, learned and thought-provoking. Its limitation, however, is that it is intellectual and, as such, can only benefit a small elite. Nonetheless, it is progressive and hopeful, and it leaves no doubt about the necessity for much hard work still lying ahead.

One of the latest serious efforts to study the problem of the Arab-Islamic heritage and the challenges of modernity was the symposium organized by the Center for Arab Unity Studies, a private social sciences research and publishing institute in Beirut established in 1977 whose director-general is Khayr al-Dīn Ḥasīb. The symposium was held in Cairo between September 24 and 27, 1984 and was attended by about one hundred participants representing the younger, as well as the older, intellectuals of the Arab world and included two non-Arab scholars: Yasumasa Kuroda who spoke on Japanese modernization and Satish Shandra who, by proxy, spoke on change and development in India. The proceedings of the symposium were published in 1985,[144] and included fourteen invited research papers, each followed by several commentators (except for one which arrived late), and each followed by discussions from the floor. To conclude the symposium there was one session of open discussion on the Arab future in the context of the general theme of the meeting.

I believe that the symposium has successfully contributed to the clarification of the intellectual trends in the Arab world today, some of which have been presented in this chapter. It also demonstrated the absolute necessity of continued free intellectual dialogue (rather than mutual exclusion) between conflicting views in order to reach a solution to the major issues confronting Arab society. There was insufficient discussion of the international order and how the Arabs should relate to it so that their economic dependency on it might be reduced while accepting its inevitable presence and reciprocal effectiveness. The symposium allowed a discourse among Arab intellectuals, and discussion occurred on issues relating to the Arab-Islamic heritage, social justice, the political order, Islam and the cultural question of modernization. But little was said about how intellectuals might seek union with the Arab masses, from whom they have been widely separated, nor was much said about Arab women or about ethnic and religious minorities in the Arab world and their place in the new order to be. Furthermore, the symposium did not offer practical ways by which the intellectuals might be able to synthesize their approaches and transform them into policies to be followed by Arab governments.

The symposium has eminently demonstrated that there is an intellectual crisis in the Arab world, indicated not only by the lack of consensus but also by the lack of an acceptable method to reach consensus with regard to Arab culture in the modern world. Political repression and the tenuous legitimization of political power are other indicators of the crisis. They are also factors in prolonging its duration and deepening its dimensions.

Chapter Three

The Modern Relevance of Islam and the Qur'ān

That Islam is an inalienable component of Arab culture is not only a historical fact of the greatest significance, but it is also a socio-psychological factor that continues to this very day to be of the utmost importance on the existential level. Secularistic Arab modernists who have ignored this truth or made light of it have continuously seen their projects dashed on its reality. More recent Arab modernizers have begun to accept this truth, though many thinkers among them disagree with regard to the extent it should be allowed to dominate the modernizing process.

Against a background of rising Islamic resurgence, typified intellectually by a Muslim Arab thinker like Sayyid Quṭb of Egypt, this chapter will attempt to portray the thought of other Muslim Arab writers who, while recognizing the absolute need for Islam in modern Arab society, have opted for varying liberal interpretations of it which they deem more suitable to the present age than the traditional ones. Of those thinkers, I will concentrate on some of the writings of Muḥammad al-Nuwayhī, Ḥasan Ṣaᶜb, Muḥammad ᶜAmāra and Muḥammad Arkūn (Mohammed Arkoun).

Let us first begin with Sayyid Quṭb (1906–1966) whose writings in several printings have become very popular after his death, including those posthumously published for the first time. A leading member of the Society of the Muslim Brothers, he is one of many Arab writers calling for a reconstruction of society along lines conforming to Islamic doctrines, his distinction being his powerful style and his latterly uncompromising insurgent attitude and bold frankness that led to his long incarceration and, eventually, to his trial and execution.[1]

One notices a radicalization of Quṭb's thought between the earliest of his book on this subject, *al-ᶜAdāla al-Ijtimāᶜiyya fī-l-Islām* (*Social Justice in Islam*)[2] published in Cairo in 1949, and the last before his death, *Maᶜālim fī-l-Ṭarīq* (*Milestones*)[3] published in Cairo in 1964, and passing through his thirty-volume work *Fī Ẓilāl al-Qurān* (*In the Shade of the Qur'ān*)[4] published in fascicules between 1952 and 1965, the first thirteen volumes of which he revised. His basic beliefs remain the same, but whereas in the earlier period he proposes the Islamic system of life as a better alternative to the prevailing nation-state systems or societies developing in the Arab world and elsewhere, in the later period he rejects those systems and societies, and condemns them as ungodly, un-Islamic and as part of what he begins to call the modern *jāhiliyya*.

This concept of modern *jāhiliyya* is pivotal in the understanding of Sayyid Quṭb's radical thought.[5] *Jāhiliyya*, as is well known, is the term used initially in the Qur'ān and later by Muslim historians and others to denote the pre-Islamic period prior to the divine revelation of the Qur'ān in the seventh century. In Sayyid Quṭb's writings, it ceases to be only a past, historical period of ignorance of God before Islam and becomes, in a pejorative usage, a human condition, a state of mind, a quality of society, a way of life whereby the Islamic system in any age or land is ignored and whereby human beings, even if they call themselves 'Muslims', deviate from the Islamic way prescribed by the Qur'ān and the Prophet's teachings.[6]

This usage of *jāhiliyya*, developed from the writings of Abū-l-Aᶜlā Mawdūdī (d. 1979), considers as evil many prevailing aspects of modern life, including those in the Arab world imitating Westerners or imbued with the values of the West, whether they are beliefs, customs, laws and institutions, or arts, literatures, philosophies or people's visions.[7] Apart from modern science and technology, deemed generally acceptable, most, if not all, other disciplines of intellectual pursuits, including the humanities and the social sciences, are considered in this view to be inimical to the general religious understanding of life and specifically to the Islamic world view.[8] In fact, there are only two kinds of culture in the world from this perspective: the Islamic culture and the *jāhilī* culture.[9] Between them, there is constant struggle which is basically a struggle between belief and unbelief, between faith in God and polytheism.[10]

The Western way of life condemned by Sayyid Quṭb is not only that of the secular democracies of the West, whether capitalistic or socialistic, but also that of the communist nations, which he sees as basically established on atheistic propositions and the belief in materialism and economic determinism, thus reducing human life to the pursuit of food, drink, clothing, shelter and sex.[11] All these are *jāhilī* systems, in Quṭb's opinion, because they adopt human values apart from God's guidance as prescribed in the Qur'ān and detailed in the Sharīᶜa, and because they set up a purpose for life other than that of God. *Jāhilī* systems include also those of India, Japan and other Asian polytheistic systems, as well as African ones. Christian and Jewish communities are equally *jāhilī* because of their deviation from the revealed truth by allowing the political order in their countries to arrogate to itself powers to legislate what is right and wrong, and thus to trespass on God's exclusive domain.[12] Muslims who accept a similar political order, that operates apart from God's injunctions and introduces alien elements into the Islamic system, are similarly *jāhilī*.[13] The confession of Muslim faith, *lā ilāha illā-llāh* (There is no god but God), is a declaration daily repeated by Muslims that "there is no governance except that of God, there is no legislation but that of God, there is no sovereignty of anybody over others because all sovereignty belongs to God."[14] This is the *ḥākimiyya* (governance) of God which is the only antidote against *jāhiliyya* and its evils.

Sayyid Quṭb believes unequivocally in the superiority of the Islamic system over all others and in its ability to lead humanity to happiness, prosperity, peace and justice on earth in preparation for the hereafter. He believes Islam is good for all peoples, in all places and all times. He argues that the Islamic system has room for models compatible with the needs of different modern societies and their continuous change.[15] Though Islamic law, the Sharīᶜa, is immutable as prescribed in the Qur'an and the Prophet's teachings, its interpretation by human beings through the instrumentality of *fiqh* (jurisprudence) is flexible and responsive to modern needs and problems. Reinterpretation is thus possible, provided it remains within the encompassing intentions of the Sharīᶜa, so that human excesses are prevented and foreign cultural elements excluded.[16]

In order to implement the Islamic system in a modern world considered to be *jāhilī*, Quṭb advocates the emulation of the Prophet Muḥammad by adhering to his method when he led the first Islamic community from the ignorance of God and the social order of the *Jāhiliyya* to faith in God and the social order of Islam, which was resoundingly victorious after long struggle. The core of the future believing *umma* (community) is therefore a group of committed individuals, the *jamāᶜa*, who are dedicated as a vanguard (*ṭalīᶜa*) to the realization of the Islamic society and willing to separate themselves from unbelievers.[17] This *jamāᶜa* is the Party of God (*Ḥizb Allāh*) that becomes conscious of itself as it opposes all other groups or people who do not share its belief in God.[18] It separates itself from them in an act of *hijra* (dissociation) in order to consolidate the *jamāᶜa*, inculcate the faith, and prepare for the *jihād* (struggle). Victory comes after continuous and steadfast struggle with the unbelievers and the eventual establishment of a new political order that affirms God's sovereignty and implements His prescriptions.

Sayyid Quṭb does not specify the form of the Islamic political order or the limits of its geographical expression. But in his many writings, he has described the ideal characteristics of such an order. According to him, the Islamic political order is based on two fundamental ideas deriving from universality in conceiving of the world, life and man: (1) the idea of the unity of mankind as to race, nature and origin; and (2) the idea that Islam is an eternal system for the world, meant to continue throughout the future of mankind.[19] This political order, he affirms, rests on the basis of justice (*ᶜadl*) on the part of the rulers, obedience (*ṭāᶜa*) on the part of the ruled and consultation (*shūrā*) between the rulers and the ruled.[20] Whatever its form or name, it must fully implement the Sharīᶜa. He says:

> Every political system that implements the Islamic Sharīᶜa is an Islamic political system whatever its form or name. And every political system that does not implement the Sharīᶜa is not recognized by Islam, even though it is run by a religious [Islamic] hierarchy or bears an Islamic name.[21]

Sayyid Quṭb believes the Sharīᶜa to be the ideal system by which individuals and societies all over the world can prosper and live happily. The individual is liberated through it from servility to mundane values and fears, from dependence on any deity or person, and is totally committed to God and a just society that God instituted.[22] In this society, there is human equality and there is no discrimination against any believer because of race, gender or class. Distinctions between men and women in inheritance shares and in other legal matters prescribed in the Sharīᶜa are necessary, we are told, due to the dispositions of each based on the different biological functions which nature gave each, and the corresponding duties required of each as a consequence, but by no means do they constitute a detraction from the spiritual equality of men and women or from the human rights of the person guaranteed by the Sharīᶜa.[23] In this society also, there is mutual responsibility among its members and a common duty of social solidarity (*takāful ijtimāᶜī*).

For example, between an individual and his famiy there is an obligation of mutual support, and between the individual and his society there is a bond of cooperation for the benefit of the whole and the protection and well-being of the individual.[24] Quṭb concludes:

> [Islam] gives the individual full liberty within limits which do not harm him and do not obstruct the group. It also gives the group its rights and at the same time charges it with responsibilities in return for these rights, so that life may go on a straight and even path, and reach its higher goals which the individual and the group equally serve.[25]

Without going into further details of Sayyid Quṭb's view of Islamic society, it is clear that his thought is highly idealistic. It does not recognize that although an individual knows his duty, he may not necessarily perform it—even if he is continually exhorted. Neither historical evidence nor knowledge of human behavior supports the view that an idealistic plan for a system, however elaborate and thorough, does by itself or by exhortation guarantee its implementation in real concrete terms. The proof of that is Sayyid Quṭb's thought itself, which considers the modern age to be one of *jāhiliyya*, implying that after fourteen centuries of Islam, even countries and societies whose people today call themselves Muslims are not truly Islamic.

Furthermore, it is evident that Sayyid Quṭb's thought is ahistoric, in that it does not recognize the factors of time and place in the development of Islam but rather presents it dogmatically as a monolithic and complete system from its inception. Disagreements among Muslims are therefore seen to be a result of their lack of faith or their deviation and perversity, rather than genuine human differences that are inevitably bound to appear, as they did in history even among sincere and pious Muslims, and especially in interpreting Islam as it moves through time and place. Thus, by excluding the possibility of pluralism among Muslims, let alone in a society where Muslims and non-Muslims live together, rational debate is excluded, and dogmatism is embraced—a fact which eventually leads to social fragmentation and likely violence because of difference of opinion.

The necessity for the freedom to express one's opinion has been emphasized by several modern Arab thinkers, but centuries of oppressive rule in pre-modern times and under colonial domination have left a legacy of distrust of government by the Arab people. Even among Arab intellectuals today, there is a certain reservation regarding the extent of free expression they as individuals feel they can afford before they arouse the wrath of the political authorities or the religious establishment. The increase of power that has been made available to contemporary Arab governments by their control of the mass media, the bureaucracy, the military and police forces through the mounting use of modern technology has made Arab intellectuals even more wary. Sayyid Quṭb himself—the bold, free spirit that he was—may be considered a victimized intellectual in ᶜAbd al-Nāṣir's Egypt, but his dogmatism is unfortunate and does not help to solve the problem of freedom in Arab countries. Free debate is an essential requisite of any desired progress in the Arab world or anywhere else.

The Egyptian scholar, Muḥammad al-Nuwayhī, has repeatedly argued that Arab intellectuals should rise to the leadership role that is their duty in public discourse. His condemnation of their diffidence in this respect goes as far as saying they are responsible, because of insufficient activity, for the apathy of the Arab masses to a revolution in many traditional values and concepts that need to be changed. He asserts that change in the socio-economic and political spheres, which most Arab governments are bent on, does not by itself achieve societal transformation, if it is not accompanied by a conviction that the ethical values and concepts which support the old, traditional order are also in need of change.[26] And it is the Arab intellectuals who are capable of advocating a cultural revolution in this field, but they should be ready for a long and arduous battle against the coercion of government bureaucracies, reactionary forces in society and established interests.[27]

Al-Nuwayhī believes that a revolution in religious thought is essential for any comprehensive Arab cultural revolution, as any new thought in Arab countries is always opposed on religious grounds, regardless of whether it addresses religion, ethics, politics and the system of government, or economics and the system of production and distribution of wealth, social customs and traditions, or science, philosophy, art, language and literature.[28] This is so, he believes, because of the place of religion in the life of the Arab people and their belief in its priority and inviolable perfection. An attempt is therefore needed to explain to the people the essence of religion and to introduce a radical change in their understanding of its role in society.[29] He limits himself to Islam in his writings because he knows it best, as he says, and because it is the religion of the majority in the Arab world.[30]

Al-Nuwayhī believes that Islam began as a progressive and revolutionary religion, but that it has turned, since the ages of decadence, into a tool for restricting the intellect and rigidifying society. He adduces two causes for this: (1) the rise of a class of people (the *ᶜulamā'*, *rijāl al-dīn*) who monopolizes the interpretation of religion and claim they alone have the right to speak for it and make pronouncements about what opinions and doctrines agree or disagree with it; and (2) the belief of this class that the religious sources and texts have regulations and teachings that are binding and cannot be amended or changed, whether they deal with doctrine or with matters of everyday life.[31]

Al-Nuwayhī asserts that this development is an extraneous accretion, since Islam recognizes no class of people like that of a priesthood in other religions. He admits the need for specialists in Islamic learning but he objects to their claim to infallibility, which prompts them to refuse discussion, accuse intellectual opponents of unbelief and atheism, seek to prohibit the publication of books objectionable to them, obtain government confiscation of such books if published, persecute their authors and incite the authorities and the common people against them.[32]

Furthermore, al-Nuwayhī argues that the earlier religious sources and their regulations and teachings are not immutable in any categorical and absolute manner. The claim of the *ᶜulamā'* that these sources constitute a perfect and comprehensive system which is useful without change for all people in all times and places is not accepted by al-Nuwayhī. When these men refer to the Qur'ān to support their view, he challenges their interpretation. For example, he suggests that S. 6:38, the Qur'anic passage that says, "We have neglected nothing in the Book," does not mean that God mentioned everything in the Qur'ān, as they claim, but that the Book intended in this context is the Preserved Tablet (*al-Lawḥ al-Maḥfūẓ*) which is with God from eternity and contains the Qur'ān as well as all creation and decrees for everyone and everything.[33] And when the *ᶜulamā'* refer to such passages of the Qur'ān as S. 16:89, "And We have sent down on thee the Book explaining all things," or S. 12:111, " . . . a detailed exposition of everything," or S. 5:3, "Today I have perfected your religion for you, and I have completed my blessing upon you, and I have approved Islam as your religion," al-Nuwayhī counters that the reference here is only to the principles of religious doctrine, and not also to matters of everyday life, as they claim.[34] He objects strongly to those who claim the Qur'ān is a record of all sciences and all fields of human knowledge. Recognizing the breadth, the multiplicity and the intricacies of modern science and learning, he accuses them of adopting the position of those who take leave of the human intellect and propagate social stagnation and a backward-looking, reactionary Islam.[35] Likewise, he objects strongly to those who claim the Qur'ān, the Sunna of the Prophet and the Islamic legal schools have the answers to all questions and the solutions to all problems. He declares such people to be ignorant on two counts, first because they show they know nothing about the extent and complexity of modern legal sciences, codes and systems; and secondly, because they show they have no idea about the history of Islamic law itself, which passed through many stages of growth and change, and exhibited vitality and flexibilty in its ages of ascendancy.[36]

Al-Nuwayhī points to the fact that the verses dealing with legal matters in the Qur'ān hardly exceed five hundred and that the crimes for which punishments (*ḥudūd*) are specifically prescribed in it are only five. Leaving aside discussions on differences of interpretation and on the extent of actual implementation of these laws in Islamic history, al-Nuwayhī argues that the Qur'ān does not prescribe punishments for most of the major crimes it forbids, now called felonies, let alone the misdemeanors or minor infractions of modern legal terminology. This reality shows that the majority of Islamic rules are more like ethical values than laws in the accurate sense of the word.[37]

When the Sunna of the Prophet, i.e., his sayings and deeds, are added to the Qur'ān as a source of more legal details, furthered by the practice and sayings of his Companions and their Followers and the teachings of the early Muslim jurists, al-Nuwayhī still argues that the legal system thus constructed is far from being one to answer every question and solve every problem until resurrection day, as is claimed. Rather, he turns this fact around to support his argument. If the Qur'ān contained comprehensive legislation, it would not have needed the additional prescriptions of the Sunna and its explanatory or expansive details. And if the Qur'ān and Sunna both constituted an exhaustive Islamic legislation, the Muslims would not have needed the practice and sayings of the Companions and their Followers. And if all these sources had been enough, Islam would not have needed the various legal schools, including the four main ones still prevailing, that arose to respond to the differing needs of society.[38]

Al-Nuwayhī adds that the history of Islamic law shows Muslims even adopted certain non-Muslim laws and institutions from the territories they conquered with regard to novel matters, especially those concerning the judiciary, the political and administrative systems, the army, the finances, the postal system and other legal aspects of social organization.[39]

Al-Nuwayhī admits that Islam, unlike some other religions, is not only concerned with the spiritual salvation of man in the hereafter, but also with life in this world, in which it wants human beings to have happiness, prosperity, justice, equality and dignity. God could have legislated every necessary detail for that but wisely refrained in order to dignify man with the use of his intellect and freedom. Thus, in addition to the principles of religious doctrine and the rituals of worship, Islam has provided two things: (1) it set up the sublime ethical ideals that Muslims should strive to achieve but it left them free to choose the means to these ideals in accordance with their changing needs and circumstances; and (2) through Qur'ān and Sunna, it provided the Muslims during the lifetime of the Prophet with a *minimum* of civil legislation which they urgently needed at the time, on account of the sudden and staggering change occasioned by the rise of Islam.[40]

Al-Nuwahī emphasizes that this legislation was only a minimum and that the Prophet was often reluctant to give further legislation, even when asked, lest it fetter Muslims in later times.[41] He also emphasizes that in matters of daily life, the Prophet accepted the suggestions or even the corrections of his Companions. The well-known *ḥadīth* regarding the Prophet's objection to the manual pollination of palm trees (*abr al-nakhl*) is quoted by al-Nuwayhī to show that the Prophet corrected himself, when the following year's crop of dates was bad because the palms had been left to natural pollination on his advice, and he said, "I am only a human being. When I order you in a matter of religion adhere to it, but when I order you in a matter of personal opinion, I am only a human being" or, in another version, he said, "You are more knowledgeable [than I am] about matters of your world."[42] Al-Nuwayhī argues that modern Muslims are also more knowledgeable about matters of their modern world and that they have the right, even the duty, to legislate for it in order to complement the rules of the Qurān, provided they remain bound by its sublime moral aims and ethical ideals.[43]

Al-Nuwayhī goes a step further and invokes the action of ᶜUmar ibn al-Khaṭṭāb (d. 644), who clearly stopped applying certain injunctions of the Qur'ān because the circumstances of his day were different from those of the Prophet (d. 632). The two examples he invokes are ᶜUmar's cessation of punishing theft, temporarily contravening S. 5:38 during the year of famine, and his stopping of the payment of a portion of the *zakāt* to "those whose hearts have been reconciled" to Islam (*al-mu'allafati qulūbuhum*), as stipulated in S. 9:60. Al-Nuwayhī extols this as an act of courage and wisdom on the part of ᶜUmar and refuses to justify it on any other ground but ᶜUmar's correct understanding of the spirit of Islam and his living logic which evolved in accordance with developing circumstances.[44] Basing his view on Muḥammad ᶜAbduh's distinction between *uṣūl* (roots) and *furūᶜ* (branches) in religion, the former being matters relating to doctrine, worship rituals and ethics and the latter matters relating to human transactions and social relations, al-Nuwayhī agrees with ᶜAbduh and his followers of *al-Manār* school that *uṣūl* may not be changed but that *furūᶜ* may be, in accordance with the needs of changing circumstances.[45] The classical legal principle of *maṣlaḥa* (public interest) of the community is also adduced in support of this stance.[46] Not satisfied with generalities, al-Nuwayhī takes up, as an example, the question regarding the woman's legal share of inheritance which, according to the Qur'ān (S. 4:11 ff), is half that of the man. He notes that it is not a matter relating to doctrine or worship but rather to everyday life and social organization. He also notes that the circumstances that necessitated this inequality in the past, by placing additional requirements and obligations on the man, do not obtain in modern times. He therefore calls for a change in the implementation of the Qur'anic prescription after proper studies of the situation,[47] a change that may very well amount to ignoring the injunction of the sacred text in this regard.

This is a very courageous call. Radical as it is, it is in line with al-Nuwayhī's argument from the data of Islamic history he selected, and with his own understanding of the essence of religion and the modern Arab need for change in this matter. He recognizes that Islam has a societal component, relating to the organization of the world, in addition to its spiritual component relating to salvation or perdition in the next. He does not want to secularize this world, for he still wants it to be inspired by the sublime ethics of Islam, and to remain mindful of its doctrines of faith and its worship rituals. But in his new understanding of Islam based on a creative interpretation of Islamic history and religious texts, he disallows the claim that Islam has a comprehensive and final system organizing all the worldly affairs of humanity, and he encourages Muslims to seek their own solutions to modern problems and their own answers to modern questions without the need for authentication from past tradition, but in the abiding spirit of Islamic ethics, even if there may arise occasions when it is necessary to discontinue the implementation of certain Qur'anic prescriptions.

Another Arab thinker who envisages the possibility of discontinuing certain Qur'anic prescriptions if the need arises is the Lebanese scholar Ḥasan Ṣaᶜb. In his book *al-Islām Tujāh Taḥaddiyāt al-Ḥayā al-ᶜAṣriyya* (Islam Facing the Challenges of Modern Life) he says:

> Nobody can make us abandon our intellect in understanding the Qur'ān in a new way in light of our unprecedented new conditions. If we see a need to stop the implementation (*waqf al-ᶜamal*) of any one of its [the Qur'ān's] texts, God has given us this right. For He wants His words to be the source of our action and not our inaction, a cause of our success and not our destruction.[48]

Ḥasan Ṣaᶜb does not argue for this position from historical precedent, as al-Nuwayhī does, but from a theological viewpoint that takes seriously the Qur'anic concept of man as a vicegerent (*khalīfa*) of God on earth (S. 2:30, for example) and as a free being capable of arriving at the Truth under God by his own reason and senses (S. 13:1–4, for example). As a result, he conceives of Islam as a ceaseless becoming, as a permanent dynamism, as a continuous intellectual revolutionism, the ideological framework of whose civilization can always be creatively renovated with the help of creative minds. Whereas modern Western civilization, for him, is in essence mainly rational and scientific, Islam is metaphysical and its civilization mainly religious—a fact which, he says, is at the origin of the challenges of modern life that Islam is experiencing. Only creative minds can allow Islam to rise to those challenges, but they must act freely to rediscover the true spirit and essence of Islam in order to build a new Islamic civilization.[49]

The aim of Islam through Qur'anic revelation and the Muḥammadan message is, Ṣaᶜb affirms, to awaken the consciousness of man in all its ontological and teleological dimensions. He says, "After God, man is the goal of the existence of all that is; and together with God, man is the acme of the movement of all that will be."[50] This view of man presupposes the limitless ability of man for perfection, to be achieved with the help of revelation, i.e., through dialogue with God Who is Himself Absolute Perfection.[51] Belief in this ability is the basis of all religious, civilizational, economic or social rebirth according to Ṣa^{c}b.

In this perspective, Muslim man is a creating man because he takes on the moral qualities of God. He creates in freedom, love, justice and mercy. His dignity lies in righteous action which makes use of nature, redeems history and orients its movement to its divine goal.[52]

Ḥasan Ṣa^{c}b emphasizes the importance of human action as an Islamic value. But he says it is only a means, not an end. Like God's action, human action in the correct Islamic understanding is creative and good, and its end is to transcend human necessity in order to achieve perfection in freedom. The correct Islamic view of social, political and economic issues in any age is consequently a futuristic, progressive view and not a past-oriented, reactionary one. It differs from that of others because it is not worldly, racial, national, class-biased or materialist but rather universalist, humane and spiritual. In Ṣa^{c}b's view of Islam, man makes history and is the goal of history and of all economic, social and political effort. After the Prophet's death, many Muslims misunderstood this reality and confused means with ends. Ṣa^{c}b says that man must now return to God by freeing himself from all the institutions that this misunderstanding has brought about; he must create new social, political and economic institutions that free him. With the guidance of God's liberating revelation, with the perspicacity of the intellect God bestowed on him, with the energy of the creative will God gave him, and with the power of the mastery over nature God granted him, the Muslim should face the social, political and economic problems of this age in a creative, Islamic way. This is his human responsibility, and to bear it is to bear the Trust, the *Amāna* (S. 33:72), which God offered man and which man accepted.[53]

Ṣa^{c}b thus sees the Muslims being called upon in modern times to build a new Islamic civilization which is as near as possible to their ideal City of God. The wisdom of Muslim ancestors and the lessons learnt from their historical experience should be taken into consideration, but other human non-Muslim experiences should be permitted to enhance their efforts. A spiritual, democratic structure should result, in which there is no distinction between Muslim and non-Muslim, between a man and a woman, because God does not make such distinctions. The command of God in Islam is that there be love, mercy, charity, justice, brotherhood and freedom. He does not command that Islam be declared state religion. Virtue should govern and man's action should be what gives him value. This is the truth of Islam as Ṣa^{c}b sees it. But he is aware that there is a deep chasm between the ideal truth of Islam and its concrete reality. "The Islamic truth is mercy, freedom and justice; but the Islamic reality is tyranny, servitude and injustice. The Islamic truth is liberation, civilization and progress; but the Islamic reality is reification, fragmentation and backwardness."[54] He attributes this to the fact that God commands but it is man's responsibility to act:

> All human progress is due to God's command and man's responsibility. [Progress], therefore, belongs to us as it does to all human beings. Our first responsibility today is to make what is ours potentially—belong to us actually.[55]

As a social scientist, Ḥasan Ṣa^{c}b is aware of the grave societal problems of the Arab world that delay and, in some cases, obstruct progress. But he firmly believes in the priority of spiritual and moral regeneration as the spark of any action leading to social, economic and political progress and the building of a new Islamic civilization. Nothing for him is more necessary than modernizing the Arab mind itself. A comprehensive cultural revolution is needed in order to move the very soul of the Arabs and their whole being in a new creative way.

He formulated this message succinctly in his book *Taḥdīth al-^{c}Aql al-^{c}Arabī: Dirāsāt ḥawl al-Thawra al-Thaqāfiyya al-Lāzima li-l-Taqaddum al-^{c}Arabī fī-l-^{c}Aṣr al-Ḥadīth*[56] (Modernization of the Arab Mind: Studies on the Cultural Revolution Necessary for Arab Progress in the Modern Age). Recognizing "the organic, dynamic relation between thought and life, between concept and behavior,"[57] he sets out to analyze the underdevelopment, the contradictions and the incoherence in Arab society caused by the modernization of certain aspects of Arab life and behavior before modernizing Arab culture and thought which, in his view, must be given priority. He generally subscribes to the postulates of modernization theory, yet he does not want to restrict development to a narrow economic meaning, but rather wants to place it in a wider civilizational context of cultural and structural progress. Modernization, for him, is a necessary stage in the growth of the human personality and of its mastery over nature and the self through science and technology. For it is this growth of the human personality to its full potentials in free, creative and happy contact with others that is the goal of civilization, modernization, development and progress.[58]

Ḥasan Ṣaᶜb discusses several requisites for the modernization of the Arab mind that should lead to the growth of the Arab personality. Among these are the following: (1) a methodological reorientation to life aiming at the making of things rather than of words, implying a determined and concerted effort at development based on rationality and on the application of modern science and technology in the use of material resources;[59] (2) a change of the Arab leadership's vision and the adoption of a comprehensive modernization strategy or, if need be, a democratic replacement of the leadership itself by a committed elite aware of its historic message of pioneering all-round development and directing the modernization process;[60] (3) a structural change of Arab institutions, and primarily the political institutions, to embody the dynamic and innovative needs of modernization;[61] (4) the modernization of Arab education and the preparation of the basic human elements that will build up the new Arab-Islamic civilization and sustain it in future generations by transforming the contemporary Arab from an imitating being to an innovative being;[62] (5) the modernization of the Arab media of communications, and the establishment of an information policy that aims at educating and mobilizing the public in all matters relating to the process of development.[63]

All these requisites are, in Ṣaᶜb's view, interrelated and complementary. But the requisite which underlies them all and is indispensable for the modernization of the Arab mind is the modernization of the Arab value system.[64] He affirms that cultural values are strongly related to religion, to the point where they are often indistinguishable. Any discussion of their relation to development and modernization is therefore bound to discuss religious renewal. In the case of Islam, which is the basis of the Arab cultural value system, there is need for a new understanding of the Qur'ān in a methodical manner that leads to new *ijtihād*.

Ṣaᶜb believes that the divine word of the Qur'ān created a new message, a new law, a new community and a new civilization. It was the rallying focal point of all the historical, geographical, social, economic and political factors combining to bring about the rise of Islam in the seventh century. Therefore, Islam cannot be understood apart from the unique power that moved it, namely, the power of the creative divine word, for so long as this word continued to be creatively effective in the human soul and in human society and history, Islam continued to grow and expand and make progress. The most wonderful aspect of the miraculous character of this word, in Ṣaᶜb's view, is that it is a divine command for constant dynamism. As "the Book of Dynamism," the Qur'ān, for Ṣaᶜb, is the wondrous image of the dynamism of divine creativity, and its command for dynamism is the only thing that does not change. Everything else is in constant motion and continuous change.[65]

The dynamism of divine creativity is transferable to humans, since God breathed into man of His Spirit, made him His vicegerent (*khalīfa*) on earth and gave him the Trust (*Amāna*) of creativity. As a result, the divine word is not only dynamic and creative but also liberating: belief in God is not absolute slavery to Him, as is incorrectly believed, but it is rather absolute freedom in Him. Ḥasan Ṣaᶜb understands this freedom in God, not as Muslim mystics have done, because in their understanding it remains individual and aims at personal self-renewal and self-creativeness. He understands it rather as a commitment to God to be duty-bound with Him in the constant creation of everything, since, as Muḥammad had said, man should put on the qualities of God and, like Muḥammad in the episode of the *Miᶜrāj* (Ascension to Heaven), man should not be satisfied with only the vision of God, but should also fashion anew everything on earth in its light,[66] as the Prophet did after the *Miʿrāj*.

Ṣaʿb believes that this new understanding of the Qur'ān and of the truth of Islam will engender a stronger and deeper renewal in Islamic thought and life than there has ever been before, because it will be the basis for endless dialogue between God and man, between man and man and between man and nature. Ṣaʿb contends that the prevailing Muslim belief in Islam as an unchanging law that regulates all thought and life is wrong,[67] for Islam in his view offers itself as a method of continuous renewal, creative adaptability, dynamic interaction and dialogue. This is most evident in the Islamic concept of *ijtihād*, which was practiced even in the lifetime of the Prophet, and later by his Companions and their Followers, and later still by a growing number of Muslim jurists. *Ijtihād* should not be understood merely as a jurisprudential process of deriving new legal prescriptions by reasoning; for, Ṣaʿb believes, it is much wider and deeper than that and is related to the spirit of Islam and its adaptability to changing human conditions and needs, proceeding, as it does, from the creative dynamism of the divine Qur'anic word.

Ṣaʿb recognizes the existence of different juristic opinions on *ijtihād*, some of which limit its practice and others which permit it in all matters except religious doctrines and rituals prescribed in the Qur'ān. But he subscribes to its absolute necessity for Islamic renewal, and he believes every Muslim has a right—even a duty—to exercise *ijtihād* if he has the scholarly qualifications to do so.[68] He even says that every Muslim is called upon to qualify himself for *ijtihād* by learning and righteousness. In his opinion, *ijtihād* should remain the means of the Muslim community to retain the creative dynamism of Qur'anic revelation. As for the manner in which this *ijtihād* is to be socially organized and whether it should be exercised by individual scholars, learned councils or representative bodies, that is up to the Muslim community to decide by consensus or majority vote. Likewise, the Muslim community is free to decide on the kind of needed political rule agreeing with its customs and interests, and on all legislation regarding public and private law, all of which can be changed to accommodate changing conditions and needs.[69]

There is a great affinity between Ḥasan Ṣaᶜb's interpretation of Islam and the views of Muḥammad ᶜAbduh (d. 1905) and Muḥammad Iqbal (d. 1938) whose works he often cites, but he also draws upon the opinions of such disciples of Ibn Taymiyya (d. 1328) as Ibn Qayyim al-Jawziyya (d. 1350) and Najm al-Dīn al-Ṭūfī (d. 1316) with regard to the scope of *ijtihād*, as well as upon the opinions of Ibn Ḥazm (d. 1064) with regard to the principle that *ijtihād* is a duty of the commoner and the scholar, each practicing it according to his ability.[70]

There is no doubt that Ṣaᶜb has been able to emphasize liberalizing and liberating elements in Arab culture that should be revived, strengthened and developed in the modernization efforts of contemporary Arabs, but there is no doubt also of his commitment to the view that contemporary Arabs should develop a new outlook on life and acquire modern science and technology as a basis for development. His major contribution is that he cogently presents Islam as a belief system endowed with permanent dynamism through the Qur'ān and with intellectual creativity through *ijtihād*, and he presents man as God's instrument on earth to continue this dynamism and this creativity in freedom, love and justice.

There are several other Arab thinkers who, like Ṣaᶜb, point to what they believe to be prevailing misconceptions which Muslims have unadvisedly perpetuated as the truth of Islam and which, in their view, should be corrected in the contemporary renewal movement. One such thinker is Muḥammad ᶜAmara of Egypt who has devoted most of his intellectual activities to the study of modern Islamic reform efforts and the assessment of their historical moorings in what he considers to be the correct and authentic interpretation of the Qur'ān and the Prophet's teachings. In one of his works, *al-Islām wa-l-Sulṭa al-Dīniyya*[71] (Islam and Relgious Authority), he squarely faces the sensitive issue of religious authority in Islam and its relation to the political order.

ᶜAmāra disagrees with the increasingly vociferous individuals, groups, parties and organizations who claim to speak for Islam and who call for the establishment of an Islamic state. He does not mention by name any one of those in the Arab world, since it appears he does not want to antagonize them but rather to win them over. He actually invites them to permit enlightened

Islamic reason to judge objectively according to the data of the Islamic heritage itself and the lessons of Islamic history regarding this matter.[72] Yet he quotes the Pakistani thinker Abū-l-Aᶜlā Mawdūdī (d. 1979) and strongly criticizes the concept of *ḥākimiyya* (governance) of God which Mawdūdī's writings have helped to propagate in the Arab world through translations and Sayyid Quṭb's elaborations.[73] ᶜAmāra is thus indirectly criticizing Sayyid Quṭb and the several radical and militant offshoots of the Muslim Brothers who have taken him as their mentor.

ᶜAmara says that, apart from the Shīᶜa, all trends in Islamic thought hold that no individual or body of individuals has the right to issue prescriptions claiming them to be divine. He asserts that no human being has religious authority to claim he speaks in the name of God and has the right of uniquely knowing and interpreting the opinion of Heaven, be that in matters of religion or of worldly affairs. This is the case, he affirms, whether the person making such claim occupies a religious post or holds political office, and it is equally the case whether the claim is made by one individual or by an intellectual or political organization.[74] ᶜAmāra argues that accepting the religious authority of an individual or an organization implies accepting their putative infallibility—a quality which, he says, Islam denies all human beings with the exception of Prophet Muḥammad who, even then, was infallible only in the religious aspect of his call.[75]

To emphasize the latter point, ᶜAmāra refers to the *ḥadīth* on the manual pollination of palm trees (*abr al-nakhl*) in which Prophet Muḥammad concludes that he is merely a human being, i.e., that he is subject to error and correction in matters relating to this world (regarding which others may be more knowledgeable), but that Muslims should adhere to his teachings in matters of religion.[76] ᶜAmāra sees here a distinction which Islam makes between religion on the one hand and politics and worldly affairs on the other. He refuses to qualify this distinction as a separation of religion from worldly affairs. It is a distinction (*tamyīz*) of spheres, he says, not a separation (*faṣl*).[77]

Furthermore, he notes how the early Companions of the Prophet almost purposely insisted on denying the nascent Caliphate to the Prophet's heirs, at least initially, in order to keep it as a political post clearly distinct from the Prophet's religious authority in people's minds. He also notes how Abū Bakr, the first Caliph, considerd the post to be devoid of the infallible divine revelation given to the Prophet and admitted he might err in performing his caliphal duties and thus pleaded for correction when in error.[78] Other Companions and later leaders of Islamic thought practiced *ijtihād* but none claimed the holiness of religious authority (i.e., infallibility) for his opinion.[79]

ᶜAmāra concludes that the Islamic position in this matter crystallizes two principles:

First, that Muslims accept in faith the religion divinely revealed in the Qur'ān and seek the help of the Sunna (the Prophet's praxis) in order to understand it, always guided by rationality in interpreting a sacred text and reconciling—without forcibleness—any apparent disagreement in it with reason, and always assured that the Sunna is free from fabrication and corruption so long as its content is in agreement with the Qur'ān.

Second, that in politics and other matters relating to this world not dealt with in the Qur'ān by a text and in detail, Muslims adjudicate personal opinion and *ijtihād*, their criterion being the public interest of the community and the avoidance of any possible harm to it, but always mindful of the general ethical ideals and universal principles laid down in the Qur'ān.[80]

After a survey of historical instances, ᶜAmāra expresses his belief that Islam, far from being a theocracy, affirms the lay (*madanī*) character of political authority and emphasizes its human quality insofar as assuming it depends on consultation (*shūrā*) with other humans, on selection and public acceptance by humans and on the fact that the ruler is responsible to a community of humans.[81] Yet Islam, in his opinion, does not call for separation between religion and the world because it does take a definite position regarding certain matters of the world and establishes a number of universal principles and general divine commendations for social life as high ideals to be pursued.[82] Separation between state and religion is unthinkable and impractical, according to ᶜAmāra, since religion is never realized in a vacuum but in human thought and behavior like all other human intellectual constructs with which it has to coexist. Hence it is more correct to say that Islam rejects the idea that the temporal and the religious authorities should be unified and endorses the idea that they should co-exist. Islam distinguishes between them but does not separate them.[83]

ᶜAmāra argues that it is an intellectual error to exclude religion as one of the factors influencing society, if this exclusion were possible at all. He affirms, on the other hand, that giving a religious character to politics and the system of government is an attempt totally alien to the spirit of Islam.[84] For Islam, in his view, distinguishes between the community of religion and the community of politics, the former being made up of Muslim believers, the latter of citizens of various faiths, as is clear from the example of the Constitution of Medina drawn up by Prophet Muḥammad himself in which the Muslim believers were referred to as one *umma*, and the Jews of the tribe of Banū ᶜAwf and other Jews in Medina were included in it as *umma* along with the believers.[85]

ᶜAmāra gives examples from what he called "a dark page in the history of Muslims"[86] in which he cites caliphs from various historical periods (and governors acting on their behalf) who arrogated to themselves religious authority and presumed to rule by divine right, imposing doctrines and eliminating opponents by brute force. He explains the genesis and development of the Shīᶜa as a protest movement against such human injustice and as a call for the establishment of divine justice through the rule of the God-chosen infallible *imām* descended from the Prophet. According to ᶜAmāra, Shīᶜī Islam eventually ended up—like Sunnī Islam—in excluding the people and the community of believers from political power of which they ought in fact to be the source and the basis.[87] He argues, with Muḥammad ᶜAbduh (d. 1905), that no person in Islam has religious authority over others, nor has anyone the right to impose doctrines or prescribe religious rulings, not even a caliph, a *qāḍī*, a *muftī* or a *Shayk al-Islām*. The authority that anyone of those has is a lay authority circumscribed by Islamic law.[88] It is basically an authority to advise and guide and call to what is good, but never to coerce. Yet this is also the duty of every commoner in Islam.[89]

As for political authority, it rests with the people. Islam has not laid down a specific political order for Muslims because the logic of its being good for all times and places requires that this be left to the people to formulate and to change in accordance with the evolution of the human mind and the interest of the community, within the framework of the general commendations and universal principles of Islam,[90] and in the light of the experience of other civilizations.[91] ᶜAmāra concludes that those who claim that Islamic revelation comprises a political, social, economic and administrative order for Muslim societies, and that humans have nothing but to implement it without recourse to human will are, whether they intend it or not, putting the creativity of the human mind out of action and giving up an important distinguishing feature of Islam.[92] Furthermore, those who, contrary to the teachings of Islam, call for the unification of the temporal and the religious authorities are, for him, merely resorting to an age-old ambition of all despotic, tyrannical authorities to disguise their despotism and their tyranny by clothing them in a religious wrapping in order to use religion as a weapon against the people who seek their right, nay their duty, to keep their rulers accountable, and against the people who want to practice their rights to legislate and remain the source of all power and all authority.[93]

Thus, ᶜAmāra's professed aim is to enlighten Muslims and expose a prevailing misconception perpetuated by what he considers to be erroneous human interpretation of scripture as well as willful, manipulative designs of rulers. Another such misconception is the treatment of non-Muslims in a Muslim society which ᶜAmāra touched upon lightly here, and which he dealt with frankly and in detail in another book entitled *al-Islām wa-l-Waḥda al-Qawmiyya* (Islam and National Unity), [94] the first printing of which (11,000 copies) was sold out in ten days.[95] The book appeared in Cairo in 1979 at the height of communal tensions between Muslims and Copts in Egypt during Sādāt's presidency and was alternately praised and condemned. Its aim was to show that Islam—as correctly understood from the Qur'ān and the Prophet's teachings—was tolerant of Christians and other non-Muslim believers, that discrimination against Christians and others was unjustly and wrongly instituted by the Muslim state in certain periods of Islamic history for mundane and unfair purposes, that Christians and others rightly rebelled against such discrimination several times in history but that they were on the whole loyal citizens, many of whom gave distinguished services to the Muslim state and remarkable contributions to Islamic civilization. He stressed that religious pluralism which is accepted in the Qur'ān (S. 11:118; S. 16:93; S. 42:8) is a fact that will remain with mankind challenging Muslims and other believers to compete for righteousness and good deeds (S. 2:148; S. 5:48) and to co-operate with one another in brotherhood within the framework of national unity.

The ideological commitment of cAmāra to Egyptian (and pan-Arab) national unity and to the concept of the equality of all citizens may have given direction to his thought. But his interpretation of relevant Qur'anic texts and selected historical facts to support his position is plausible, if untraditional. His basic belief is that God-given religion is one in essence and that religions differ only in rituals.[96] Hence, his conviction that members of all religious communities should be equal.

For his part, the Algerian scholar Muḥammad Arkūn (Mohammed Arkoun), of the Institute of Arab and Islamic Studies at the Sorbonne (Paris III), has been calling for a totally new approach in his extensive writings in French and their latterly increasing Arabic translations.[97] While he generally appreciates the contributions of Orientalists to the study of Arab and Islamic culture and history, he believes they are limited by their philological method and their historicism grounded in nineteenth-century positivism. The social sciences and the humanities have undergone tremendous development and innovative change since the 1950s which, in his opinion, most Orientalists have not caught up with. Similarly many Arab thinkers, in his opinion, are behind the current Western approaches, either lingering in historicist writings or in traditionalist and apologetic ones, locked up as most of them are in ideological debates.

Unlike the Moroccan scholar, cAbd Allāh al-cArwī, who considers historicism (*al-tārīkhāniyya*) to be a necessary stage for contemporary Arab thought to pass through so that it may transcend traditionalism,[98] Muḥammad Arkūn believes Arab thought should rather directly and immediately embark on the stage of historicity (*al-tārīkhiyya*) in order to liberate itself and historical study as much as possible from ideological influences of all sorts.[99] By understanding the historicity of human existence and by applying the latest multidisciplinary methodologies of the historical sciences, sociology, anthropology, psychology, linguistics and semiotics to the study of Arab-Islamic history and culture, contemporary Arabs would not only achieve a clear comprehension of their past and present in order to orient themselves successfully to the future, but would also be contributing to these modern sciences themselves, correcting and advancing them by testing their validity. This is what Arkūn professes to be doing.[100]

The basic thrust of his writings is the deconstruction of the prevalent conceptions of Arab-Islamic history and culture as anything but the product of human action in time and space. His analytical method aims at going behind these conceptions to expose their reality as mere constructs of the human mind reacting to specific conditions in a specific period and a specific place. His writings attempt in various treatments to show the epistemological underpinnings of human thought itself, the purpose being to exhibit its limits and nature as grounded in a particular language and a particular historical social environment. Arkūn's ultimate goal is certainly not a solipsistic attitude to knowledge but an emphasis on the historicity of any knowledge. Applied to Islam this emphasis aims at a process of demythologization, which many Muslims find to be very disturbing because it appears to be undermining the foundations of their faith. Arkūn, however, believes it allows Muslims a real understanding of their culture as a product of previous generations and thus encourages them to contribute to it and change it to respond to modern needs as their ancestors had done in their time.

Using epistemological analysis, especially as developed by Michel Foucault regarding knowledge and power, Arkūn believes that in Islam it is urgent to show how manifestations of meaning have been transformed into ideological categories and ranked according to the choice of dominant class, the imperatives of historical conditions or the weight of a stereotyped tradition.[101] It is therefore necessary in the modern age to unveil the disguise mechanisms of the traditional culture and unmask the real truth, as opposed to purely psychological truth.[102] Arkūn's aim is to establish methods of scientific thought in the study of Islam as manifested in history. His intellectual openness to the new methodologies of the social sciences and the humanities is not, he assures us, a precipitate adoption of "fashionable" ways but rather an attempt to give an example of what today's *ijtihād* should be that would be faithful to the spiritual and intellectual tension of the great thinkers of classical Islam, yet one that would also establish a rational and intelligent break with the logical procedures, the epistemological postulates and the conceptual apparatus of those same thinkers.[103] This is imperative today because contemporary Islamic thought is going through unprecedented, new historical change the like of which it never witnessed in the ages of early *ijtihād*. And since every age has its own difficulties and problems, as well as its concomitant methods and intellectual attitudes to suit them, Islamic thought today is obliged to rethink and to write on questions of *ijtihād* and all that is related to criticism of knowledge and its foundations.[104] Arkūn believes that the corpus of traditional Islamic knowledge that has reached present-day Muslims has been built on foundations of a cognitive system which was gradually developed in response to the socio-economic and political conditions of the early centuries of Islam. The persistence of this cognitive system, in his view, is not due to its exceptional epistemological validity or its incomparable ontological moorings, as religious reasoning would have people believe, but rather because of the continuity of the socio-economic and political conditions that have governed the exercise of thought in Arab-Islamic society.[105] This cognitive system has been able to lay down the parameters of what is thinkable (*le pensable*) and to forge the mental tools and linguistic mechanisms to express it clearly. Arkūn defines the thinkable as follows:

> The thinkable of a linguistic community in a given period is what is possible to think of and render explicit with the aid of the available mental equipment.[106]

What is unthinkable (*l'impensable*), therefore, is what is not possible to think of and render explicit in the same period and in the same socio-cultural area: either because of the limitations of the cognitive system and current modes of intelligibility, or because of ideological constraints that are risky to break out of unless one is ready to pay the price, or because the intensity of thought reaches regions of the ineffable or the unfathomable opaqueness of being, as in poetic or prophetic discourse.[107] Examples of unthinkable areas of Arab-Islamic thought given by Arkūn include the critical study of (a) the Qur'ān after it had been canonized by ᶜUthmān, (b) the received Ḥadīth collections of al-Bukhārī and Muslim and (c) the Sharīᶜa after al-Shāfiᶜī laid down the principles of Islamic jurisprudence.[108] Arkūn adds, however, that what is unthinkable at a certain time or in certain circumstances may become thinkable when ideological constraints are lifted and scientific conditions of free research are realized, *ijtihād* thus becoming possible, as in modern times; but he believes that, in Arab society today, political will and deep-rooted beliefs of the masses still obstruct free thought.[109] One area of the unthinkable is what Arkūn calls the unthought-of (*l'impensé*)[110] which is a wide and important area modern thinkers should explore, now that they have new methodological and conceptual approaches to reach new horizons in the understanding of Arab-Islamic culture and history.

Arkūn aims at a twofold objective: (1) to enrich the history of thought by highlighting what is at stake cognitively, intellectually and ideologically in the tensions among the many schools of thought; and (2) to dynamize contemporary Islamic thought by drawing attention to the problems it has repressed, the taboos it has set up, the limits it has drawn and the horizons it has ceased to look at or forbidden to view—all, in the name of what it has progressively imposed as the only truth.[111]

Arkūn's attempts at what he considers to be the dynamizing of contemporary Islamic thought has appeared to many traditional Muslims as the dynamiting of Islam itself. He is himself aware of this danger of being misunderstood and tries to warn against it in his writings.[112] He believes, however, that the objective truth is that those who most vehemently reject Western culture (and his own approach) are usually those who know nothing about the progress of scientific knowledge and the modern achievements of the social sciences and the humanities since 1950 and the real conditions in which they have been achieved.[113] He notes, for example, how he has been condemned by those who read the Arabic translation of his French description of the Qur'ān as a discourse of mythical structure.[114] He says that concepts like "discourse," "myth" and "structure" have not yet been thought of properly in contemporary Arab thought, and that discussion with his opponents on such matters leads to no good results if they cling to traditional philology, narrative linear history and the Qur'anic use of the concept of *usṭūra*[115] (myth, as untrue legend) whereas he understands myth in the anthropological sense as a symbolic story that reveals an inspiring truth which is a live force within a culture or subculture.

And yet he had to respond to his detractors in the 1984 Cairo symposium convened by the Center for Arab Unity Studies where a paper of his on "The Heritage: Its Content and Identity, Its Positive and Negative Characteristics"[116] was read on his behalf in his absence. His written response[117] decries the obligation which a Muslim Arab has always to resort to, wasting valuable time in order to proclaim his true faith and his respect for the current ideological postulates underlying Muslim people's perception of historical, social, psychological and cultural reality, if he is not to be considered as a renegade or an unbeliever by them. Arkūn declares historicity to be still in the realm of the unthought-of (*l'impensé*), even among many Arab scholars, and he urges them to keep abreast of the latest developments in contemporary knowledge if they are not to fall into tragic misunderstandings. He also urges them to study the Qur'ān in the light of the new methodologies developed recently in the disciplines of history, linguistics, sociology, anthropology and others as a basic initial step or point of departure for a new, critical understanding of the Arab-Islamic heritage and the Arab-Islamic past as a whole.

He recognizes that, because Arabs today are fighting Western imperialism and Zionism, they need a combatting ideology which they readily find in their old Islamic religious and cultural heritage. But he believes that this combatting ideology uses the Islamic heritage as a motive for political mobilization of the Arabs against Western imperialism and Zionism more than for effective scientific research that would unveil the present-day bearing of Arab-Islamic culture and values which, unmasked, would be shown to be related to a medieval mentality no more functional in modern times.[118] Arkūn also recognizes the fact that this ideology is endorsed emotionally by the rapidly multiplying Arab masses, particularly in the ever-growing urban centers now becoming increasingly crowded, as much by natural growth as by continuous flow of migrants from rural areas. Urbanization in Arab society, as in all the world, continues to move ahead to the detriment of agricultural sectors. Though not as fierce as in other parts of the world, this Arab demographic movement is causing socio-cultural dislocations whose psychological effects are reflected among Muslims in the recrudescence of fundamentalist attitudes which function as sure, proven ground for identity and struggle for rights in the uncertainties of a changing society.[119] Rather than allow himself to be submerged in this surge, the scholar—according to Arkūn—should use the analytical tools provided by the most recent achievements of the social sciences and the humanities to study the situation and make it understood by the people so that it may be transcended, and a better future may be ushered in.

Arkūn has certainly established himself as one of the few scholars with deep insight into the conditions of contemporary Arab-Islamic culture, based as he is in a sound understanding of the Arab-Islamic heritage and history and a firm knowledge of the latest developments in the social sciences and the humanities. His writings are generally respected in scholarly circles in the Arab world and in the West, in spite of the exasperation of some scholars[120] with the lack of progress in the application to Arab-Islamic studies of the methodologies he advocates. One would like to see Arkūn devote more of his daring writings to the further application of those methodologies to substantive problems in Arab-Islamic studies and explore more areas of what he calls *l'impensé*, the unthought-of, in Arab-Islamic culture and history as he has eminently done, for example, in works on Miskawayh, al-Tawḥīdī and many others.[121] But Arkūn may well be justified in emphasizing method, for method is still one of the major problems in Arab-Islamic studies, the solution of which is the gate to new knowledge. The entrenched philologist-historicist approach has to be transcended, as well as the established traditional apologetic one, before new knowledge can begin to make headway. But new knowledge means new power, and those in positions of power at present continue understandably to resist change, hence Arkūn's persistent resort to continual, sometimes repetitious, elaboration of the methodologies which, he believes, will introduce change.

In the meantime, he continues to apply his methodologies wherever possible to produce intrepid and thought-provoking conclusions, and a growing number of younger Arab scholars are beginning to be inspired by his writings.

Chapter Four

Dependency and Cultural Liberation

Although legally independent, the Arab countries are acutely aware that they are dependent on forces outside the Arab world for many aspects of their national life. The international order emerging especially after the Second World War aligned clusters of countries in a dependency relationship with either U.S.A. or U.S.S.R. The Bandung Conference of 1955 attempted a bold idea when it created the movement of non-aligned nations and achieved some successes. However, the reality remained starkly clear that the two superpowers had a dominating influence in large spheres of international relations. Despite ideals set forth by the United Nations charter, military might and economic strength were undeniable factors in international politics and diplomacy in which U.S.A. and U.S.S.R. enjoyed the lion's share. The emergence of China has not yet introduced a significant change in the world order, and it may well be some time before any major change happens in this regard.

Arab thinkers who have given attention to this situation have viewed it from various angles. There are those who invoke Islam as a potential power that can stand up to both the capitalist system led by U.S.A. and the communist system led by U.S.S.R. They do not speak of Islam as a religion only, but as a culture and a civilization endowed with social, economic, political and legal institutions that insure prosperity, peace and justice for all. The Islamic system is destined, in their view, to eliminate all others in the world if Muslims only implement it properly and are united in their endeavors. There are other Arab thinkers who believe this to be an unrealistic, even naïve vision of things and who advocate a practical approach that recognizes the possibility of being aligned with one or the other of the two superpowers. They are no less zealous for Arab independence or for Arab identity, but they accept given international conditions either pragmatically or ideologically. And there are others still who believe Arabs should creatively develop a new identity for themselves by freeing their consciousness from the retarding influences of their own glorious but unattainable past as well as from their present undignified subservience to others. They would like to be authentic in remaining Arab, but only in a way that would also permit them to be truly modern. Only by being genuinely *modern Arabs* do they hope to have an important role in the international order in which their cultural specificity would be recognized, their political weight felt and their contributions accepted and integrated. To be *modern Arabs*, they admit, entails wide-ranging and even drastic change that will take a long time to achieve but which should be undertaken in spite of many internal and external deterrents.

This chapter will study some of the writings of those Arab thinkers who have given some thought to the global conditions of the Arabs, among them Hishām Sharābī, Anwar ᶜAbd al-Malik, Jalāl Amīn, Samīr Amīn and ᶜAbd al-Kabīr al-Khaṭībī. Other writers may be also invoked but the concentration will be on these five who have made clear analyses of the situation, some of them venturing intrepidly into areas of theorization.

Hishām Sharābī is a Palestinian who has written in English and Arabic. He is now professor of history at Georgetown University and has been living in the United States almost continuously since 1947. His books on various aspects of Middle East politics, particularly with regard to the Palestine question, Arab nationalism and revolution, are well known.[1] He has also written on Arab intellectuals and their encounter with Western culture.[2] More recently he has become interested in the study of Arab society, its institutions and value system with particular concern in its stunting influences on the psycho-social growth of the younger Arab generations.[3]

Hishām Sharābī recognizes the traditional, authoritarian and coercive structure of contemporary Arab society. He analyzes it soberly and with the grand strokes of a master, though he is not a sociologist.[4] He uses Marxist categories of analysis, in spite of the fact that he does not subscribe to a Marxist ideology. He also uses anthropological and sociological concepts in his analysis. His main interest is to study the intellectual history of the Arabs in modern times and, for this purpose, he marshals all analytical tools that provide a deeper understanding of prevailing Arab conditions.

In his most recent contributions, Hishām Sharābī speaks of *neopatriarchy* in contemporary Arab society.[5] This is a term he coined to denote an analytical concept (a) helping to formulate a theory about socio-cultural affairs in Third World countries including the Arab world and (b) at the same time helping to refer to their socio-historical reality.[6] In the social sciences, the term patriarchy is used to denote "a form of family organization in which the father is the formal head and the ruling power in the family. The authority of the father is absolute and final. . . ."[7] Hishām Sharābī believes that this has been not only the dominant form of the family in Arab tradition but also that this authoritarian state of affairs informs all other aspects of traditional Arab culture. All authority in the Arab-Islamic tradition, whether it is political, social, religious or intellectual is absolute and final; it is also exercised in a hierarchy of power that flows from top to bottom. The social structure which ensues with its culture, its institutions, its values, its attitudes and ways of behavior is what he calls "traditional patriarchy."

Neopatriarchy is something else. As an analytical concept for a theoretical formulation, neopatriarchy in Sharābī's view "occupies the space between traditional patriarchy and modernity." As a socio-historical reality, neopatriarchy for him denotes "a concrete historical reality, describing a social entity neither purely traditional nor authentically modern, but a hybrid formation combining both."[8] Sharābī believes neopatriarchy is a unique product of imperialism and of decolonization. It is when traditional patriarchy in the countries of the Third World is combined with imperialism, as these countries are colonized and later decolonized, that neopatriarchy arises and establishes its unique socio-political structure in them. This is what has happened in Arab society in the last two centuries according to Sharābī. Neopatriarchy is nothing but a traditional patriarchy that has been corrupted and combined with distorted modernity. The corrupting factor in this regard is not the traditional patriarchy as such but rather its dependency relationship with imperialism in which the latter finds its historical tool and expression.[9] Sharābī emphasizes that dependency in Third World countries is more than a mere result of aggression, domination, repression, despoliation and dispossession by external forces: it is more than political, economic and military hegemony practiced by the center over the periphery. It is also a relationship of cultural domination. Dependency is thus an internal cultural state of being in Third World countries, and it is this quality of it in its psycho-social facets that characterizes neopatriarchy.[10]

Sharābī defines neopatriarchy by the following social characteristics: (a) *social fragmentation*: it is the family, the tribe, the religious group or the ethnic group (rather than the nation or civic society) that constitutes the basis of social relations; (b) *authoritarian organization:* it is power, coercion and patriarchal authority (rather than co-operation and equality) that govern all social relations, from the level of the family up to that of the state; (c) *absoluteness of models*: in work, in politics and in daily life there is a closed and absolutist consciousness based on transcendental concepts, metaphysics, religious revelation, and a closed mind (rather than diversity, pluralism, egalitarianism, openness); (d) *ritualistic practices*: behavior is based on formalities, customs and rituals (rather than on spontaneity, innovation, and creativity).[11]

Sharābī believes that neopatriarchal Arab society has reached a state of crisis, being unable to cope with the inner (social) conflict and the pressures of the external (political) world. Its thought could not manage the opposition between the demands of modernity (*ḥadātha*) and the requirements for the preservation of authenticity (*aṣāla*), and thus slid into religious defensiveness, now visible in the socio-political upheaval characteristic of contemporary movements of Islamic militancy and resurgence. He adds:

> Secularist doctrines (reformism, liberalism, socialism) had not been able to strike deep roots in neopatriarchal soil, not so much because of their intrinsic inapplicability to Arab social structures, but because of the distortion to which these doctrines were subjected in their translation into neopatriarchal forms.[12]

Sharābī concentrates on the thought of the "cultural critics" of contemporary Arab society: al-Jābirī, Arkūn, al-ᶜArwī, Adonis and others whose writings, in his view, form the first radical critique of neopatriarchal culture and society, challenging their basic foundations and rendering them open to analysis and criticism. These new critics, whether living in the Arab world or outside it, are increasingly co-operating among themselves, forming professional associations, establishing human rights and women's organizations, convening conferences on Arab socio-cultural issues and in many ways posing a threat to the political and religious forms of Arab neopatriarchy. Yet, in Sharābī's view, inasmuch as they are still concerned with *problematizing* rather than with *theorizing* their subject matter, their writings remain largely negative and represent only "a first stage of autonomous self-consciousness." He says:

> Criticism as such may be considered only the first level of a process in which *synthesis* (autonomous perspective, coherence, unity) and *creativity* (independent vision, original theory, "going beyond") form the higher levels which the critical movement must embrace to achieve genuine and independent self-consciousness.[13]

Sharābī recognizes the difficulties those Arab cultural critics have before achieving full cultural liberation. He notes, for example, that despite their efforts to transcend the West, its intellectual categories provide the implicit models of their thought. Furthermore, the Arabic language they use does not fully translate the Western discourse into the Arab cognitive system, this being an impossible task, and their didactic modes of discourse impose prescriptive considerations on their writings, making them lose sight of the need for theoretical formulations. More seriously perhaps, Sharābī points to the apparent lack in Arab structuralist and post-structuralist critiques of space for political revolution as an unconditional necessity because they focus on language and textuality. He insists on a comprehensive theory to be developed by the Arab intellectuals because otherwise, the formalistic orientation of structuralism and deconstruction ends up as a fragmented project delighting in deconstructive play, whereas it has the possibility of undermining the neopatriarchal discourse from within.

Hishām Sharābī's theorizing is helpful in the way it places contemporary Arab thought in the context of historical and societal change. His notion of neopatriarchy, however, even as he defines it himself, cannot be said to be uniformly applicable to all parts of the Arab world, since each is at a different stage of social evolution due to internal and external factors, the form of its neopatriarchy being unique to iself; much less can Sharābī's notion of neopatriarchy be said to be uniformly applicable to all parts of the Third World. Only when one accepts the possibility that its content may be different in various areas can it be a useful analytical concept denoting a state of sociocultural being, corrupted in varying degrees by imperialism and constituting a hybrid existence between tradition and modernity.

The Egyptian thinker Anwar ᶜAbd al-Malik (Anouar Abdel-Malek) has introduced a new element in contemporary Arab discourse on dependency and cultural liberation. A Marxist and a well-known figure in the Egyptian National and Progressive Movement until he left Egypt for France in 1959, he is the author of important books on contemporary Arab thought,[14] Egyptian and Arab society[15] and more recently on geopolitics and the sociology of imperialism.[16] Some of his publications have appeared in English, Japanese, Spanish, Italian, Portuguese and Turkish translations in addition to those originally published in Arabic and/or French. ᶜAbd al-Malik has been research professor in sociology at the Centre National de la Recherche Scientifique in Paris. He has also been co-ordinator of the United Nations University's "Project on Socio-Cultural Development Alternatives in a Changing World" in Tokyo.[17]

Anwar ᶜAbd al-Malik believes that the world order set up at Yalta in 1945 and dominated by U.S.A. and U.S.S.R. in two respective spheres of influence has been finally shaken and that the balance of power in the world began to change between the years 1949 and 1973. In his opinion, the emergence of the People's Republic of China in 1949 introduced a third superpower in world politics, and the potential of the independent Afro-Asian nations was demonstrated in 1973 by the victory of Vietnam over U.S.A. and by the successful Arab oil embargo against U.S.A. and other Western nations which had supported Israel in its October war with Egypt and Syria in that year.

ᶜAbd al-Malik notes that the relations between the two superpowers, U.S.A. and U.S.S.R., have gradually changed in this period because of the emergence of China and other Afro-Asian nations, strengthened by growing Latin American tendencies to non-alignment. According to him, those superpower relations passed through three phases:

(1) The first was the cold war phase between 1947 and the end of the Korean war in 1952. After the Yalta conference of 1945, there was a short period of euphoria following the establishment of the United Nations Organization. But that was soon succeeded by the formation of NATO and the Warsaw Pact, as well as by the vicious armed struggles against the socialist revolutions and the national liberation movements in Asia and Africa. The aim of the cold war was twofold: (i) to stop the progress of the socialist revolutions and national liberation movements and (ii) to preserve the status quo in Europe socially, politically, and ideologically.

(2) The second phase stretched from 1952 to 1971 and was called peaceful co-existence. Having determined that nuclear confrontation was scientifically out of the question, U.S.A. and U.S.S.R. limited themselves to political, economic and ideological struggle, thus avoiding all direct military collision. Meanwhile radical change was happening in Asia, Africa and Latin America led by such great personalities as Jamāl ᶜAbd al-Nāṣir, Sukarno, Sékou Touré, Nkruma, Nehru and the Algerian FLN. This was the age of Afro-Asian solidarity, followed by that of the Three Continents. The influence of the two superpowers was diminishing so they concentrated on mutual understanding to preserve their respective powers.

(3) The third phase was that of détente inaugurated in 1972 at the initiative of President Nixon and General Secretary Brezhnev. U.S.A. felt it had to open up to

> China and the Arab world, and U.S.S.R. felt it had to have time to rebuild itself after the Nazi war attrition and catch up with the technological and economic progress achieved by the capitalist West led by U.S.A. Détente allowed both superpowers to work towards such ends.[18]

Thus, the world today has three, not two, superpowers according to ᶜAbd al-Malik, and U.S.A. and U.S.S.R. have recognized this fact and have gradually readjusted their interrelationship accordingly. He prefers to look at the global situation in terms of civilizational circles. There is first the circle of Western civilization whose center is U.S.A. and it tries to dominate the southern half of the globe, especially South America, Africa and the Pacific Ocean, its tool of influence being Western nuclear strategic hegemony. There is secondly the circle of Western socialist civilization whose center is U.S.S.R. and its influence stretches to Eastern Europe, the Mediterranean, North Africa and the Middle East, South Asia and especially the Indian Ocean, its tool of influence being peaceful co-existence and economic aid to developing nations. There is thirdly the civilizational circle of the socialist East whose center is the People's Republic of China and its influence extends to the socialist states of Asia and to the Asian continent generally, its tool of influence being the new civilizational pattern that flows from "the Long March" to "the Cultural Revolution" and leads into the movement of "the Four Modernizations."[19]

ᶜAbd al-Malik recognizes the identical elements of Western civilization that exist in both U.S.A. and U.S.S.R. and in their respective circles. In spite of differences in their internal systems, these two civilizational circles remain Western in their outlook and at variance with the civilizational circle at whose center is China. Both Western circles emphasize civilizational patterns of life whose essence is production and consumption based on material gains achieved since the fifteenth century, whereas the outlook of the Eastern civilizations emphasizes other aspects of life. The new center of world power developing in the latter, particularly since 1949, is gradually offering a new civilizational project to humanity.[20]

It is obvious that, although he is a Marxist, ᶜAbd al-Malik leans toward China and not the Soviet Union. He still considers the latter as a friendly world power whose support developing nations like the Arabs should seek and he lauds its great achievements as the first socialist state in history. Yet he interprets world history in such a way as to explain that the upcoming forces of change in the world are inevitably moving in the direction in which China and its civilizational circle are heading.

In an important article published in 1979, ^{c}Abd al-Malik introduces the concept of "historical surplus value."[21] The Marxian concept of surplus value derived from the Marxian labor theory of value is considered by ^{c}Abd al-Malik to be too limited a concept for the analysis of the global situation. It only explains the last stage of capital accumulation within a particular society in the world whereby the capitalists exploit the proletariat of that society and accumulate the surplus value of labor, paying workers subsistence minimum wages and thus maximizing bourgeois income. ^{c}Abd al-Malik expands the concept of surplus value to include the historical exploitation of the Three Continents (Asia, Africa and Latin America) by Europe and the West generally at least from the fifteenth century. He contends that it was this exploitation that has given societies in the Western civilizational circle the historical surplus value which has helped their capital accumulation and afforded them the economic and military power to impose Western hegemony and to establish the historical structure of the world order that has served their interests.

He explains that the historical surplus value has been formed in three waves. The first one consisted in the conquest, plunder, penetration and occupation of the Arab-Islamic region beginning with the medieval Crusades, followed by modern European colonization and continuing with contemporary Zionist aggression. The second wave stormed the African continent with colonization, and took a particularly fierce form in human attrition through the slave trade. The third wave destroyed the societies and civilizations of the "Indians" in Central and South America and subjected them to the Spanish and Portuguese empires.

Thus within a period of several centuries, Europe and the West were able to destroy the centers of power in the East, and generally in Asia, Africa and Latin America, and succeeded in accumulating capital from the material riches of the Three Continents, controlling their human resources and cultures, and using them for the advancement of the upcoming Western national bourgeoisies. ᶜAbd al-Malik emphasizes that the historical surplus value was never limited to the economic sphere, however important were matters like amassing raw materials, energy sources, land, control of cities, ports, networks of communications and transport across the oceans. All these were the means to insure world hegemony and pave the way for the Industrial Revolution. Meanwhile, the technology of communications helped to concentrate the movement of ideas, theories and concepts from the "center" to the "periphery." ᶜAbd al-Malik says:

> The result was a unique accumulation at the "center" which reached its peak in the concentration of the formation of social theory and of modern intellectual trends generally in the seats of Western hegemony. Hence, it was impossible for the periphery—Asia, Africa, and Latin America—to develop in any way except according to the method suggested or imposed by the various schools of thought in the hegemonic West.[22]

Thus, early colonization which led to classical imperialism and to the higher form of imperialism in our age, namely, hegemonic imperialism, insured not only what has come to be known as the traditional international order which found its modern expression between 1815 and 1945 and more definitely at Yalta, but it also insured that any thought about it should be in accordance with its own self-image and in the service of its own interests.

As explained above, ᶜAbd al-Malik believes that this traditional international order has been shaken since 1949 and that the balance of power has begun to change. A new world order is coming into being in which Asia, Africa and Latin America will be recognized and will have a dialectical relation with the advanced societies in Europe and North America, capitalist as well as socialist. The Three Continents should expect a long struggle but they should depend on themselves and mobilize all their natural and human resources in a manner that opens the way for intellectual creativity from within them, instead of following the methods now prevalent in what is called the "transfer" of technology and the "transfer" of knowledge. Regions like Japan, the

Indian sub-continent, the Arab world, Brazil, Iran, South-East Asia including China in the forefront, will increasingly be factors in the reconstruction of new patterns of power in the world leading to an "alternative scenario" which balances them against the prevailing Western hegemony.[23]

ᶜAbd al-Malik stresses intellectual creativity in the endogenous cultures of the Three Continents.[24] Liberation from Western hegemony should not only be political, military and economic; it should also be cultural and based on creativity from within those cultures. This necessitates a deep and full understanding of the endogenous cultures by their own peoples, and not as interpreted to them by Western specialists, Orientalists and the like.

The special reality of each national social unit should be carefully studied by its own people in order that they may arrive at a genuine knowledge of its distinguishing features, i.e., its specificity (*khuṣūṣiyya*) which has helped that human society to persist over the centuries. ᶜAbd al-Malik has argued in his social dialectics that this is the result of the interaction of four factors:

(1) The manner in which the necessities of life are produced (Economics)

(2) The manner in which that human society continues to exist (Sexual life and family organization)

(3) The manner in which a system of political authority is formed (The State)

(4) The manner in which man relates to time (Philosophy, Religion, and Ideology).[25]

ᶜAbd al-Malik sees distinctive cultural areas within each of the larger civilizational circles into which he divides the world.[26] Between the Western civilizational circle made up of Indo-European cultures and the Eastern civilizational circle at whose center is China lies the area of Islamic culture and civilization extending from Morocco to the Philippines, and within it lies the Arab world at whose heart is Egypt.

Part of the larger Islamic area, the Arab cultural area has all the elements of cultural unity. But within it, there are societies with varying degrees of national cohesion. Some of these societies have retained national unity for generations. Egypt, according to ᶜAbd al-Malik, is the oldest national unit in history. Other old national units, within the Arab world are Yemen and the Maghrib. One old national unit was torn up by Western imperialists after the First World War into five states (I presume he means Syria, Lebanon, Palestine, Jordan and Iraq) and from it issued the idea of pan-Arab unity. And there are other areas in the Arab world which are not homogeneous as far as national solidarity is concerned.[27]

Based on their cultural unity, which is a reality, these Arab societies should aim at unifying the struggle of the popular masses despite their diverse national and geographical formations, in order to achieve Arab unity, liberation and renaissance (*nahḍa*). This is a complex process which cannot be limited to one political organizational form, yet it is part of the renaissance of the peoples of the Eastern civilizational circle and their movement towards human and socialist liberation.[28]

Understanding the specificity of the national or societal unit is essential, in ᶜAbd al-Malik's opinion, for its progress on the path of liberation and unification, because such understanding discloses the unseen elements of the group's continuity over the centuries which must then be used and reinforced in order to achieve success.[29] In the case of Egypt as a national unit, for example, ᶜAbd al-Malik believes that its specificity as a society lies in its long-standing national heritage of political centralization and military control because of its geographical features and location.[30] ᶜAbd al-Malik also believes that Islam is an essential element of this specificity of Egyptian society[31] as it is also of the whole Islamic cultural area, including the other parts of the Arab world.

For him, however, Islam is not merely a monotheistic religion. It is an historical experience which many societies underwent as a culture, a religion, a philosophy of life, a political system and a shield against foreign aggression and domination. It has fused vital elements from all pre-Islamic cultures within it and has given the peoples of the areas in which it spread an indelible identity. Political and cultural Islam, therefore, is the main framework from which progressive Arab thought ought to draw its inspiration.[32]

ᶜAbd al-Malik rejects the reactionary interpretations of Islam but he calls for the cultural and political liberation of Muslims from Western hegemony by highlighting Islam as an authentic aspect of their identity and integrity within the Afro-Asian liberation movement. He has no specific prescription regarding the manner in which Islam as a political and cultural phenomenon may be separated from its religious and legal content. Whether this is possible or desirable is an issue which he does not discuss. In fact, he ignores it completely as he offers his views on political Islam as a mobilizing force[33] and on what he believes to be total harmony between Islam and Arabism.[34]

ᶜAbd al-Malik is an original Marxist thinker, but his big ideas do not deign to bother with details of truth or facts of history as much as is needed in order to be established on strong grounds. His argument is specious, prompted as it is by ideological convictions and political commitment. It allows wishful thinking to appear as actual reality. China, for example, is not the superpower he claims it to be. It may truly have all the potential of one, but to construct a geopolitical vision as though it were already a superpower confuses hope with reality. Furthermore, his thought is much too deterministic to leave human will any reasonable scope for freedom of action. His concept of a nation's or a society's specificity, for example, gives too much weight to factors of geography and physical environment, and less to the possibility of human action. His division of the world into civilizational circles with a varying number of cultural areas within each is too neat to accord with historical development; besides, he confuses circles with areas, and civilizations with cultures in his several writings on this matter, and one is left with a jumble of ideas.[35] Furthermore, it is questionable whether countries belonging to one civilizational circle or one cultural area do necessarily form a harmonious bloc for geopolitical purposes. Yet when all is said and done, one must acknowledge the power of ᶜAbd al-Malik's writing to create a desire among people of Third World countries to foster their own cultural liberation which would rid them of the ethnocentric domination of Western frames of thought.

Let me now turn to an Egyptian economist, Jalāl Amīn (Galal A. Amin), who has distinguished himself by paying attention to the change in Arab culture and society attendant upon the introduction of economic change in policies of development in the Arab world. He formerly taught economics in the Faculty of Law at ᶜAin Shams University in Cairo, and is now professor of economics in the Department of Economics at the

American University in Cairo. He has published books and articles in Arabic and English on economic and monetary theories,[36] on socialism and Marxism,[37] on the economic and social problems of the Arab world[38] and more recently on the socio-cultural effects of development and economic change.[39]

In his writings, Jalāl Amīn has questioned many prevailing economic theories and argued against their assumptions. His basic position is that these theories and assumptions (like many other aspects of the social sciences) have been developed in the West, by Western thinkers, and for Western societies. To apply them indiscriminately in the Arab world through policies of modernization introduces a disrupting factor in Arab society and a distorting influence on Arab culture. All that is achieved by these policies is a further integration of the Arab world in the world economic system, to the advantage of the powers controlling it and to the detriment of the majority of the Arab masses.

At bottom, Jalāl Amīn cannot agree with the intellectual and cultural assumptions of development theory which postulates that the aim of economic activities in Third World countries should be to close the gap between themselves and the industrialized countries of the world, the latter being the model to be emulated. Third World countries, whether called poor and backward, or—euphemistically—undeveloped, underdeveloped or developing, are so rated in relation to Western countries of the capitalist (U.S.A.) and the socialist (U.S.S.R.) varieties and according to Western criteria. Third World countries, on the other hand, have their own cultural values which posit other aims of life, not all necessarily related to economics and economic achievement. Furthermore, the means suggested to close the gap by financial and technical aid from the "developed" nations to the "developing" nations is, in his view, only a means to perpetuate and increase the gap and render Third World countries even more dependent, to say nothing about the damage done to their social and cultural fabric.

Jalāl Amīn is not against development as such, but he is against *dependent* development which, according to him, only exacerbates the problems of Third World countries. Furthermore, he is against development which does not take into consideration the social and cultural values of the country concerned and concentrates on growth in the economic sector with little or no regard for anything else.

Jalāl Amīn has articulated his ideas in a scholarly critique of the development philosophy underlying the United Nations resolution adopted by the General Assembly on May 1, 1974 and calling for the establishment of a 'New International Economic Order'.[40] He criticizes its presupposition that there is only one pattern of development and only one road towards progress and general well-being, namely, the Western one. He argues that the present conditions of Third World countries are not a mere stage to be transcended or an inferior state to be improved in terms of the experience of developed countries. He emphasizes that closing the gap between developing and developed countries is not, nor should it be, the goal of Third World countries. Only a small minority of urban dwellers with high incomes and continuous contact with Western culture may think so; the majority of the population rarely aspires to anything beyond clean drinking water and slightly more adequate diet and shelter. Furthermore, in view of economic realities this goal of closing the gap is either impossible to achieve or too remote in the future and continuously receding.

Jalāl Amīn also criticizes the strategy of development through foreign aid advocated by the U.N. resolution. The experience of Third World countries is that foreign aid on the level of governments, whether bilateral or multilateral, ends up serving the interests of the giving rather than the receiving parties. The latter are usually required by contract to spend a large proportion of the foreign aid to purchase technical services and equipment from the former. Their dependency on the giver becomes greater because of interest to be paid, new demands on further services and equipment, and the imbalance of the developing economy engendered by the foreign aid itself. Foreign investment by multinational corporations and other private agencies in Third World countries is similarly shown to be to the benefit of the investors who profit from the cheap labor and the consumer markets made available to them and who are unconcerned about the economic and social dislocations they cause to their hosts. Jalāl Amīn concedes there may be economic growth in certain cases but he argues it is usually not the kind really needed by the host country or it is one pulling the country in an undesirable direction or one that does not profit the majority of the population. Heavy reliance on foreign aid and foreign investment accentuates economic and social dualism in a poor country and does not help to eliminate the gap between it and rich countries, but rather increases it.

Apart from all these economic disadvantages of dependent development in Third World countries, which Jalāl Amīn carefully documents,[41] he argues that it not only integrates the poor countries into the Western economic system but gradually also into its value system.[42] The goods and services imported in the process of dependent development in a developing country are functionally related to the general cultural level of developed countries, where they satisfy real or imagined needs and where their prices are compatible with average incomes. In a poor country the prices of these goods and services are out of proportion with the country's average incomes, and marketing them not only increases income inequality but also cultural dualism, since sections of the population begin to acquire new tastes for previously unknown products and nonexistent needs. This often cuts invisibly into the ethical values of the developing country. For example, in Arab countries where people attach much value to strong family ties, goods and services that provide the young with separate homes and entertainment help to change this value; similarly, where stability and a slow tempo of life are considered to be wise, high-speed means of transport and constant change of fashion introduce new values. Western goods and services thus help to tear apart the patterns of the Arab way of life by changing taste; and when taste is changed, it is not possible for one thus affected to judge whether the new way is an improvement on the old. Jalāl Amīn concludes that the U.N. resolution is not merely calling for faster development but really for more rapid Westernization of the Third World and he doubts whether that leads to a better life.

Third World countries, Jalāl Amīn suggests, are better advised to follow a policy of *independent* development, whereby they rely on themselves, their resources and cultural ways first and foremost. Development for them should mean an increase in the welfare of society as a whole and not of an extremely narrow section of it; it should also be an enhancement of all aspects of life not merely an increase in economic output. In order to be able to do that, Third World countries have to undergo a period of self-imposed isolation, as did England and Germany at one time and Japan, Russia and present-day China later on, in order to achieve balanced economic development within their borders and thus be able to contribute to civilization. Some Third World countries have indeed succeeded in establishing the beginnings of industrialization in periods of involuntary isolation as did Argentina, Brazil, Mexico and Chile during the two world wars and in the interwar period, as did Egypt, Syria and Iraq—specifically, not when they depended on foreign import and foreign aid but when these were both virtually unavailable.

Jalāl Amīn says that most Third World countries are under the wrong impression that they cannot go it alone.[43] Yet, he asserts, all they initially need is to free their political will; for they have the labor force and much of the capital. A large part of what is termed 'technical aid', 'the entrepreneurial element' or 'managerial skill' claimed to be lacking in a Third World country can be acquired and developed from its own human resources. Some may not be needed at all, and that which is really needed but is unavailable may be obtained on better conditions if the country regains its freedom to bargain or, in other words, realizes the extent to which the industrialized West is dependent on the Third World for its own prosperity.[44]

Jalāl Amīn believes isolation and self-reliance in independent development are crucial for the Third World if its nations are to preserve their culture, their way of life and their civilization. He says:

> What has been happening in the Third World is neither development nor modernization but nothing more nor less than a dramatic encounter of civilizations in which the weaker civilizations have been paying a very heavy price.[45]

In other writings, he calls what has been happening "a civilizational invasion" (*ghazw ḥaḍārī*) and he advocates repelling it.[46] He concedes that Arab-Islamic civilization in the past has accepted influences from other civilizations, but he says it has done so by selecting elements from foreign civilizations that would enrich its own and it has done so from a position of strength and superiority. Modern Arabs, he emphasizes, are weak today and many of their intellectuals suffer from an inferiority complex in relation to Western civilization. They are thus liable to accept blind imitation of the West or, at best, have an apologetic attitude toward it, forgetting that it is still possible for the Arabs to have all the criteria of creativity and that they can still make new contributions to civilization.[47]

Jalāl Amīn is confident that because the Arabs had a powerful and prosperous civilization not so long ago, they can resist and repel the current civilizational invasion of the West. He says:

> The collapse of the Arab nation before the civilization of the West does not go back to more than two hundred years. Arab values and customs are still strongly rooted in no less than three quarters of the population who have not yet known urban living. The Arabs are still ready to regain their self-confidence at the return of some hope to them that their conditions can change to the better.[48]

He believes that half the battle is won if the Arabs are psychologically convinced that the invading civilization is not necessarily more advanced than theirs, and that Western values are not necessarily indicative of greater progress than theirs. They should distinguish between what constitutes doubtless human advancement in Western civilization and what is merely an expression of a particular culture in it; for much of what is believed to be aspects of real human progress in Western civilization is nothing but special 'applications' which a specific culture generated, namely, the culture of European or American society, and they have no universal value to be considered good for all places and times.[49] Jalāl Amīn warns that Arabs should not close their door to the products of the human intellect and its progress, whether Eastern or Western, but they should certainly close it to the products of any Western or Eastern seller who would sell them these as fruits of human progress while they are really no more than an expression of the seller's special ambition or even, as is often the case, symptoms of his special diseases.[50] According to Jalāl Amīn, Arabs should basically believe in themselves and the integrity of their culture. However, they ought to remain open-minded and acquire elements from any culture when these constitute real contributions to human progress. Whatever they acquire, they should fully assimilate and make their own, in their own manner so that it may serve their purposes. They should learn from the Chinese who have adopted Marxism without doubting their own special view of things. Their Marxism, therefore, is different from that of the Soviet Russians and, whatever they call it, they practice it in their own way to serve their purposes.[51]

In the take-off stage of any economic renaissance, there has always been a psychological factor, as Jalāl Amīn explains. It is unfortunate that, in searching for economic development, economists have overlooked this factor almost completely and have concentrated on its superficial results, such as the rise in the level of savings and investments or the development of the techniques of production. This psychological factor is related to the nation's cultural identity and feeling of self-worth. Jalāl Amīn says that Arabs must not allow anyone to make them doubt the values of their own culture, for therein lies the key to the psychological energy that brings about their renaissance. His opinion is that this latent energy can burst forth only through religion which, in the case of the Arabs, is Islam. To those who say it should be reinterpreted to encompass the requirements of modern life, he says this is a risky venture and may lead to contrary results, namely, the loss of confidence in the perfection and distinctiveness of Islam. He therefore warns: "Beware lest our attempt to restore glitter to gold should cause any scratch in it."[52]

The preservation of the special civilizational values of any nation as a basic element of the concept of development should not merely mean the addition of a civilizational aim to the material goal of raising the average income and satisfying material needs. Jalāl Amīn considers such preservation to be "a condition for the achievement of the material goal itself, and perhaps its basic condition."[53]

It is probably here, more than anywhere in the argument of Jalāl Amīn, that there is lack of detail and clarity. As a social scientist, he knows very well that change in the material life of a human group is bound eventually to affect its moral and spiritual life. Unless he is against any and all change, which I don't think he is, one does not see how Jalāl Amīn reconciles socio-economic change with his idea of Islam as gold to be preserved from scratches. One would have liked him to elaborate on this point and discuss specifics.

Samīr Amīn, an Egyptian political economist, is an internationally known Marxist writer. Born in Cairo in 1931, he received his higher education in Paris where he obtained a *doctorat d'état* in economics in 1957. He became senior economist at the Economic Development Organization in Cairo (1957–1960), then technical adviser for planning in Mali (1960–1963) before accepting academic positions as professor of economics (1963–1970) at the universities of Poitiers, Paris and Dakar for various periods. He then assumed the post of director of the United Nations African Institute for Economic Development and Planning in Dakar, Senegal.

His publications are numerous and wide ranging. A comprehensive bibliography of those of his works available in French and English (1955–1980) has been specially compiled and appended to the English translation of his *L'Economie arabe contemporaine* (Paris: Minuit, 1980).[54] His intellectual influence in the Arab world, particularly in leftist circles, has been increasing with the translation of some of his major works into Arabic.[55]

It was in the 1970s that Samīr Amīn's international fame took off after he assumed his U.N. position as director of the African Institute for Development and Planning, and with the publication of his two major works: *L'Accumulation à l'échelle mondiale: Critique de la théorie du sous-développement*[56] in 1970 and *Le développement inégal*[57] in 1973. He came to be known as one of the leading world thinkers analyzing capital accumulation and the phenomenon of underdevelopment on a global scale, from the viewpoint of dependency theory, which he sharpened and solidly based on a Marxist-Leninist-Maoist foundation, expanded upon and applied to the political economy of the Third World, particularly Africa.

As one critic, Anthony Brewer, said:

> . . . [Amin] has tried to link together a range of subjects that had previously been studied in virtual isolation from each other: modes of production, class structures in the periphery, the pattern of international trade and specialization, the formation of international prices, the (economic) problems of national development in the periphery, the periodisation of capitalist development and so on.[58]

For the purposes of this book, his views on the Arab world in the light of his global outlook are presented.

Whether in his studies of particular parts of the Arab world such as *L'Egypte nasserienne*,[59] which appeared in 1964 under the pseudonym of Hassan Riad, and *L'Economie du Maghreb*,[60] which appeared in 1966 in two volumes, or in his studies of the whole Arab world, such as *La Nation arabe: Nationalisme et luttes de classes*,[61] published in 1976 and *L'Economie arabe contemporaine*, published in 1980, Samīr Amīn views the balkanization of the whole Arab world by imperialist design as part of the historical circumstances leading to its underdevelopment and dependency status. In his writings on the future transformation of the Arab world, he insists on regional planning and unification, not in an effort to implement a nationalistic project of unity, but in the belief that this is the only practical way available to the Arabs to correct the wrongs of the past and begin to achieve self-centered development and a better life for the broad Arab masses. The separate development of each individual Arab country will lead nowhere, even if there is relative growth in it, so long as each Arab country remains dependent on the world capitalist system. In his view, real transformation begins when Arab fragmentation is overcome. He stresses the need for what he calls *les grands espaces* in order to achieve the integration of the region as a whole, permitting it to pool its natural resources and manpower. Otherwise, there might be at best what has been called "growth without development," a situation—in one country—created and maintained from the outside world without establishing the inside structures necessary for self-centered national development based on the internal dynamism of that country. This kind of growth may benefit a small upper class, but it will eventually slow down and leave that country in poverty and in submission to the external forces of imperialism.

Samīr Amīn views each of the Arab states as separately integrated into the world capitalist system, each in its own particular way, based on its historical experience with imperialism. Now that each is legally independent within borders earlier imposed by the colonial powers, each continues to evolve separately in its internal structures as well as in its external relationships with other Arab states and the world at large. Inter-Arab trade remains negligible and the bulk of Arab trade is with foreign countries of the capitalist system. Statistics show that the ratio of exports and/or imports to the Gross Domestic Product is much higher for the Arab world than for any other region of the Third World, the implication being that the Arab economy is more externally oriented than the economies of the rest of the Third World, hence more dependent too.[62]

Samīr Amīn explains that there are historical reasons why this is so. He believes that the Arab world's evolution was "blocked" by the aggressive expansion of European capitalism and its development into a world system, beginning with the rise of European imperialism in the latter part of the nineteenth century and continuing with the contemporary hegemony of the West and the predominance of U.S.A. This expansion has been facilitated by the internal structures of the countries of the Arab world where the social order was weakened by centuries of stagnation.

Samīr Amīn advances several theses about the history of the Arabs, about the socio-economic and political factors shaping them into a nation, and about European capital accumulation and unequal development in the world. Some of his theses still need extensive research in order to substantiate them. Nonetheless, he argues as though they have been substantiated in his mind and he presents bold opinions in this regard.[63]

He says that, because of the arid or semi-arid nature of the Arab region, agriculture in it has always been weak, with the exception of Egypt and possibly Iraq in certain periods of history. Arab civilization, in his view, did not develop on the basis of agriculture but rather on the basis of trade relations, external long-distance ones as well as internal domestic ones grafted on them. The period of Arab unity under the Umayyads and the early ᶜAbbasids was the mercantile product of a class of merchant-warriors who integrated the Arab world of the time and took advantage of its trade position in relation to three continents. When the growing bourgeoisie of Europe circumvented the Arab trade intermediaries by new ocean routes leading to new geographical discoveries, the decline of Arab trade invited national Arab disintegration. This facilitated the eventual integration of the Arab world into the imperialist system which, *ipso facto*, accentuated Arab disintegration.

In this social structure of the Arab world, Samīr Amīn believes that the urban centers have been dominant in political matters, the rural areas being always marginal and usually distinguishing themselves by separate linguistic, ethnic or religious identities (Berbers, Maronites, ᶜAlawīs, Shīᶜīs), except in Egypt in which the peasantry were more integrated in the national entity for ages before the Arab conquest. No feudalism grew in the Arab world as in Europe and no bourgeoisie parallel to that of Europe. Similarly, no proletariat and no capitalist class developed until European imperialist intervention began to distort the pre-colonial Arab social structure.

According to Samīr Amīn, the transformation imposed by the capitalists of dominant imperialism lies in the nature of the class alliance they have made in the Arab world for the purpose of their own development. Imperialism allies itself with classes of people in the Arab world who benefit from the integration of their country into the world system. These classes gradually develop into local bourgeoisies because of accruing benefits while serving imperialism and controlling the country for that purpose. They mainly consist of a comprador bourgeoisie and of the big landowners who develop into what Samīr Amīn calls a *latifundist* bourgeoisie. The latter are not feudal in the European sense but they do control the use of land for purposes of imperialist exploitation, and they introduce whatever land and agrarian reform is needed in order to entrench themselves as the rural ally of imperialism. As the local bourgeoisies grow stronger, they become a statist bourgeoisie and they force themselves upon imperialism as its main ally in the new modalities of the international division of labor. Capitalism in the Arab world, now a periphery integrated into the world system, begins to develop but it remains dependent on that of the imperialist center. Light industries and mining, where possible, are permitted to grow as long as they do not impede the designs of the imperialists but rather advance them. A proletariat begins to develop in the Arab world and, like the poorer peasantry, it begins to feel alienated from its products because it has no control over them or over the developing mode of production.

This is generally the situation in the Arab world as it enters the second half of the twentieth century in Samīr Amīn's analysis. Meanwhile, an Arab petty bourgeoisie has developed and it begins an anti-imperialist struggle which it aims at the national bourgeoisies as well as at imperialism. The Arab proletariat and poorer peasantry give it the leadership in this endeavor, particularly as it claims to hold socialist aims, as in Egypt under ᶜAbd al-Nāṣir, Syria or Iraq under the Baᶜth Party and Algeria under Bū-Midyan. The Arab petty bourgeoisie takes control but cannot achieve anything more than state capitalism which remains dependent on the world capitalist system. It is no less a state bourgeoisie than the national bourgeoisies it replaced in several Arab countries and accused of being collaborationist allies of imperialism.

Samīr Amīn believes that the Arab communist organizations have failed in leading the Arab proletariat and poorer peasantry. The reason, in his opinion, is that Arab communists have toed the Moscow line, without accurately analyzing the global interests of the U.S.S.R. and without lucidly understanding the new situation caused by the internal evolution of the latter. As a new class society and as a new superpower, the Soviet Union's policy is to support state bourgeoisies in opposition to Western and especially American imperialism, the idea being that an alliance between the U.S.S.R. and Arab state capitalism tends to weaken the alliance between U.S.A. and Arab private capital. The new class society of the Soviets, requiring an increasing centralization of capital, is considered by Samīr Amīn as better suited to the development of the productive forces, hence the Soviet Union's interest in supporting Arab state capitalism and affording it the necessary aid for rapid industrial development at a rate that cannot be matched or wanted by Western imperialism. Samīr Amīn sees the possiblity of a new type of imperialism developing in the future led by the Soviet Union, a sort of "social imperialism" that will gradually replace the classical forms of imperialism. With the decline of American imperialism, there will be a rise in the centralization of capital in U.S.S.R. and similar systems, and a preponderance of statist forms of capitalism in its peripheries.[64] This is not a desirable outcome in Samīr Amīn's view since it does not lead to the liberation of the Arab masses, but rather to the Soviet domination of the Arab world, if not the whole Third World, unless it is opposed.

He notes the growing crisis of Western imperialism resulting from rising tensions about economic interests between U.S.A., Japan and Europe on the one hand, and the relative concessions Western imperialism has increasingly to make to Third World countries to lure them away from U.S.S.R. on the other hand. He also notes the rise of the People's Republic of China as a socialist model that succeeded in establishing itself on the periphery of the imperialist center while adopting a version of Marxism other than what he considers to be Soviet revisionism. He therefore suggests that Third World countries, including the Arab world, should learn from this model. He concedes the Chinese experience cannot be reproduced in the Arab world, but he points to the universal principles it contains and urges the Arabs to find specific solutions based on similar principles.[65]

The conditions of Arab disunity under statist bourgeoisies and imperialist dominance cannot continue indefinitely, in Samīr Amīn's view. Furthermore, the Arab world or any of its countries cannot hope to develop a full-fledged capitalist system as a partner of Western imperialism using the resources of Western technology, Arab oil wealth and Arab cheap labor. He believes that "Japan was the last country ever to achieve full development by the capitalist road, because it was the last ever to launch its development before the formation of imperialism."[66] Autonomous capitalist development in the periphery of the imperialist world system is now irrelevant for, in his opinion, it will never reach what Rostow calls the economic "take-off point" because the capitalist center will always ensure the unequal development of the periphery for its own survival. In his opinion, only one way remains open for the Arabs to break out of their "blocked" evolution: it is the way of a socialist revolution which will gradually bring about Arab unity as a necessary step while the Arab masses are being simultaneously liberated.

To achieve this, Samīr Amīn proposes the formation of a broad anti-imperialist front in the Arab world led by an Arab working class that must be ideologically and organizationally autonomous and in close alliance with the impoverished Arab peasantry. Under such leadership, all internal and external forces will be marshalled to oppose imperialism. Using flexible tactics, its strategy should aim at a full disengagement from the world capitalist system. This will be a difficult and long-lasting task, particularly because the Arab world's integration into the capitalist system is very advanced, much more than China's ever was, especially when considering the powerful factor of the Arab oil contributing to it. But disengagement is indispensable and Arabs will have to renounce Western patterns of consumption and, to some extent, of Western technologies and to understand that these are not neutral. Through their liberation from these patterns, the Arabs will affirm socialist relations of production that are the very content of popular power.

Regional planning will be more feasible in this context and Samīr Amīn suggests it should be based on strictly self-centered pan-Arab development to solve the problem of weak agriculture and industry. Accepting Arab diversity, industry should be localized in areas of lowest agricultural potential and used to develop agriculture in areas of highest potential.[67] Summing up he says:

> This kind of strategy leads to Arab unity. Not that this could be achieved immediately, of course. That would be neither necessary nor useful, in fact it would be dangerous. A long tradition which respects regional particularities is a far better strategy. A collective mutual aid aimed at reinforcing the autonomy of the whole and the interdependence of its constituent states is the only road to popular and socialist Arab unity.[68]

Samīr Amīn recognizes that no program of any political force within the present-day Arab world corresponds to this strategy but he asserts it corresponds to the objective interests of the Arab peoples who, if unheeded, will turn to a populist revolt —the example of revolutoinary Iran being there to prove it.[69]

Is Samīr Amīn's thought utopian? Is he unrealistic? These are questions which may be answered differently by different persons, depending on one's point of view and class position in society. I believe his thought is logical, but it allows itself a number of wide and sweeping generalizations, particularly in his later books, which have a strong theoretical content. In his earlier books, fully documented and supported by statistics, his approach is more empirical, undergirded though it is by the same theories. There is a lot for intellectuals, scholars, policy-makers and the masses of the people in general to learn from his writings. That is why he remains an important contributor to contemporary Arab thought as well as to modern thought in the world generally.

The last Arab thinker to be presented in this chapter is ᶜAbd al-Kabīr al-Khaṭībī (Abdelkebir Khatibi). A Moroccan born in 1938, he received his higher education in France and returned in 1964 to Rabat where he is now a professor at Muḥammad V University. A sociologist by training, he is also a creative writer who has written plays, novels and poetry in addition to an autobiography and literary criticism and history.[70] He has also written studies on popular culture in the Maghrib with innovative insights,[71] as well as an acute criticism of Zionism and its supporters among French leftists.[72] His call for intellectual pluralism in Arab thought is well argued in one of his latest books.[73]

Al-Khaṭībī calls his approach "double criticism."[74] It is basically an in-depth criticism of Moroccan (and Arab) thought on the one hand and of Western thought on the other, the purpose being to delineate a new path for the renewal of Arab culture as well as to de-center Western thought and establish the pluralism of all human thought.

He depends heavily on the philosophical theories of Jacques Derrida and Michel Foucault whose works he considers to be indispensable for discourse analysis. From the former, he borrows the notions of deconstruction and difference; from the latter, the concept of episteme. And he plunges into the archeology of modern knowledge to deconstruct it from stratum to stratum in order to show the ethnocentrism of the West and the cultural dependency of the Arabs.

For him, the West is not only the capitalist, imperialist West which imposed on the world its own view of itself and the world in the course of its colonial expansion and rise to power and through its advancement in science and technology. It is also the Marxist West which continues to maintain there is only one universal path on which all peoples of the world should go to reach the final goal of communism. Both systems suffer from an undesirable logocentrism, an ethnocentrism which creates its own discourse as a self-sufficient speech which consciously and unconsciously builds up the idea that the West is the center of the world.

Although the capitalist, imperialist West has permitted decolonization of the Third World to proceed, peoples of the Third World, in al-Khaṭībī's view, have not yet achieved a decolonization of the mind in order to promote a system of thought that can criticize the ideological apparatus of the still-dominant West and establish a plurality of discourses for the world. And although Marxism presents itself as being against imperialism, its traditional analysis of other societies outside the European experience groups them under the label of "the Asiatic mode of production." This is a deficient label, according to al-Khaṭībī, because it is too general and does not distinguish the multitude of conflicting systems in Asia or Africa, one pre-colonial society like Morocco having a patriarchal system, a tribal system, an artisanal and mercantile capitalist system, a rural seignorial system and the Makhzen.[75] Furthermore, al-Khaṭībī draws attention to the fact that Marx himself wrote that the English colonization of India had a double mission, "one destructive, the other regenerative: the annihilation of the old Asiatic society and the laying of foundations for Western society in Asia."[76] Al-Khaṭībī suggests that Marx can be read as calling for the destruction of native tradition outside Europe so that a Westernized and capitalist system may be regenerated in order to prepare, when it collapses, for the advent of communism. Al-Khaṭībī does not want to reduce Marx's thought to a mere ethnocentric strategy, but wants rather to show its failure, as Western thought, to recognize the Other and wants to demonstrate its single-minded will to unite the world on the basis of one universal system.

This deconstruction of both Western systems, in al-Khaṭībī's opinion, should go hand in hand with the affirmation of a "thought of difference," what he calls *pensée-autre*. The Third World has not begun to build up this unthought-of system of thought, and underdeveloped societies can be more appropriately called "silent societies." To allow these societies to develop speech that can be heard, they should not merely echo Western thought as they have done since decolonization. They should rather resort to the subversion of the Western systems, they should decolonize their own mind and uproot Western thought from the central place within it, they should claim their right to speak and act according to their own selves and their own cultures, and they should de-center the West from the central place it has assigned itself in the modern world. All this should be done "by operating in the sphere of a plural and planetary 'thought of difference' that struggles against its own reduction and domestication."[77]

Third World peoples should also apply deconstructive analysis to their own cultures in order to be able to speak authentically as themselves. They should realize that their knowledge has been circumscribed and distorted by Western thought in the first place. But they should also realize that it has been shaped, even in precolonial times, by ideologies implicit in historical realities, each people in the Third World having their own specific matrix of influences.

Taking contemporary Arab knowledge, ᶜAbd al-Kabīr al-Khaṭībī believes it is stamped by an ideology of Islam. This knowledge should be subjected to deconstruction in order to show that its concepts are historical products that have taken their particular structures in relation to a specific way of thinking and specific events in time and space. All attempts to consider the Arab-Islamic heritage sacred should be dropped because they blind one's critical awareness by the illusion of a nostalgic return to past glory.[78] History should be considered as a continuous critical exercise of all that defines Arab existence here and now, and this attitude to it should shake the foundations of the ideological system dominating contemporary Arab knowledge.[79] While it is useless to make this Arab knowledge pass through all the stages Western thought has experienced, it is likewise useless to believe that it is possible to establish an integrative relationship between it and the old Arab knowledge of the heritage.[80] A radical rupture should take place before it can affirm its difference from the dominant past. Al-Khaṭībī puts it this way:

> Contemporary Arab knowledge cannot, without experiencing a radical rupture, escape its own theological and theocratic foundations which characterize the ideology of Islam and of all monotheism.[81]

In order to bring about this rupture, Arabs should know their heritage very well and love it. Any rupture or change in it should be done with a deep sense of responsibility and true criticism. The plural elements within it should be recognized as such by contemporary Arabs. In Morocco, for example, the Moroccan person carries within him all his pre-Islamic, Islamic, Berber, Arab and Western (colonial) past. These elements of his heritage that form his identity should not be neglected. Thought should be given to the possibility of uniting all these elements, but each should be allowed its share of distinctiveness and the whole should also allow free movement. This plural identity emphasizes the idea of difference, and this disturbs Arab leaders because it constitutes danger to theology which is built on the principle of unity encompassing all believers.[82]

According to al-Khaṭībī, the Arab world as a whole is not a unity that can be enclosed within one ideological system, it is rather a plurality. The current idea of unity based on linguistic, religious and ancestral foundations cannot by itself define modern Arab identity. It should be deconstructed lest it continue to burden the Arabs, along with any theology or ideology that believes in the absolute One.

Expanding on this idea of the absolute One, the Moroccan writer Muḥammad Binnīs (Mohammed Bennis), who translated some of al-Khaṭībī's French writings into Arabic, says:

> This theological vision of the subject acting in history and civilization is anchored in our consciousness and in our unconscious. We see this subject spreading its rays across the totality of the Arab world. It is personified socially in the father, politically in the tribe, and culturally in the echo of the latter and its extensions. It is even seen disguised under new terms such as [national] unity, socialism, liberty, democracy, terms that are thus transformed, on the basis of the sociocultural givens of the present Arab world, into simple metaphors of the One, because the One does not submit to plurality, change, or difference.[83]

The theological/ideological obsession with the One, both as conscious and unconscious experience, transforms all desiderata into metaphors of the One. Plurality is unthinkable and unthought of, and the reality of plural societal manifestations of

Arab life is ignored or considered wrong in the Arab conscious and unconscious mind. This is because the idea of plurality is based on accepting the "thought of difference" and on accepting the other as he or she is. That does not happen in the Arab world where everything has to be fused into the One or its metaphysical transformations in Arab society, according to al-Khaṭībī. The contemporary Arab episteme, i.e., the whole field of contemporary Arab knowledge at all societal levels, has to be subjected to deconstruction in order to reveal its reality as a plurality. And that is what ᶜAbd al-Kabīr al-Khaṭībī believes he is doing as a sociologist and a thinker in his approach called "double criticism."

In his book *al-Ism al-ᶜArabī al-Jarīḥ*, for example, al-Khaṭībī discusses certain aspects of popular culture in North Africa: proverbs in the vernacular language, tatooing parts of the female human body, Shaykh Nafzāwī's book *al-Rawḍ al-ᶜĀṭir* on sexual intercourse, the oral folk story of "The Speaking Bird," in addition to a study of Arabic calligraphy. Apart from the latter,[84] the other four studies concentrate on the culture of the marginalized common people, a culture that is unrecognized by the elite, a culture that is usually considered forbidden—or at best—worthless and irrelevant, though it is that of the majority, whose right it is to determine their own destiny but is ignored by the elite and is often suppressed. Al-Khaṭībī's approach is not that of ethnology, which he considers to be a paternalizing outsider's approach. It is rather a forceful ideological intervention in contemporary Arab culture in order to affirm in it the thought of difference and plurality. It is also an attempt to deconstruct current theological thinking which regards certain activities of the human body as forbidden, al-Khaṭībī's aim being to call for the celebration of the pleasures of the human body, and for its liberation from false moral constraints if sociocultural liberation is also envisaged for it. The same applies to the vernacular language of the Arab people, which should be recognized as conveying the wisdom and experience of actual daily life, as opposed to the knowledge derived from books written about books.

There are other aspects of the contemporary Arab episteme which al-Khaṭībī analyzes in order to affirm the thought of difference and plurality. His strategy for a renewal of Arab culture is to start from what exists here and now. His "double criticism" approach aims at extricating Arab culture from a prevailing double dependency: (1) a dependency on the West, and (2) a dependency on an oppressive unity-oriented Arab discourse.

In their various ways, all the Arab thinkers discussed in this chapter are cultural critics of Arab society. Furthermore, they are all thinkers who view the Arab world from a global perspective and attribute much of its present-day predicament to the cultural, political and economic intrusions of the West and the manner in which the Arabs perceive the West, themselves and history. They all prescribe solutions, sometimes emphasizing one thing and sometimes another; yet they are always mindful of the necessity of change—not only in the Arab world or in the West—but also in the relationship of one with the other.

Chapter Five

Voices of Arab Women

The status of women in the Arab world has been one of the most recurrent themes in Arab society's quest for modernity in the last hundred years.[1] But whereas in the beginning women's voices were faint and shy, and too few and sparse to impress society with the urgency of needed change, they have increasingly become stronger and bolder, and more numerous and organized as the twentieth century wears on.

Arab women do not speak with one voice, any more than Arab men do or, for that matter, men and women of other nations. But they do speak with the specificity of an Arab-Islamic cultural background that affects their lives in a particular way. There is a growing awareness among them that the Arab man must change as well as the Arab woman before Arab society can achieve success in anything it endeavors to do. This is a difficult task, no doubt. But it is at the heart of the Arab struggle to build a new society.

From the extreme right to the extreme left, a succession of women have expressed their thoughts on matters related to their social and legal status, their political and economic rights and the need for change. Independent of conservative or liberal views expressed by men purporting to improve women's conditions, Arab women have presented their own case with the immediacy of those who have actually experienced inferior status and with the dignity that ought to be due to them and to all human beings.

Arab women have expressed themselves in various genres of writing: essays, studies, articles, poems, short stories, novels, autobiographies, diaries and interviews; they published their ideas in books, magazines, newspapers, learned journals and the electronic media. They have also expressed themselves in women's organizations, clubs, conferences and international meetings.[2] To study contemporary Arab thought without including women's thought is therefore misleading and incomplete.

In this chapter, the thought of a few Arab women from a range of social and political tendencies will be presented. As in previous chapters, this presentation cannot be comprehensive but it attempts to give a fair view of the intellectual contributions of these women to contemporary Arab thought. The chapter begins with an outstanding Islamic scholar, Ā'isha ᶜAbd al-Raḥmān, known also under her pen-name as Bint al-Shāṭi'; and it moves on to an Islamic activist, Zaynab al-Ghazālī, to portray the traditional background of conservative thinkers against which a number of Arab women espousing liberal thought are working. Following a presentation on the thought of Nawāl al-Saᶜdāwī of Egypt and that of the Moroccan sociologist Fāṭima al-Marnīsī, will be comment on the effectiveness of the women's movement in the Arab world.

ᶜĀ'isha ᶜAbd al-Raḥmān is reported to have once said to a person interviewing her, "I am conservative to a degree that crosses no woman's mind."[3] She meant she was extremely conservative, but her words leave the impression that a woman is not expected to be so conservative or even conservative at all. Whether she meant what she said or was only throwing a smoke screen as a Muslim woman who desired to be in the public eye but wanted also to preserve feminine modesty and propriety is a matter of speculation. Daughter of an Azhar-educated shaykh, she was born in Dimyāṭ, Egypt, and raised in a conservative home. Had it not been for her mother and great-grandfather who were relatively progressive, her father would have succeeded in obstructing the development of her career. As it turned out, she eventually became professor of Arabic language and literature at the University of ᶜAin Shams in Egypt, and sometime visiting professor at Umm Durmān Islamic University in the Sudan and Qarawiyyīn University in Morocco. She has more than sixty books to her name in addition to several hundred articles on subjects ranging from Arabic language and literature to Qur'ān exegesis and historical studies of the life and times of the Prophet and of women in early Islam.[4] Her publications include fiction as well as biographies, literary criticism and essays on public affairs with an Islamic point of view. In all her works, she exhibits an independent and critical approach but remains definitely Islamic with strong conservative leanings.

Her understanding of a woman's status in society is circumscribed by what she perceives as the correct Islamic values derived from the Qur'ān and the Ḥadīth, and practiced by the female believers of early Islam. Her detailed studies of the lives of the Prophet's mother, his wives, his daughters, his granddaughter and his great-granddaughter are not meant to be an exercise in biographical scholarship only, but also an attempt to set models for Muslim women of all times, including modern times.[5] She emphasizes those women's piety and modesty, and she highlights their devotion and loyalty to their men folk. But she also stresses their independence, at times economic and at other times intellectual, meanwhile always showing their individual character as distinct persons in their own right. She extols their capacity for sacrifice and heroism, their patience in hardship and their constant hope in God.

Within the framework of Qur'anic principles governing the relations between men and women in Islam, ᶜĀ'isha ᶜAbd al-Raḥmān sees ample latitude for women to fulfill themselves as free human beings and as believers. They have rights and duties which may in certain respects differ from those of men, but the difference does not mean inequality; it rather means distinct complementary functions in a social order that necessarily requires the input of both men and women in different modes. In matters spiritual, however, she believes Qur'anic principles show no gender distinctions, both men and women being equal in the eyes of God.

Women's liberation to ᶜĀ'isha ᶜAbd al-Raḥmān consists in their liberation from ignorance. Many Muslim women do not even know all the range of rights that Islam gives them, let alone practice those rights. And men who are not really good Muslims take advantage of this ignorance, thus abusing their own rights. Therefore, the gate to women's liberation is education and particularly in matters relating to Islam, and to women's rights and duties in the Islamic social order properly implemented.[6] To ᶜĀ'isha ᶜAbd al-Raḥmān the charter of women's liberation is the Qur'ān, not imported ideas from the West. It is the Qur'ān that says (S.4:1): "Mankind, fear your Lord, who created you of a single soul, and from it created its mate, and from the pair of them scattered abroad many men and women; and fear God by whom you demand one of another, and the wombs; surely God ever watches over you." For here, in ᶜĀ'isha ᶜAbd al-Raḥmān's opinion, is the established foundation of the Muslim woman's freedom which lies in the fullness of her being human with all attending rights and duties. A woman is a full human being in her own right, as God's creature originated with man from a single soul. Like man's, her rights are intrinsic and cannot be granted or withheld by the man, and are not conditional on his will or on whether she can bear children or not, and whether she can give birth to males or not. To acquire knowledge is an essential element of a woman's humanity so that she may fulfill herself and rise to the fullness of her human potential. This is emphasized by the Qur'ān in all the places it attributes reason to human beings and asserts God's teaching of them and His guidance.

Being free, a Muslim woman bears the responsibility of her freedom and the trust of preserving her virtue. The guardianship by her father or husband does not relieve a woman from the responsibility of her obligations or the responsibility of work and good deeds. This is an inherent responsibility for which a woman will be rewarded or punished in the hereafter, since the Qur'ān says (S.6:164): "Every soul earns only to its own account; no soul laden bears the load of another."

ᶜĀ'isha ᶜAbd al-Raḥmān insists that women should remain women and men men; their differences should not constitute rivalries or enmities but rather occasions of complementary cooperation and companionship and harmony. She insists the Qur'ān does not speak of the inequality of men and women, but rather of the inequality of good and evil, of belief and disbelief, of guidance and misguidance, of learning and ignorance. Where the Qur'ān (S.2:228) speaks of men having a degree above women, she explains that this is not an absolute right for men, but only a conditional right. The Qur'ān specifies (S.4:34) that "Men are managers (*qawwāmūn*) of the affairs of women for that God has preferred in bounty one of them over another, and for that they have expended of their property." If this condition is not fulfilled, the men's right of management is lost. The degree men have above women, therefore, does not obliterate the equality between men and women in matters of equal rights, obligations and responsibilities. Even certain messengers of God have been exalted above others in degrees, ᶜĀ'isha ᶜAbd al-Raḥmān reminds us, as the Qur'ān has it in S.2:253. Similarly, believers and those given knowledge are raised above others in degrees (S.58:11), absolute equality being non-existent. Therefore, rather than this imaginary enmity between men and women, Muslims should live according to the Qur'ān's proper relationship, as where it says (S.30:21): "And of His signs is that He created for you, of yourselves, spouses, that you might repose in them, and He has set between you love and mercy. Surely in that are signs for a people who consider."[7]

ᶜĀ'isha ᶜAbd al-Raḥmān has not been known to belong to any political party, but she has taken strong stands in political matters and expressed her opinions boldly in newspaper articles and in books. She even criticized President Sadat of Egypt to his face once for curbing the freedom of the press.[8] However, her appeal and popularity in Muslim circles rest on her scholarship and her deep insights in Qur'ān interpretation and Islamic culture, not on political stances or activities.

Zaynab al-Ghazālī is a woman of another kind. Like ᶜĀ'isha ᶜAbd al-Raḥmān, she is Egyptian and defends the rights of Muslim women in accordance with what she perceives to be the correct Islamic doctrine, and like her she is the daughter of an Azhar-educated father. But she has been an organizer of women and an Islamic activist, rather than an Islamic scholar. Early in her youth, she was an active member of the Egyptian Feminist Union, founded by Hudā al-Shaᶜrāwī in 1923. She resigned her membership in disagreement with the ideas and ideals of the women's liberation movement and, at the age of eighteen in 1936, she founded the Muslim Women's Association in order to organize women's activities according to Islamic norms and for Islamic purposes.

The Society of the Muslim Brothers, founded by Ḥasan al-Bannā in 1928, was thinking of creating a division for the Muslim Sisters at the time, and Ḥasan al-Bannā asked Zaynab al-Ghazālī to head that division and incorporate into it her new Muslim Women's Association. She and her association's general assembly rejected the offer, but promised co-operation. After the Society of the Muslim Brothers was dissolved in 1948, she gave a personal pledge of allegiance to Ḥasan al-Bannā in 1949 to support him and back his efforts to establish an Islamic state. Though he was assassinated soon afterwards, she continued her personal allegiance to his successors in the society and helped their members, particularly after they went underground during ᶜAbd al-Nāṣir's regime in the 1950s and the 1960s.[9]

In an interview at her home in Heliopolis, Egypt in 1981 Zaynab al-Ghazālī said:

> Islam has provided everything for both men and women. It gave women everything—freedom, economic rights, political rights, social rights, public and private rights. Islam gave women rights in the family granted by no other society. Women may talk of liberation in Christian society, Jewish society, or pagan society, but in Islamic society it is a grave error to speak of the liberation of women. The Muslim woman must study Islam so she will know that it is Islam that has given her all her rights.[10]

This is the core of Zaynab al-Ghazālī's thought regarding the status of women as expressed in her public lectures and her articles in *al-Daᶜwa* magazine, for which she was editor of a section devoted to the ideals of a good Muslim home. The thrust of her activism and that of her association is an educational one: to instill the doctrines of Islam in women's minds, teach them about their rights and duties and call for change in society leading to the establishment of an Islamic state which rules by the Qur'ān and the Sunna of the Prophet.

Zaynab al-Ghazālī believes that Islam permits women to take an active part in public life, to hold jobs, enter politics and express their opinion. She believes Islam permits them to own property, do business and be anything they wish to be in the service of an Islamic society. Yet she also believes that a Muslim woman's first duty is to be a mother and a wife, and that no other activity should interfere with this role of hers, for this should have priority over everything else. If she has free time to participate in public life after her first duty is fulfilled, she may do so because Islam does not forbid her.[11]

Zaynab al-Ghazālī strongly believes in the religious and social duty of being married. In her first marriage, her husband did not agree with her Islamic activism and so she got a divorce in accordance with a marriage precondition. Her second husband was more understanding and undertook in writing to assist her and never to prevent her from fulfilling her mission in the service of the Islamic cause. In her autobiographical book, *Ayyām min Ḥayātī*,[12] she tells how, though worried about her, her husband continued to support her in her activities; she emphasizes, however, that she never neglected him or her family duties, even as she continued to be president of the Muslim Women's Association, to work long hours at its headquarters and to be personally involved in the clandestine activities of the Society of the Muslim Brothers. After her second husband's death, she felt that she had done her duty in marriage and was free to devote all her time to the cause of Islam.

Like many Muslim activists disenchanted with the 1952 Egyptian revolution which many of them supported at the beginning, Zaynab al-Ghazālī considered ᶜAbd al-Nāṣir and his regime to be enemies of Islam. After some members of the Society of the Muslim Brothers were sentenced to death and many others imprisoned, she started programs to take care of their orphans and widows, to cater to the needy and unemployed among those released or at large, to help their families and in general to use her position as president of the Muslim Women's Association to do social work that was greatly needed. She also intensified her educational activities and participated in secret Islamic study groups guided by the leadership of the Muslim Brothers in prison. By 1962, she had established contact with Sayyid Quṭb in prison through his two sisters and received his approval of an Islamic course of readings in commentaries on the Qur'ān and the Ḥadīth as well as in Islamic jurisprudence. She also received from him sections of a book he was writing in prison, later to be published under the title *Maᶜālim fī-l-Ṭarīq*.[13]

Pages from this book and instructions from Sayyid Quṭb in prison, along with the set verses from the Qur'ān, would be studied by groups of five to ten young men meeting at night in the home of Zaynab al-Ghazālī or elsewhere. Discussions followed and views were established and opinions formed. With the agreement of Sayyid Quṭb and the Muslim Brothers' leadership, it was decided that this Islamic training program should continue for thirteen years, which is the duration of Prophet Muḥammad's call in Mecca before he moved to Medina and established the Islamic state. It was also decided that at the end of this period, a survey would be conducted in Egypt to find whether at least 75 percent of Egyptian men and women were convinced of the necessity of establishing an Islamic state. If so, then they would call for one; if not, they would continue their study and learning for thirteen more years—this to be repeated again and again until the nation was ready to accept Islamic rule, implementing Islamic law in accordance with the Qur'ān and the Sunna of the Prophet.[14]

When the Egyptian government became suspicious and these secret groups looked to it like seditious political cells, a crackdown on Muslim Brothers took place in 1965. Muslim Sisters were not spared, the Muslim Women's Association was dissolved, and Zaynab al-Ghazālī, among others, was imprisoned. She was brought to trial with several others in 1966 and sentenced to hard labor for life, but she was released in 1971. In the open Islamic resurgence in Egypt which became stronger after the death of ᶜAbd al-Nāṣir in 1970 and since Sadat replaced him as Egyptian president, she has continued to be an active speaker and teacher of Islam, calling for the establishment of an Islamic state as the ideal toward which all Muslims should strive in order to have a society which is divinely guided by the Qur'ān and the Sunna of Prophet Muḥammad.[15]

Zaynab al-Ghazālī's ideas regarding the would-be Islamic state are very general and lack specificity on many points. Her belief in it, however, is no weaker for that reason. She believes there is no Islamic state on earth at present, i.e., one totally bound by the Sharīᶜa and implementing it fully; not even Pakistan or Saudi Arabia qualifies to be called an Islamic state in her view. She supports the Iranian revolution and hopes its regime will soon become settled so that it can devote its efforts to solving its internal and external problems. The penal code of the Islamic Sharīᶜa should not be applied now, but it should rather be postponed until an Islamic state is established and the Sharīᶜa can be fully implemented. Allegiance should be given to an Islamic ruler by general election or by the group traditionally known as *ahl al-ḥall wa-l-ᶜaqd* who are honest, wise, experienced and righteous people who, according to her, could be chosen, appointed or elected, no specific system being involved. She believes Islam forbids that the headship of the Islamic state be a hereditary position. One who is head may be called a caliph or a president, and it is conceivable that there could be two caliphs at one time because of the expanse of the Islamic world; but the two should be united and their two armies should fight for the same cause. A caliph should have a council of advisers who are experts in various fields so that he can remain trustworthy and acceptable to the people who elected him. According to her, Islam does not accept a multi-party system because it has its own self-contained system, the Muslim people having the right in it to chose their ruler and the duty to obey him so long as he adheres to the true path of Islam. Other systems or regimes are man-made and inferior to Islam's, which is made by God. Non-Muslim believers will be treated by the Islamic state in accordance with the prescriptions of the Qur'ān and the Sunna, and non-believers likewise. Zaynab al-Ghazālī believes the Islamic system will bring justice to everyone, but Muslims must first be united. There can be differences of opinion among Muslims on issues over which their ranks will not be divided: they may differ on means but not on ends, where the goal should always remain unity.[16]

Nawāl al-Saᶜdāwī is one Muslim Arab woman, among many other women and men in the Arab world, who will differ on means and on ends with Zaynab al-Ghazālī and with thinkers or activists of her frame of mind. One of the staunchest Arab feminists, she is a medical doctor who has written several novels and short stories, some of which have been translated into English.[17] Controversial as her fiction may be, it is her books and articles on sex and on women's issues that have brought her in direct conflict with the political and the religious establishments in Egypt.

Born in 1931 in the village of Kafr Tahla on the Delta banks of the Nile, she received her medical training in Egypt and began her medical practice in 1955 in the rural areas of the country, and later in Cairo hospitals, in the fields of gynecology, family medicine, thoracic surgery and psychiatry. She eventually became Egypt's director of Public Health, but on the publication in 1972 of her first non-fiction book, *al-Mar'a wa-l-Jins* (Woman and Sex), she was dismissed from her post under pressure put on the Ministry of Health by political and religious authorities, and she was also made to relinquish her editorship of a health magazine. She worked for a while in Addis Ababa on the United Nations program for women in Africa, and later in Beirut on the women's program for the United Nations Economic Commission for West Asia. Back in Egypt, she continued her private practice and her writing, but in 1981 she was arrested on orders from President Anwar Sadat because of her controversial views on women's conditions in Egypt. On her release, she has resumed her writing and remains today as undaunted as ever.

The distinctive quality of Nawāl al-Saᶜdāwī's thought is not that it deals squarely with the physiological and psychological aspects of sex in women and men, which many in the Arab world still consider to be taboos, but also that it puts all gender relations in social, economic and political perspectives that are meant to analyze and explain the prevailing oppression in society, and particularly highlight the inferior status of women, the purpose being to subvert the present social structure and help bring about a more humane and equitable one.

In her first non-fiction book on woman and sex, mentioned above, she succinctly states her main thesis:

> The liberation of the woman is not possible in a capitalist society. The equality of women and men cannot happen in a society which distinguishes between one individual and another, and between one class and another. Therefore, the first thing that the woman should realize is that her liberation is only part of the liberation of all society from the capitalist system.[18]

In her later non-fiction books, she elaborates on this thesis in the same texts discussing the physiological and psychological aspects of sex in women and men.[19] But perhaps she has put her thought best in her book *al-Wajh al-ᶜĀrī li-l-Mar'a al-ᶜArabiyya*,[20] later edited and translated into English as *The Hidden Face of Eve: Women in the Arab World*.[21] Here, more forcefully than in the other books, she argues that the value system that subjugates women to men forms part of the basic structures of patriarchal society and is a function of the economic system of that society. A power structure is put in place to maintain and defend this system through political and social institutions, which reinforce it by the laws and sanctions associated with them. With capitalism, the system reaches its fiercest aspects of exploitation and oppression, particularly when heightened by imperialism on the world level, with its economic global domination.

As Irene L. Gendzier says, the power of this book lies in the passionate exposé of the contemporary oppression of Arab women in general and Egyptian women in particular, so that "in spite of its occasionally dubious historical generalizations," the implications of the book go far beyond the study of women in Arab society.[22] Anthropological and sociological generalizations concerning matriarchy and patriarchy may also be dubious in places, but that does not reduce the anger the book expresses at a number of cruel practices degrading to Arab women, nor does it diminish the bitter criticism leveled at the double standard of ethics practiced in Arab society which, in her opinion, discriminates against females.

There is a certain amount of ambiguity in Nawāl al-Sa^c^dāwī's thought with regard to the role of Islam in the scheme of things as seen from a feminist perspective. On the one hand, she repeatedly asserts that Islam has improved the status of women and that, in contrast with Christianity and Judaism, it afforded women a much better life. On the other hand, she also asserts that, beginning with the Caliphate of ^c^Uthmān ibn ^c^Affān, what she calls the "primitive socialism in Islam" came to an end with the growing prosperity of the new classes as "the Muslim warriors burst beyond the narrow frontiers of the Arab desert and flowed out from the burning sands into the green valleys of Syria, Iraq and Egypt."[23]

Whether the inferior status of Muslim women really started with the Caliphate of ^c^Uthmān or not, Nawāl al-Sa^c^dāwī believes that the values of religion are shaped by the economy, and she writes:

> Throughout human history the standards and values of religion have themselves been shaped by the economy. The oppression of women in any society is in its turn an expression

> of an economic structure built on land ownership, systems of inheritance and parenthood, and the patriarchal family as an inbuilt social unit.[24]

This implies that Islam's standards and values are shaped by the economy, and not by divine revelation in the Qur'ān. Further in her argument, she specifies how the influence of the economy works in shaping the moral values of society. Not excluding the moral values of Islamic society, she says:

> Moral values are in fact the product of social systems or, more precisely, of the social system imposed by the ruling class with the aim of serving certain economic and political interests, and ensuring that the situation from which that class draws benefit and power is maintained.[25]

Such Marxist ideas clearly show that she has not made up her mind whether Islam is a revealed religion or a product of human society in history.

Nawāl al-Saᶜdāwī has supported the Iranian revolution of 1979 as a people's movement that has rid Iran of the oppressive regime of the Shah as well as of American, and generally Western, influence in the country. She has also recognized the power of Islam in the success of the revolution. But she is opposed to the Iranian religious leaders who insist on having women covered in the *chador* or deprived of the civil rights they have gained over the years. She argues that such religious leaders "either do not understand Islam correctly or have accepted to serve a dubious cause."[26] And she adds:

> A religious leader is not a God, he is human and therefore liable to go wrong and to make mistakes. It is necessary that his words and actions be submitted to democratic control and critical appraisal by the people whose life he wishes to influence and even direct. He should be questioned and appraised by the women and men he is trying to lead.[27]

It is here, I think, that Nawāl al-Saᶜdāwī shows little understanding of Shīᶜism, and of Islam generally, which do not accept that the revealed laws be submitted to democratic control by the people as in a secular system, particularly if there are specific religious texts available that do not allow for personal opinions. Indeed, here lies one of the major issues in the debate between those who would establish an Islamic state and the secularizers. But Nawāl al-Sa^c^dāwī brushes it off as an issue of right or wrong interpretation, and does not contribute to the debate about the role of divinely revealed texts in a modernizing society.

On this score, perhaps the Moroccan feminist Fatima Mernissi (Fāṭima al-Marnīsī) is more direct in her belief that Islamic law governing the Muslim family should be changed to accommodate the modern economic and political transformation that is increasingly overtaking Muslim societies. As a sociologist, her research on the conditions of Arab women is mainly related to modern Morocco, but her insights and conclusions can be helpful in understanding similar conditions of Arab women elsewhere, especially where the Islamic traditional lifestyles are still prevalent, and modernity is still struggling to establish its hold.

Mernissi believes that the modernization process is putting social and psychological pressures on both men and women, and that change in their relations is bound to occur. The tensions arising in the process are caused by the ambivalent attitudes of both men and women to basically two sets of factors: (1) the exigencies of the Islamic system of values, on the one hand; and (2) the demands of the ever-changing socio-economic and political realities, on the other. She views the present age as a transitional age, and believes that the contemporary conflictual relations between men and women will eventually change into an increasing male-female rapprochement which will be more capable of facing the common problems of daily reality. Attitudes will change, in her opinion, and a new system of values will emerge in the future.

Mernissi believes that there is a state of anomie in Arab society at present.[28] As defined by Emile Durkheim, anomie is more a confusion of norms than the absence of norms; it occurs when the moral system is shaken, after having prevailed for centuries, when it does not respond to new conditions and has not yet been replaced by a new system.[29] The Islamic moral system which segregates women from men in the Arab world is being challenged, in her view, by the fact that women are increasingly entering public life and the work place, previously reserved for men. Mernissi does not see Islamic gender segregation as an isolated social phenomenon of a religious nature, but as a political expression of a specific distribution of power and authority and an economic reflection of a specific division of labor, both forming a total and coherent social order. When this Islamic segregation is shaken, the coherence of the traditional social order as a whole is put into question, especially if social reform is not able to set up an acceptable new system of values governing male-female relations.

In order to examine the content of the traditional Islamic value system with regard to male-female relations, Mernissi refers to the Qur'ān and depends heavily on al-Ghazālī's *Iḥyā' ᶜUlūm al-Dīn*. She also makes use of Mālik ibn Anas's *al-Muwaṭṭa'*, Ḥadīth collections, and a number of classical Islamic works like Ibn Hishām's *Sīrat al-Nabī* and Ibn Saᶜd's *Kitāb al-Ṭabaqāt al-Kubrā*. She cannot be said to speak with a specialist's expertise of the intricacies of Islamic law and ethics on the subject of gender relations in traditional Islamic society, but it can be fairly said that she used the material she collected in this respect with the critical attitude of a convinced feminist, employing modern sociological categories with an evident independence of judgment. She does not consider the modern Western woman as a model for the Muslim woman to emulate, for she believes both are victims of social systems that discriminate against women. Her method analyzes the male-female relation as an entity in the Islamic system, and she uses comparisons with the West only to underline the unique patterns of this relation in Muslim society.

Mernissi's main thesis is that the Islamic system is not so much opposed to the woman as to the male-female relation itself. She believes that such relation, if developed into an encompassing love involvement satisfying the physical, emotional and intellectual needs of both partners, is considered as a detraction from the male's full allegiance to God and as a threat to the totality of his commitment to the divine. Therefore, it has to be controlled and strictly regulated in order to insure God's supremacy in the social order. A corollary of this thesis is that the Islamic system, in her view, considers the woman to be a powerful and dangerous being, not a weak and inferior one.

Hence the Islamic institutions of gender segregation, polygamy and divorce are perceived by Mernissi as strategies for containing female power and danger.[30]

In her book *Beyond the Veil: Male-Female Dynamics in a Modern Muslim Society*,[31] Fatima Mernissi makes much of the concept of *fitna*, a seductive quality which she perceives Islam as ascribing to women, by which they entice men and distract them from their social and religious duties. In support of this perception, she refers to al-Ghazālī who considers civilization as a struggle to contain the woman's destructive power, the survival of society itself being dependent on institutions fostering male dominance through gender segregation.[32] She also quotes *ḥadīths* from al-Bukhārī, Muslim and al-Tirmidhī to present the Islamic view of the irresponsibility of women's attraction to men and the social danger of unsatisfied sexual desires.[33] She concludes by saying:

> What is attacked and debased is not sexuality; it is the woman who is attacked as the embodiment of destruction, the symbol of disorder. She is *fitna*, the polarization of the uncontrollable, a living representative of the dangers of sexuality and its rampant disruptive potential.[34]

Mernissi recognizes Islam's efforts to regulate sexuality in society, but she believes it does so at the expense of the dignity of the human being. In a polygamous Islamic marriage open to the possibility of divorce, the woman is not only treated as inferior to the man but she is always under the threat of either being divorced or of sharing less of her husband if he marries more than one wife. The man in such a marriage is treated as a primarily sexual being who may need up to four wives to satisfy his sexual drive and he is insured against sexual boredom by the right to divorce and remarry. The conjugal unit is thus considered as a merely sexual relation in Islam, and an unstable one at that.[35]

As modernization and economic necessity lessen gender segregation in Arab countries, and as love in a conjugal unit becomes increasingly valued and expected,[36] Mernissi concludes that Arab men and women will achieve an increasing male-female rapprochement to resolve the social and emotional tensions they feel.[37] What she calls "the seventh century laws of the family,"[38] meaning the Qur'anic principles and the Prophet's Sunna which constitute the sources of Islamic laws governing the Muslim family, will have to give way in the face of increasing modern economic and political pressures for change and a new distribution of political power and authority. The Arab ruling class, in Mernissi's opinion, is beginning to realize the necessity of utilizing all human and natural resources in the building of a sovereign future, and she believes "the Arab woman is a central element in any sovereign future."[39]

Mernissi considers Morocco's 1957 *Code du Statut Personnel* (Code of Personal Status) as an undesirable instrument, since it is nothing but the codification into a neat series of articles, sections and sub-sections of the traditional Mālikī principles of law governing the Islamic family. She would like to see Morocco and the Arab world go beyond what she considers to be a seventh-century legal system to a modern one that will derive its principles from the current needs of a changing society and continue to evolve as these needs change.

To end this chapter, I would like to note that Arab women who have publicly expressed their opinions still remain a minority of Arab women. It may also be true that Arab men who have publicly expressed their opinions are also a minority of Arab men, yet their voices carry more weight because Arab society still remains, to a large extent, a man's world. Arab women, have a long and strenuous struggle in front of them, before their voices begin to have equal weight.

Perhaps it is in literary activities that Arab women have made themselves most heard. Since poetry occupies a prominent place in Arab culture, women have sensed the importance of using it as a vehicle of their cause in the last hundred years or so. More recently, Arab women have indeed made a special effort and some of them are today in the forefront of Arab poetic achievements of modern times. The Iraqi Nāzik al-Malā'ika and the Palestinian Fadwā Ṭūqān, to name only two, have been among the major poets of the Arab world who, along with men, have forged a new direction for modern Arabic poetry. Others include the Palestinian Salmā al-Khaḍrā' al-Jayyūsī (who is also a well-known literary scholar and critic), the Lebanese Thérèse ᶜAwwād, the Syrian Saniyya Ṣāliḥ, the Iraqi Lamīᶜa ᶜAbbās ᶜAmāra, the Kuwaiti Suᶜād al-Ṣabāḥ, the Saudi Arabian Fawziyya Abū Khālid, the Jordanian Munā Saᶜūdī, and Ẓabya Khamīs of the United Arab Emirates.[40]

As Arabic fiction has been increasingly vying with Arabic poetry for first place in the literature of the modern Arab world, Arab women have contributed some of the most outstanding novels and short stories to date. Both ᶜĀ'isha ᶜAbd al-Raḥmān and Nawāl al-Saᶜdāwī, whose main interest is in another field, have written successful fiction. Among the well-known names of Arab women in this field of creative writing are Laylā Baᶜlabakkī, Laylā ᶜUsayrān, Ḥanān al-Shaykh, Emily Naṣrallāh and Rose Ghurayyib—all of Lebanon; Samīra ᶜAzzām and Saḥar Khalīfa of Palestine; Colette Suhayl Khūrī, Ilfat Idilbī and Ghāda al-Sammān of Syria; Daisy al-Amīr of Iraq; Sophie ᶜAbdallāh, Laṭīfa al-Zayyāt and Suhayr Qalamāwī of Egypt; Zubayda Bashīr of Tunisia; and Khannātha Bannūna of Morocco.[41] Some Arab women have even ventured into creative literary expression in Western languages such as Andrée Chédid, Etel ᶜAdnān, Nadia Tuéni, Claire Gebeyli and Assia Djebar, some of whose works have been translated into Arabic. Some others have made a name as literary critics of established reputation, such as the Syrian Khālida Saᶜīd, the Lebanese Yumnā al-ᶜĪd, the Egyptian Céza Qāsim Drāz and the Iraqi Ferial Jabūrī Ghazūl.

Of these literary figures, Ghāda al-Sammān seems to have achieved the widest recognition. She is a prolific writer of undaunted and uninhibited nature. Rebellious against all constraints of tradition, she has been writing since 1961 in a variety of genres that attest to her creative imagination and power of expression. Best known for her novels and her short stories, she has also written essays and free verse poems, and has given many revealing interviews to the mass media. She now has twenty-six books to her name, some reprinted several times and, since 1978, all published by her own Ghāda al-Sammān Publications of Beirut, Lebanon, though a few of her earliest books were first published by other publishers and republished later by her own press.

Ghāda al-Sammān was born in 1942 in Damascus, Syria. Her mother having died when she was still a child, she was raised in Damascus by her father, Dr. Aḥmad al-Sammān (d. 1966), a self-made man who became university professor, dean of the faculty of law, rector of the University of Damascus and finally minister of education of Syria, then held a post-retirement professorship at King Saud University in Riyadh, Saudi Arabia. A university graduate herself, with degrees in English literature, Ghāda al-Sammān started her literary career in Beirut where she lived from the 1960s until the Lebanese civil war forced her to start a new life with her husband and son in Paris, where she continues to write with ever-deepening insights into the human condition and Arab life at home and abroad.

The universe of Ghāda al-Sammān's fiction is peopled by all sorts of characters through whom she tries to portray Arab society and criticize its ills. Though coming from a rather well-to-do family, she does not sympathize with the wealthy and powerful, but rather condemns the banality and moral depravity of the Arab bourgeois classes, bent on their own self-interest, often at the cost of the nation's. Earlier in her literary career, she may have emphasized the oppression of Arab women and criticized those aspects of Arab life that put Arab women at a disadvantage, such as attitudes deprecating women, institutions unfavorable to women and values and customs supported by age-old beliefs discriminating against women, but she soon widened her vision and saw the problems of Arab women as part of a larger picture, in which Arab men were as oppressed as Arab women. Her writings began, therefore, to probe this larger picture in which social forces played havoc with the lives of both men and women. Pan-Arab nationalism and socialistic or revolutionary tendencies began to appear in her fictional world. Religious distinctions and socio-political discrimination based on religious identity as prevailing in Lebanon, for example, and fragmenting Arab societies were also decried, and Arab unity was considered to be a defense against Western and Israeli encroachments. Freedom was shown to be an absolute necessity for the Arab individual: both Arab men and Arab women were in vital need of liberation from all kinds of constraining traditions, institutions, attitudes, values and beliefs so that they could regain their lost humanity if new Arab life was to be achieved.[42]

Though powerful and often articulate and down-to-earth, voices of Arab women have been successful only to a limited extent in changing Arab society. One cannot minimize the progress Arab women have achieved in recent times, as individuals who have reached high positions in government and in the professions, and even as reformist elements who have brought about some change, at least in attitudes if not always in behavior, in regard to a number of glaringly iniquitous or abhorrent practices. Yet Arab women still have a long way to go. More and more of them are realizing that the problem is not merely one of gender conflict, though many Arab men and women still view it as such. A deeper understanding is increasingly pointing to the need for radical change that would restructure Arab society and transform Arab culture itself, thus changing the lives of men as well as women. Economic needs in Arab society are an important factor in forcing social change and creating new attitudes and behavior. But cultural transformation is a slow process, and the need for the co-operation of both genders is being increasingly perceived as necessary in order to put it on solid foundation.

Chapter Six

The Intellectual Crisis and Legitimacy

> "Theory is not like a pair of glasses, it is rather like a pair of guns; it does not enable one to see better but to fight better. Intellectuals ought to be struggling against the forms of power they are involved with: knowledge, truth, discourse."
>
> J.G. Merquior, *Foucault* (Berkeley-Los Angeles: University of California Press, 1985), p. 85.

The previous chapters have tried to present some of the major aspects of contemporary Arab thought in the last two decades or so, with particular emphasis on the Arab intellectual struggle to achieve societal and cultural regeneration. We have avoided value judgments as much as is humanly possible, and we have attempted to show that most—if not all—Arab thinkers are unhappy with the present conditions of the Arab world. Whether they are on the extreme right or on the extreme left or on the wide spectrum in between, Arab thinkers want change. The intellectual struggle is about the direction of this change and about the power it will bring to those effecting it. In this chapter we will attempt to understand the sociological and epistemological dimensions of this intellectual struggle.

To begin with, we should state that thought does not exist in a vacuum, and yet it is not merely a reflection of "reality." By reality, we mean the physical world and the system of complex societal relations, the human perception of which constitutes the initial aspect of thought. Thought and reality form a continuum in which they have a dialectical relation with each other. Thought has a certain relative autonomy as it deals with reality, although it is also determined by several factors within reality. In fact, when thought becomes conscious of itself in relation to reality, its relative autonomy may be such that it attempts to change reality according to its perceived needs and interests, its success in this attempt often being a function of the extent of its grasp of reality and of its control over it.

The realization that thought can control reality to whatever extent is, by itself, a recognition of the power of knowledge. A system of knowledge that grows, accumulates and circulates in society becomes its cultural discourse—which permeates, characterizes and constitutes the social world, its institutions, its values and the behavior of its members. Michel Foucault has analyzed the subtle relationship between knowledge and power, and he has shown that there can be no exercise of power without a certain economy of discourses that maintain and support society's perception of reality.[1] Discourses are composed of thought expressed in speech, statements, texts and other means of language communication and are generally believed by those who hold them to contain "the truth."

For a discourse to contain "the truth," it must be capable of the verbal construction of meaning in a manner acceptable to certain persons and their perception of reality. In other words, meanings are not found in verbal expressions of thought only, but are also embodied in human society and its institutions, as well as in social practices and institutional techniques. Discourse is the locus of the social production of meaning for the simple reason that speech and writing are social phenomena. Hence, a philological approach to a text or a statement is not capable by itself of elucidating its meaning; resort must be made to the methods of the social sciences in order to shed light on the relations of the text or statement to its human and social milieu in a particular moment in history.

The social sciences have recently developed several approaches in the theoretical work on discourse analysis.[2] Furthermore, recent neo-Marxist perspectives on the subject have expanded our knowledge of the relations between discourse, social psychology and the social structure in the development of ideology.[3] We shall therefore use some of the approaches of these recent studies for the better understanding of the intellectual struggle in society generally, and in Arab society in particular.

It has been observed that the social formations in a particular society have different perceptions of reality, and that they may thus tend to have different discourses. The social formation which has political power over the others tries to make its own discourse prevail and often succeeds in neutralizing all the other discourses. In this event, the discourse constitutes the ideology of that society, until it is displaced or changed. Thus, ideology is related to the process of sustaining relations of power in society by the successful construction of meanings within discourse and by the appropriation of those meanings, not only by the dominant class or group, but also by the dominated classes or groups. As John B. Thompson says, "to study ideology is to study the ways in which meaning (signification) serves to sustain relations of domination."[4]

Relations of domination in capitalist societies are directly linked with relations of production. Hence, meaning depends on class position. As Pêcheux says, "Words, expressions, propositions change their meanings according to the positions held by those who use them, which signifies that they find their meaning . . . by reference to the ideological formations . . . in which those positions are inscribed."[5] He also says that discourses exist antagonistically, inasmuch as ideological formations from which they come are themselves antagonistic. The struggle, therefore, is not merely a struggle of meanings in discourse but rather an ideological and political struggle related to class positions, and ultimately to class power and domination.[6]

Althusser had argued that ideology interpellates individuals as subjects and thus calls on them to recognize themselves as such through the mechanism of identification. Pêcheux has developed this argument further and says that individuals are interpellated as *speaking* subjects of discourse representing, in language, the ideological formation which corresponds to them, and thus they identify with the discursive formation that dominates them.[7] He further adds two other mechanisms of interpellation: the first is counteridentification, which rejects the identity inscribed in the ruling ideological practices, thus remaining more or less subordinate to what it opposes; and the second is disidentification, which works against the prevailing ideological practices in order to transform them and eventually displace the dominant ideology.[8] Pêcheux thus removes from the mechanism of interpellation the determinism of Althusser and restores to thought a measure of relative autonomy.

On the other hand, Laclau has emphasized the function of contradictions among ideological discourses and the antagonistic efforts of each to prevail through ideological struggle and transformation. The dominant ideological discourse remains prevailing so long as the social formation producing it is able to marginalize, absorb and neutralize the antagonisms of the dominated classes or groups. When it fails in times of ideological crisis, the result is a disarticulation of the dominant ideological discourse.[9]

According to Laclau, the ideological crisis is brought about by contradictions that continue to accumulate and intensify, as increasing social differentiation and economic contradictions between the dominant and the dominated classes grow and adversely affect the polity.[10] A new political discourse is articulated by the rising social force in order to displace the dominant discourse. If the new force cannot impose its hegemony within the existing institutional structures, it appeals to the people.[11] In fact, each class represents itself as the authentic representative of the 'people', of the 'national interest' and so on.[12] In Laclau's view, class struggle for hegemony is of the utmost importance because it integrates what he calls popular democratic interpellations into an ideological class discourse with the aim of winning mass support.

In other words, this is a process of legitimation. By delegitimizing the dominant class or group, the rising ideology is proclaiming its own legitimacy and aiming at domination. As Max Weber observed, every system of domination cultivates a belief in its own legitimacy and for that purpose appeals to rational, traditional or charismatic elements.[13] This appeal is generally expressed in language, it is addressed to the people and it contains the meaning which serves to sustain relations of domination. If those relations serve the interests of some people at the expense of others, as is often the case, the ideology resorts to dissimulation, concealing or denying this fact and explaining it in terms acceptable to the people.[14] Ideological discourse in any society seeks to be perceived as articulating the needs and interests of that society by using its language and cultural symbols to the utmost advantage. Its *modus operandi* should not blind the intelligent to its aim of sustaining relations of power and domination or to its aim of articulating a justification for a transformation in those relations of power and domination, in societies whose dominant ideological discourse is undergoing a crisis.

The above discussion on ideology and discourse analysis has no pretension of exhausting the topic, not even of sketching the main outlines of its concerns. The literature on it is voluminous and is still growing, consensus in it is rare, as theories on it continue to multiply, and the difficulties of objective conceptualization are evident, given the nature of the topic as an object of study replete with subjective considerations. What we have presented, however, is a practical preface in the light of which we will offer our own understanding of the state of the current ideological discourse in the Arab world and its intellectual crisis.

In the various trends of Arab thought presented in the previous chapters, is evidence of the intellectual struggle going on in the contemporary Arab world. Recent reports on events and developments in the area speak of the pressures under which Arab regimes are trying to maintain their authority as they are being incessantly criticized by groups and movements of resurgent Islam and, perhaps in a less dramatic manner, by liberal and secular forces and tendencies. While some may argue that instability which the Arab world experienced in the 1950s and 1960s is not in evidence today as we approach the last years of the 1980s (Lebanon being the exception), it is almost certain that the present stability of the Arab regimes is only transient or apparent, and that their legitimacy is still in question, since it is nowhere based on the full and genuine participation of the Arab people. In a recent book which seeks to show the resilience and durability of the Arab state and cogently presents ample evidence to support its arguments, this is the conclusion:

> For some time to come, the stability of the Arab state will continue to rest on the ability of political leaderships to exercise effective control through coercion[;] to co-opt individuals and groups into the administrative and political structure; to extend economic and social benefits to hitherto excluded sectors of society; and to satisfy the hunger of the urban middle and upper-middle classes for an increasing role in the political

> process by allowing them limited political participation and representation. As long as these functions are performed, the Arab state will continue to be resilient. But it is not the durable resilience of the system whose legitimacy is based on the full participation of the people in the body politic.[15]

It is in the context of these conditions that we must view the current Arab intellectual discourse. The contemporary Arab states have endured primarily because they have used their coercive power to control and manipulate, to repress and silence, even to forcefully remove and liquidate opponents. But they have also been concerned with their legitimacy, and have tried to gain the grudging acquiescence of their restive populations when they were unable to obtain their willing acceptance. And so they have co-opted individuals and groups into their institutions and included them in extended benefits and permitted them a measure of limited political participation. But they have not created *civic society*, nor have they permitted one to develop. The vocal ones among those who would not be coopted into these systems are either in prison or in exile. The latter, especially those in Paris and London, have developed their independent forums, associations and Arabic journals and newspapers supported by the growing Arab communities outside the Arab world and by Arabs in the homeland, with whom the exiles aim to remain in touch. The Arab regimes that own and run state-controlled radio, television and print media that disseminate their ideology wish to control the Arab media in exile too. In recent times, they have even attempted to co-opt some intellectuals in exile by cajoling them to return home, by inviting them to lavish inter-Arab conferences and festivals, or by offering them other enticements. When the Arab regimes fail to win them over, they try to pressure the governments of the host Western countries (so far unsuccessfully, one must quickly add), to help them in their coercive attempts or the regimes themselves start publications and activities abroad and at home to counteract those of their exiled opponents.[16]

Within the Arab world itself, some of the political regimes permit opposition more than others, but then only within certain limited bounds and never allowing the opposition to challenge the existence of the regime. Outside these limited bounds, the regime's punishment is sure to be meted out quickly, and as violently as King Ḥusayn's treatment of the PLO men in the Jordanian events of Black September in 1970, President Sādāt's treatment of the Egyptians in the antigovernment riots of 1977, King Khālid's treatment of the Saudi Muslim extremists in the takeover of the Grand Mosque of Mecca in 1979, President Asad's treatment of the Syrian Muslim Brothers in the rebellion of Ḥamā in 1982, and the Algerian government's treatment of the people's riots of October 1988, to mention only some of the violent events of suppression in the area. This is not to say that an Arab regime (or any other for that matter) should not defend itself if its existence is threatened, but that the opposition is usually throttled so effectively that it is sometimes pushed to adopt violent means. The dissidence permitted by an Arab regime is normally so benign that it is hardly worth mentioning except as a token of that regime's openness and tolerance. Human and civil rights of individuals and groups under contemporary Arab regimes are severely curtailed and often completely ignored.

The sense of bitterness and indignation associated with this repressive atmosphere has been captured in poems, novels and short stories as well as in articles, books, conference proceedings and so on.[17] Irony in this respect has made Nizār Qabbānī write a sarcastic article entitled "We who undersigned with our hoofs" in the Paris Arab weekly, *al-Mustaqbal*, in which he says, in part:

> We, the Arab sheep, who undersigned with our hoofs, having put our trust in God's grace, may He be praised and exalted, and having written our will and insured our heads with the American Life Insurance Company against being cut off: Have decided to write to our Master the Sultan and his consort Qamar al-Zamān. . . .
>
> We have discovered . . . that the Arab sheep, metaphorically called the Arab masses, are deprived of all rights granted by the United Nations, the International Red Cross, and the Societies for the Prevention of Cruelty to Animals. . . .
>
> We, the Arab sheep, whose eyes have been extinguished so that they may not see, whose horns have been sawed off so

that they may not butt, whose brains have been washed so that they may not think;

We, the Arab sheep, traveling from terror to terror, who are forbidden from using the telephone, from going to the Post Office, and from buying tickets for travel by sea, land, or air;

We, the Arab sheep, whose meat is used broiled in official ceremonies, and whose skin is used tanned in the footwear industry; . . . .

We, the Arab sheep, who have been condemned to remain sheep until the Day of Judgment and who are required not to complain, argue, or object:

Do hereby wish, in all respect, to explain to the meat contractors supplying our Lord the Sultan, his consort Qamar al-Zamān, their children, grandchildren, and their cats, dogs, monkeys, and parrots . . . that our flesh is not sufficient for their Grand Banquet. . . .

And until we meet in the next world under the protection of the Forgiving and Merciful [God], we urge you to take good care of our children.[18]

In view of mounting governmental repression in Arab countries in the 1970s and the 1980s, it was not surprising to see a group of thirty-five Arab intellectuals of various ideological convictions, from different Arab countries and overseas, meet privately between April 1 and 4, 1983 in Tunisia to discuss ways of confronting it. They decided to call for a larger meeting but were denied permission to hold it in any one of the three Arab countries they chose: Egypt, Jordan and Kuwait. So they held it in Limassol, Cyprus on December 1 and 2, 1983. As a result, a permanent pan-Arab organization called the Arab Organization for Human Rights was set up.[19] A fourteen-member board of trustees and a seven-member executive committee were established with offices in Geneva, and a secretariat in Cairo when the Egyptian government relented. Although not the only Arab organization of its kind, this more important organization, financed entirely from non-governmental private contributions and membership fees from Arab individuals at home and abroad, pursues a vigorous monitoring and defense of human and civil rights in all the Arab world, and takes all possible measures to pressure Arab governments for redress of abuses and respect of international human rights agreements. It has been well received by the increasingly politicized Arab publics.[20] It publishes a newsletter and a non-periodic journal, it investigates violations of human and civil rights, makes personal and written representations to Arab authorities, holds periodic conferences and co-operates with similar organizations in Arab countries and in the world at large.

All these activities indicate that contemporary Arabs are no longer willing to put up with governments who would not respect them as human beings with rights. If in the 1950s and the 1960s they acquiesced in the suppression of their rights in the name of national security and especially on account of the struggle against Israel, or for the proclaimed purpose of economic development and the establishment of Arab socialism, or as a supposed requirement to achieve pan-Arab unity—now they know that none of those aims would justify the suppression of democratic freedoms which are fundamental goals in themselves, and none of those objectives could be achieved in any case without the democratic process.

It may be argued that those Arabs who feel so are only a minority, consisting of the articulate and educated elite of the urban middle and upper-middle classes. Even if this argument is correct and the silent majority of the population (as in most countries of the Third World and elsewhere) is passive and does not want to be involved in politics for fear of trouble, this does not speak well of the legitimacy of Arab regimes. No regime can forever continue to exercise power if it does not have legitimacy, and the political leaders of the Arab world know that fact very well, and constantly try to win the acceptance of their populations, or at least their acquiescence to their leadership, by all palliative means possible, but not by according them their human and civil rights, including the right of full and genuine political participation and representation.[21] Arab regimes continue to be authoritarian and coercive, though most may appear to be stable and durable.

The demographic changes in the Arab world aggravate the situation. It is now estimated that the Arab world has about 200 million people. Its urban population has swelled from 27.7 percent of the total in 1950 to 46.8 percent in 1980 and has continued to grow. By the year 2000 it is expected that almost six out of every ten inhabitants of the region will live in cities. This urban growth is not only the result of natural reproduction but also of the exodus of rural dwellers to cities in search of better work opportunities and services.[22] In individual Arab countries, most urban populations are concentrated in a few large cities: one third of Syria's population lives in Damascus, one fourth of Egypt's lives in Cairo. In the Gulf states, the urbanization is particularly pronounced: approximately 80 percent of Bahrain's population lives in cities, over 90 percent of Kuwait's, more than 87 percent of Qatar's and 80 percent of the United Arab Emirates.[23] The Maghrib at the other end of the Arab world shares similar trends: about 45 percent of Moroccans, approximately 50 percent of Algerians and more than 50 percent of Tunisians are now city-dwellers.[24]

This rapid urbanization is having a deep and adverse effect on the quality of Arab life. The overcrowding conditions, which have not been effectively met with good planning and wise development by the authorities, have multiplied the problems. The housing shortage, the traffic jams, the inadequate water and sewage sytems, the electricity outages, the inefficient public transportation and communications systems, the insufficient health and education resources, the unemployment: all intensify the ravages of poverty and increase the stress of living for the majority of Arab city-dwellers.

As the conditions of the poor deteriorate in the growing urban centers rendering city life more and more difficult, the wealthy are able to leave for the new suburbs, abandoning the inner cities to the poor. Shantytowns on the outskirts are still the blight of many an Arab city and although in some, as in Baghdad, these shantytowns have been removed by the authorities and replaced by modern housing units, in Cairo many of the poor, estimated to range between 250,000 and 900,000 continue to live in old cemetery vaults and tombs in the City of the Dead.[25] The daily awareness of the gulf between the rich and the poor, visibly represented by the sumptuous hotels, new office buildings, high-rise apartments, shops full of imported consumer products adjacent to shabby neighborhoods and scenes of staggering deprivation must be a trying experience, if not a potentially explosive one.

The modern cities of the rich Arabian Gulf may have been spared some of those problems, as the new cities have little in common with their abandoned or almost vanished traditional sites. Their extravagance, however, leaves the impression that their authorities think the oil wealth is inexhaustible. They have not planned for an eventual future without oil, nor have they given thought to the human problems of imported manual and unskilled workers and of significant minorities of segregated foreigners in their midst. Some of these cities seem to be facing a developing problem of drug addiction, especially among the affluent young men and women in their populations, though this is not widely discussed or studied for the purpose of finding solutions.

The overall picture of recent demographic changes highlights the fact that rural populations have been all but neglected in the Arab world and that urban populations have not been adequately served. They are both, largely, young populations, 45 percent of whom are under the age of fifteen.[26] For the most part too, they are illiterate populations: 70 percent of those over the age of fifteen in the early 1970s were illiterate (about 60 percent of males, and 85 percent of females), though this percentage is rapidly decreasing.[27]

Arab society exhibits differentiation; it is not monolithic or uniform as a whole, and it is changing quickly and drastically. Unable to control its destiny, repressed, underdeveloped, repeatedly defeated and constantly oppressed, the Arab populace is in a state of alienation from itself and its rulers. The Arab political regimes for their part do their best to remain in power, only involving the populace when it is advantageous to do so, but mostly using it, abusing it and always serving the interests of the ruling classes. Their dependency on the West exacerbates the situation, and their inability to stand up to the challenges of Zionism and Israel compounds their difficulties.

Contemporary Arab thinkers would be worth nothing if they did not call for changing those bad conditions. But thought is grounded in reality, and whatever discourse they have created expresses the ideology that that reality has given birth to, in its dialectical relationship with thought. The relative autonomy of thought dictates that Arab society should extricate itself from its present alienation and take control of itself and its destiny.

The methods and means suggested by each individual Arab thinker speak of his class position, of how he reacts to the prevailing ideology as a subject. His discourse expresses his ties to an identity, basically his identification with a social formation, with a group or a class. If a member of the ruling elite, he supports the ideological discourse of his ruling group or class, with which he identifies. This is why Arab regimes seek to co-opt Arab thinkers into their systems and thus tie them to the dominant ideology with which they want them to identify. If the thinker is a member of the Arab populace and rejects cooptation by the regime, he is psychologically resorting to another mechanism of interpellation. He now articulates an antagonistic relation to the dominant ideology of the Arab regime, he rejects being interpellated by it as a subject, he resorts to the mechanism of counteridentification, rejecting the identity inscribed in the ruling ideological discourse and its practices. However, he remains subordinate to what he opposes in that his discourse still recognizes the ideological discourse of the Arab regime he opposes, but he does not identify with it. This is the case of many Arab thinkers in the wide spectrum between the extreme Right and the extreme Left.

As for the extremist Arab thinker, he resorts to still another mechanism of interpellation, namely, that of disidentification. His discourse displaces the Arab individual from the position of subjectivity and disrupts the functioning of the dominant ideology; it works against the practices of ideological subjection by the Arab regime and aims at the displacement of the prevailing ideology. The extremist Arab thinker's aim is the deconstruction of the dominant ideology represented by the prevailing Arab regime and its practices and institutions. He does not recognize it, he does not identify with it or with any of its practices and institutions, he does not acknowledge its legitimacy, he does not accept its claim to authority as legitimate or rightful power, he does not admit to the logic of its discourse: because if he does any of those things, he will be participating in the reproduction of the dominant system as a whole. His disidentification seeks to achieve total ideological transformation.

The difference between the extremist Arab thinker on the Right and the extremist Arab thinker on the Left is that the former conforms to a past-oriented ideology which he believes originates in God and divine revelation, while the latter creates a new ideology which he believes originates in man and his societal needs, with emphasis on economic and social justice. And each wants his own ideology to replace the current dominant one.

In all this struggle, each of the Arab regimes tries to absorb, marginalize and neutralize any attempt at displacing its dominant ideological discourse and its control over Arab society. It may succeed for a time and appear durable and stable. The success of each regime depends on its ability to deal with change in the social world and the ideological discourse; it also depends on the magnitude and force of this change at any particular conjuncture of history and how it meets the change. The Arab regime may resort to coercion, repression, censorship, cooptation and the extension of limited economic, social and political privileges to individuals or groups. It may ally itself with other Arab and foreign regimes to strengthen itself. It may gain a new lease on life through these and other means, but it will not achieve legitimacy and real stability until the Arab people in its domain obtain all their human and civil rights, including all the freedoms and full participation in the democratic process of government. The importance of the Arab people with regard to the lasting legitimacy of any Arab regime necessitates the notion that no ideological discourse will succeed unless it authentically represents them. That is why the political discourse of the various Arab thinkers, speaking from various class positions, consists of antagonistic articulations in which each represents itself as the authentic discourse of 'the people'. As Laclau says, each class represents itself as the authentic representative of the people, of the national interest and so on. The undeclared aim of each Arab thinker, therefore, is to win support of the Arab masses by popular democratic interpellations into the discourse of his own class. Only that ideology which captures the will of the people by actually changing the social world in the service of all the people will eventually achieve hegemony in a legitimate manner.

All the signs indicate that there is an ideological crisis in the Arab world. Part of a more general crisis in the economy and the polity of the Arab countries, it originates in the intensification of the contradictions and the accumulation of conflictual situations in Arab society. The increasing social differentiation which has enlarged the gap between the rich and the poor has heightened the economic contradictions between the dominant and the dominated Arab classes. The dependency of the Arab regimes on the West has, in many instances, engendered stronger ties by the dominant Arab classes with the West as a means of strengthening themselves against the dominated classes and postponing an eventual encounter with them. The dominant Arab classes have become increasingly unable to neutralize the antagonisms of the dominated Arab classes, and their dominant Arab ideology is beginning to crack and be increasingly unable to win the continued acquiescence of the members of the dominated Arab classes.

Arab nationalism in the 1930s and the 1940s, during the struggle for independence, helped the pan-Arab movement to grow even stronger in the 1950s and the 1960s during nation-building after independence, and made the call for all-Arab unity part of the dominant ideology in the Arab world. Though some Arab regimes may have differed with Jamāl ᶜAbd al-Nāṣir, the Baᶜth Party and other leaders and movements advocating pan-Arab ideas, their ideology on the whole accepted the premises of Arab nationalism based on the commonness of the Arabic language and Arab culture among the population of the region, and on the socio-economic, political and strategic advantages of pan-Arab unity. Islam was generally considered as a component of Arab culture and was believed not to prevent Arab nationalism from remaining basically a secular movement supported by Muslim and non-Muslim Arabs. The dominant classes in the Arab world instituted this ideology and the dominated classes, as interpellated subjects, subscribed to it as an appealing ideology of 'the people'. The League of Arab States took it for granted and, though it recognized the legal independence of each Arab state, its charter encouraged mutual agreements of further co-ordination and unification. Socialist ideas of one sort or another were grafted on the ideas of Arab nationalism but, in those Arab regimes which implemented them, they turned out to be policies of state capitalism serving the interests of the dominant bourgeois classes.

Disenchantment grew stronger among the Arab people as neither Arab unity was achieved nor socialist dreams of better life for the lower classes were realized. The defeat of the Arab regimes in the war of June 1967 against Israel laid bare the hollow character of the dominant ideology in the Arab world. The growing class differentiation between the rich and the poor, particularly in the rapidly-growing Arab cities, sharpened the economic contradictions in Arab society and intensified the need for change. The rural newcomers in the Arab cities, the growing numbers of younger Arabs in the cities and elsewhere, the lost and alienated masses of people caught in drastic change, all needed to find meaning to their lives as individuals and as groups. The dominant discourse spoke less and less to them. The dominant Arab classes represented in the Arab regimes became increasingly unable to neutralize the antagonisms of the dominated classes. The dominant ideology of Arab nationalism, and of Arab 'socialism' where it was implemented, were in crisis because of the more general crisis in the Arab economy and polity which the Arab defeat of 1967 aggravated. The times were increasingly ripe for another ideology to articulate the needs and interests of the new rising social forces in Arab society, an ideology which would appeal to 'the people', bring meaning to their lives and give them hope in improvement.

This was the ideological situation in the Arab world, until the 1970s and the 1980s ushered in resurgent Islam as an ideology. It is not that Islam was not there all along, but its sociopolitical and legal dimensions were not prominent in ideological discourse. The Society of the Muslim Brothers in Egypt and later in some other parts of the Arab world brought in those dimensions in the 1930s and the 1940s; but in the 1950s and the 1960s the Muslim Brothers clashed with the regime and its dominant ideology and they were suppressed in Egypt, though in other Arab countries, like Jordan, they continued to operate. Following the Arab defeat in 1967, the Arab regimes and their dominant ideology began to be increasingly discredited for having failed to achieve their aims. By the early 1970s, Islam as a comprehensive ideological discourse began to loom as an appealing system of ideas and beliefs to increasing numbers of Muslim Arabs searching for secure moorings in a rapidly changing world and for a means to oppose the prevailing Arab regimes. Not only the Society of the Muslim Brothers but several offshoots of it and similar movements began to have growing influence over sections of the Arab public. The Islamic discourse was familiar to these people, its language and symbols were not alien, its claim to divine authority appeared religiously compelling to them, its drive to political ascendancy seemed justified under the circumstances. The success of the Iranian revolution in 1979 in establishing an Islamic Republic gave Islamic resurgence a boost everywhere. Today, in the 1980s, the Islamic discourse has numerous adherents in several Arab countries, including Egypt, Jordan, Syria, Lebanon, Kuwait, Tunisia and the Sudan.[28] Though not organizationally unified in these countries and others, its aim everywhere is to displace the dominant ideological discourse and achieve political hegemony. But it does not go unchallenged, even in Egypt where it seems to be strongest.

A cursory look at the current newspapers in Cairo, for example, reveals daily debates on their pages between supporters of Islamic resurgence and their opponents. Magazines and journals prominently feature writings of thinkers defending one or the other of the opposing sides. Books on both sides of the argument abound in the bookstalls of the city. Radio and television programs present interviews and heated discussions on the issues at hand. The Egyptian university campuses offer daily reminders of Islamic resurgence. The Egyptian parliament itself is often the forum of arguments on the subject, as well as legislation that takes Islamic resurgence into account. And the debate goes on.

A well-known Egyptian thinker, Fu'ād Zakariyyā, keeps reminding his co-religionists that the current Islamic discourse is an ideology which does not represent all Muslims and that it does not really present Islam itself. He explains that it is a politically-motivated discourse whose aim is to keep the Arabs (and other Muslims) retarded in the modern world, occupied with useless arguments and impossible goals, and irrationally concerned about matters that distract them from the real problems to which they ought to give attention. He says that this Islamic ideology has created a special kind of Islam unknown in earlier history, and he calls it Petro-Islam in reference to the support it receives from certain oil-rich Arab regimes. Their purpose, he says, is to preserve their dominance in their own societies and elsewhere, keep the oil wealth in the exclusive possession of the dominant classes and unshared with their own Arab people and other Muslims in the world, and to sustain their profitable relations with the dominant capitalist West and their place in its world economic system.[29]

Fu'ād Zakariyyā enters the debate with a strong plea for rationality.[30] He declares he wants to keep a running dialogue with the members of the Islamic movements and he hopes the media will give them equal time. His purpose is that this important subject be given its due public attention so that those men and women who listen to the dialogue may understand both points of view before deciding how to orient their lives. His observation is that those who join the Islamic movements have not usually been given such an opportunity: they know only one point of view and believe it is true; they depend on quotations from holy scripture and other texts, accept blindly interpretations offered by their leaders and repeat these endlessly in their arguments without using their own reason.[31]

Fu'ād Zakariyyā subjects some of the ideas of the Islamic movements to scrutiny and finds them wanting. He points to their belief in what they call the governance of God and argues that this is an impossible proposition because any governance, whatever the source of its authority, is mediated and implemented by human beings. For him, therefore, Islam is what Muslims have made of it in history; it is not some ahistorical system beyond human experience.[32] It is how those Muslims in history have interpreted the Qur'ān and the teachings of Prophet Muḥammad in their daily lives that constitutes Islam. Furthermore, those Muslims who were in positions of governance were subject to all the frailties of being human and thus there were occasions when they committed errors and injustices, though there were also occasions when, like other people, they achieved feats of great significance. Therefore, the hope that if an Islamic government is established in Egypt or anywhere it will be perfect and will provide peace, justice and prosperity for its people is a false hope. There can be no guarantee of perfection for any human government. Zakariyyā says that past Islamic history proves this fact as well as recent Islamic history, but members of the Islamic movements reply that any failures in this respect have been failures of human beings, not of Islam. For Zakariyyā, this is complete disregard of history and shutting one's eyes to lessons offered by reality.[33]

The claim by the Islamic movements that the religious texts of Islam are good for all times and places is rejected by Fu'ād Zakariyyā as another ahistorical proposition. The religious texts that make up the Sharīᶜa are finite, in his opinion, whereas historical and societal changes are infinite, and thus there is contradiction in the claim itself. Finite rules cannot apply to infinite cases. If, as a way out of this contradiction, Islamic movements restrict themselves to general principles in the religious texts and consider them to be good for all times and places, leaving the particulars to be worked out by every generation, many obstacles arise such as how to determine what parts of the religious texts belong to general principles and what parts belong to particulars, especially as some of these particulars are specified in the religious texts and relate to important human matters such as the rules of inheritance, marriage and divorce, which are historically subject to change.[34]

Fu'ād Zakariyyā accuses the Islamic movements of not having a specific plan for society as a whole and that their concern is limited to the individual, as if the total of individuals makes up a society. Even then, their concern is addressed to the form rather than the content of Islam, such as their insistence on observing religious rituals and responding to religious commands and prohibitions that hardly affect public life. This includes the undue concern of Islamic movements with what they consider to be proper dress for men and women, their fussiness about the performance of prayers and other religious duties and their finicky imposition of gender segregation. The veil for women, the robe for men with a length reaching midway between the knees and the feet, and beards but no moustaches—all these are seen by the Islamic movements as basic to being good Muslims.[35] Zakariyyā does not accept that these dress codes are to preserve propriety and morality, as purported by the Islamic movements, but that they are themselves an expression of excessive concern about sex, giving it more importance in life than it actually has, to the extent that the real problems of bread, shelter, justice and security disappear.[36]

Fu'ād Zakariyyā concedes that religion may have a mobilizing power among Muslims, as it did in the first stages of the Iranian revolution of 1979. This power, however, can be manipulated to push society backward, as indeed it has been in Iran, Egypt and some other countries; and, although it may be called a revival or an awakening, one should discern its true nature. The fact that most Muslims in the world are illiterate masses lacking rationality and political consciousness and living under conditions of oppression, tyranny, repression and violence makes Islam seemingly the only power to move these masses and mobilize them to stand up to their oppressors.[37] But Zakariyyā warns that this should only open doors to further developments and reactions, rather than revert to backward-looking movements.

Faraj Fūda is another Egyptian intellectual who has entered the debate staunchly defending secularization and democracy, and criticizing the Islamic movements that call for the Islamization of society. Like Zakariyyā, Fūda says that these Islamic movements have no specific plan for society and no thought-out program for running it. They call for the instant implementation of the Sharīᶜa and naively assert that implementation will immediately result in a good society whose problems are all solved.[38] Fūda accuses these Islamic movements of not knowing the complexities of societal relations in modern times, which cannot be dealt with by the Sharīᶜa, and of ignoring the lack of agreement among Muslim jurists themselves with regard to many important aspects of the Sharīᶜa, not least being the criteria and procedures of electing the head of the Islamic state and the constitutional problems concerning the people's rights of being consulted and the extent of their control of the government. He also accuses them of not really knowing Islamic history, the details of which would show that their ideal Islamic state has never been achieved in the past, even under the earliest Muslims who knew the Prophet personally and were fully conversant with the principles of the Sharīᶜa.[39]

The idealization of the Islamic past as a model for Muslims to invoke and revive, like the idealization of the Sharī'a as a panacea for all Muslim society's ills, is in Fūda's opinion a dangerous and misguided attitude which he opposes and seeks to correct. In his book, *al-Ḥaqīqa al-Ghā'iba* (The Absent Truth), he concentrates on the Islamic past and, though not a professional historian, he marshals sufficient compelling and documented evidence from classical Muslim historians like al-Ṭabarī, al-Mas^cūdī, Ibn Sa^cd, al-Balādhurī, Ibn Kathīr and others to support his claim that the Islamic state was not a perfect state, as believed by the Islamic movements today. He concludes:

> The truth is that Islam as state has been a detraction from Islam as religion and it has been a burden on it; for Islam, as God wished it to be, is a religion and a doctrine, and not government and power. The truth also is that human beings are human beings in all ages; and in this regard the periods of the Rāshidūn, the Umayyads, the ᶜAbbasids, and our own modern age are all equal. Talk about paradise on earth is prattle of no value, scum of no use, and falsehood of no avail.[40]

Fūda makes great efforts to disabuse the Islamic movements' followers of any illusions about the claimed perfection of even some of the earliest Muslims, many of whom are considered saintly. Though a Muslim himself, he does so in order to show that these early Muslims, like all others in history, are only human beings subject to the frailties of the human condition. Right from the beginning of his book, he warns that his discourse is a discourse about the world, politics and government, though it may appear to be a discourse about religion, doctrine and faith.[41] Even some of those ten Companions of the Prophet who were given the good news of deserving Paradise are not spared in his account derived from the classical sources, and doubts are cast about the great wealth they amassed after Islam; he mentions them by name: ᶜUthmān ibn ᶜAffān, al-Zubayr ibn al-ᶜAwwām, Saᶜd ibn Abī Waqqāṣ, Ṭalḥa ibn ᶜUbayd-Allāh and ᶜAbd al-Raḥmān ibn ᶜAwf and he mentions the considerable amounts of money and property they left at their death, though earlier, as Emigrants from Mecca to Medina, they hardly possessed anything.[42]

Again basing his work on the classical sources, Fūda gives an account of the correspondence between the fourth Caliph ᶜAlī ibn Abī Ṭālib and his cousin, the great and pious scholar of Islam ᶜAbd-Allāh ibn ᶜAbbās, who was governor of Baṣra for him and who was reported to him by its treasurer Abū al-Aswad al-Du'alī to have embezzled the monies under his command. The correspondence shows that Ibn ᶜAbbās initially denied the accusation but refused to be accountable when asked to give a detailed treasury statement of income and expenditure. When later pressed, he submitted his resignation, still refusing to be accountable, and declared that in his eyes ᶜAlī's shedding of the Islamic community's blood in his quest for power and rule was of graver enormity than the embezzlement of all the wealth of the world. Ibn ᶜAbbās then collected the balance remaining in the treasury of Baṣra and, under the protection of his maternal uncles from Banū Hilāl, left the city, despite minor armed engagements with its people, and settled comfortably in the Holy City of Mecca. ᶜAlī sent him one more letter asking him to relent and return the monies embezzled or face God's punishment as well as ᶜAlī's necessary measures in due course. Ibn ᶜAbbās's response stated that his right to the monies of the treasury was greater than ᶜAlī's amounts taken from it, and in a final letter he said that if ᶜAlī did not stop his shenanigans he, Ibn ᶜAbbās, would take the monies to Muᶜāwiya to help him fight ᶜAlī.[43]

Fūda also discusses the civil wars that plagued the nascent Muslim community in Arabia after the death of Prophet Muḥammad, and how Muslims killed Muslims during the Caliphate of the Rāshidūn, three of the four Caliphs themselves being victims of assassination, despite the freshness of the message of Islam in the hearts and minds of the people.[44] He argues that it was politics and other mundane matters that swayed the leaders of the Muslim community as well as the people: although there were many saintly believers among them who based their actions on the Qur'ān and the teachings of the Prophet and although the Sharīᶜa was fully implemented, neither justice nor peace and order necessarily ensued, and neither good government nor a happy and peaceable community automatically followed.[45]

Fūda points to many other documented acts and events in the Caliphate of the Rāshidūn, then moves to the Caliphate of the Umayyads[46] and later the ᶜAbbasids[47] to prove that the Islamic state was never an ideal government and that the Sharīᶜa was manipulated by the leaders according to their needs and their perception of the requirements of society. His call, in modern times, remains for a democratic and secular state in which religion is separated from politics for the benefit of both, religion *and* politics.[48]

Other Egyptian intellectuals whose discourse argues against the Islamic movements include Maḥmūd Amīn al-ᶜĀlim, Ghālī Shukrī, Muṣṭafā Marᶜī, Zakī Najīb Maḥmūd and others in a variety of approaches. The Islamic movements have their own intellectuals who spread their beliefs by means of the written word, such as ᶜUmar al-Tilimsānī, ᶜUmar ᶜAbd al-Raḥmān, ᶜAbd Allāh al-Samāwī, Fahmī Huwaydī, Ṣalāḥ Abū Ismāᶜīl, Jūda Muḥammad and others from various Islamic movements. Sometimes the written word is not printed but rather handwritten and clandestinely distributed among the votaries such as *al-Farīḍa al-Ghā'iba* by Muḥammad ᶜAbd al-Salām Faraj[49] and *al-Tawassumāt* by Shukrī Muṣṭafā[50]. In addition, they also resort to propagating their discourse orally through sermons in mosques and talks in social gatherings. Furthermore, they disseminate it through several series of popular cassettes, such as those of Shaykh ᶜAbd al-Ḥamīd Kishk and Shaykh Muḥammad Mutawallī al-Shaᶜrāwī, the better to reach the illiterate or semi-literate among the Muslim masses hungry for feelings of belonging in the midst of their alienation, and yearning for improvement in their miserable conditions by their support of the Islamic movements opposing the regime and promising a utopian society.

Outside Egypt, the Islamic discourse tries likewise to attract the Muslims in several Arab countries and win them over to the Islamic ideology as the ideology of 'the people'. In this discourse, Arab regimes are presented as ungodly, un-Islamic, even anti-Islamic, and therefore not legitimate. The quality and strength of the Islamic opposition to these regimes depends on the type of group advancing the discourse and on the local circumstances within each particular country. One cannot say the Islamic discourse is the same in all Arab countries. It is not even the same within any one country like Egypt.[51] But as Islamic ideology, its aim is to interpellate the people, displace the dominant ideology and take possession of the state—though methods and approaches may differ from one group to another and from one country to another.[52]

Although the Islamic movements are nowhere in the Arab world capable yet of taking possession of the state, even in Egypt where they appear to be most rampant, their discourse testifies to an evident disarticulation of the dominant ideology in the Arab world. The intellectual struggle is rife with the social and economic contradictions between the dominant and the dominated classes in Arab society, accentuated by the increasing dependency of the Arab regimes on the West, the ally and protector of Israel. The intensification and the accumulation of these contradictions are aggravating the political crisis within each Arab country and in the Arab world as a whole, because there is no solution on the horizon. What still looms large on the horizon is continuing underdevelopment and poverty, continuing dependency, continuing national fragmentation on the pan-Arab level, continuing socio-economic and ethno-religious and gender differentiation within each Arab country, and continuing social disintegration and confusion of ethical norms everywhere. The atmosphere is one of alienation in which the Arab people are unremittingly subjected to an authoritarian social structure, governmental coercion and repression, violation of human rights and dignity, and lack of genuine popular participation in political, economic and social decision-making.

These are the real problems in the Arab world and they cannot be solved by the utopian and other-worldly hopes of the Islamic movements, nor by the repressive policies of the Arab regimes. If, because of the Arab dependency on the West and the Arab economy's absorption into the world capitalist system, the growth and evolution of modern Arab society has been stunted by the destructive aggressiveness of Western colonialism and imperialism, "blocked" (to use Samīr Amīn's term), or turned into a "neopatriarchy" (to use Hishām Sharābī's term) so that it is neither purely traditional nor authentically modern but a hybrid formation combining both—then the solution is not by ignoring this fact and hailing back to a supposedly ideal past which cannot be recaptured; nor is it by suppressing this fact and stifling the voices of social and cultural critics who point it out. If, because of the checkered history of the Arabs in modern times, in which dominance within the Arab region continued to remain in the hands of a small class or group whose interests allied it with foreign powers exploiting the region and its people

—then the solution is not in preserving this system by allowing desultory palliative reform of the 'liberal' or 'socialist' or 'Islamic' type, and propagating an ideology of false hopes; nor is it in strengthening the system by providing it with the coercive force of the most modern arms and the latest technologies and methods of controlling the masses and their minds. The solution lies rather in a total and radical transformation of the system within the region and in a drastic redefinition of its relation to the world order outside it along lines suggested by some of the Arab thinkers discussed earlier in this book. The solution lies indeed in nothing less than a comprehensive restructuring of Arab life. This is the challenge that contemporary Arab thought should face up to, and this is the reality whose dynamics Arabs everywhere should understand in order to extricate the Arab world from it.

The Arab sociologist, Ḥalīm Barakāt, who is a professor at Georgetown University's Center for Contemporary Arab Studies, has come to a similar conclusion at the end of his book *al-Mujtamaᶜ al-ᶜArabī al-Muᶜāṣir: Baḥth Istiṭlāᶜī Ijtimāᶜī*, which is one of the most penetrating and insightful studies of contemporary Arab society recently published.[53] Although he recognizes the existence of powerful objective factors threatening the present political, economic and social structures in the Arab world and menacing to engulf Arab society in a comprehensive revolution, he also correctly recognizes that other necessary factors are absent. Among the most important of those are popular revolutionary movements and leaderships that can mobilize forces and take the initiative at the opportune moments. Barakāt relates this lack to the means which Arab regimes have used to contain revolutionary movements by isolating them from the populace, by terrorizing the masses, by co-opting potential opposition and by turning traditional institutions (especially religion and family) against all radical change. Thus, the Arab regimes have been able to impose themselves, strengthen their positions, distract the Arab people from basic issues and preoccupy them exclusively with securing their daily livelihood.[54] In the collective studies edited by Dawisha and Zartman, this process has been studied in detail to explain the resilience and enduring nature of the Arab states.[55] The price in human suffering and alienation has not been discussed, as though stability at all costs is worth anything in and of itself.

The realization of a comprehensive revolution in the Arab world is an arduous and long-term task, Barakāt says, but it is inevitable and necessary as an issue of destiny if the Arabs are ever to transcend underdevelopment, stop the process of their own extinction, achieve justice and freedom and contribute to the enrichment of humanity—including the humanity of their enemies.[56] Against it there are many gigantic odds, but the vision of it can enthuse the people and unify them in their long and continuous struggle if, inspired by good leaders, they are agreed on its goals. The duty of Arab intellectuals is to define those goals and foster agreement on the basic issues. They should not allow themselves to be co-opted by the regimes, distracted by side issues or numbed by partial reforms or utopian ideas. They should seek to bridge the present gap that isolates them from the masses. Their discourse must be within the reach of the people, it must speak the language of the people, its content must articulate the aims and hopes of the people, and it must be formed in conjunction with the people—their discourse must indeed be organically that of the people. Only an ideological discourse like this will succeed in democratically winning the people, giving them identity and restoring meaning to their lives, and strengthening their struggle to stop their national fragmentation, end their conditions of underdevelopment and dependency, and usher in the societal transformation they desire.

It is obvious that at present there is no such national ideological project in the Arab world. The ideological disarticulation is so pronounced that Arab discourses today are at cross purposes. This crisis has led a number of intellectuals to organize themselves in professional associations and service societies, but their influence is still minimal. The Islamic movements are taking advantage of the situation and trying to fill the void at the grassroots and to use the mobilizing power of Islam, but their traditional backward-looking vision is an antonym of modernity;[57] furthermore, they are being used by reactionary forces in the Arab countries and abroad to preserve the present order of things favorable to them.

Meanwhile, the Arab regimes are coasting along, biding their time, muddling through—and enduring. Their legitimacy will remain in question until the societal contradictions are resolved.

But, as they say, the darkest hour is that before the dawn. And, as Hisham Sharabi says, "To fight the pessimism of the intellect, one must hold fast to the optimism of the will."[58]

Notes

Chapter Two

1. For two reports and a criticism of the conference in Arabic, see *al-Ādāb*, Nov. 1971, pp. 82–85.

2. See the conference proceedings in *Mu'tamar al-Aṣāla wa-l-Tajdīd fī-l-Thaqāfa al-ᶜArabiyya al-Muᶜāṣira* (Cairo: ALECSO, Directorate of Culture, 1973); and *al-Ādāb*, Nov. 1971, pp. 2–27 where six of the eight conference papers are published.

3. Zakī Najīb Maḥmūd, "Mawqif al-Thaqāfa al-ᶜArabiyya al-Ḥadītha fī Muwājahat al-ᶜAṣr," *al-Ādāb*, Nov. 1971, p. 6.

4. Muḥammad al-Mazālī, "al-Aṣāla wa-l-Tafattuḥ," *al-Ādāb*, Nov. 1971, pp. 13–17.

5. Ibid., p. 16.

6. Ibid., p. 17.

7. Shukrī ᶜAyyād, "Mafhūm al-Aṣāla wa-l-Tajdīd wa-l-Thaqāfa al-ᶜArabiyya al-Muᶜāṣira," *al-Ādāb*, Nov. 1971, p. 2.

8. Ibid., p. 3.

9. Ibid., pp. 4–5.

10. Ibid., p. 5.

11. See the complete conference proceedings in *Azmat al-Taṭawwur al-Ḥaḍārī fī-l-Waṭan al-ᶜArabī: Waqā'iᶜ Nadwat al-Kuwayt mā bayn 7 - 12 Nīsān (April), 1974*, ed. Shākir Muṣṭafā (Kuwait: Alumni Association, Kuwait University, 1975). A large part of the proceedings was also published in *al-Ādāb*, May 1974, and in *al-Maᶜrifa*, June 1974. For an English report and analysis see John J. Donohue, "Crisis and Culture: The Kuwait Colloquium," *CEMAM Reports 1974* (Beirut: Dar El-Mashreq, 1975), pp. 1–4 and 16–24.

12. See *al-Ādāb*, May 1974, pp. 2–5 and *al-Macrifa*, June 1974, pp. 292–302. For an English translation of the conference declaration see John J. Donohue, trans., "Final Declaration," *CEMAM Reports 1974*, pp. 5–15.

13. *al-Ādāb*, May 1974, p. 3. Author's translation.

14. Ibid.

15. Ibid.

16. Ibid. "Al-Ḥadātha wa Qaḍiyyat al-Taqaddum wa-l-Takhalluf," pp. 6–9.

17. Ibid., pp. 10–12 and 149–150. See also Ṭayyib Tīzīnī's criticism of Maḥmūd's concept of civilization in *al-Ādāb*, June 1974, pp. 13–15.

18. *Al-Ādāb*, May 1974, "al-Abcād al-Tārīkhiyya li-Azmat al-Taṭawwur al-Ḥaḍārī al-cArabī," pp. 13–24 and 111–112.

19. Ibid., p. 14.

20. Ibid., p. 15.

21. Ibid.

22. Ibid., pp. 16–22.

23. Ibid., p. 112.

24. Ibid., "al-Takhalluf al-Fikrī wa Abcāduh al-Ḥaḍāriyya," pp. 30–37.

25. Ibid., p. 30.

26. Ibid., p. 36.

27. Ibid., pp. 36–37.

28. Ibid., p. 38.

29. Ibid.

30. Ibid., p. 39.

31. Ibid., "al-Khuṣūṣiyya wa-l-Aṣāla," pp. 41–43.

32. Ibid., pp. 46–47.

33. Ibid., p. 50.

34. Ibid., p. 51. For this and other views of al-cĀlim, see his *al-Wacy wa-l-Wacy al-Zā'if fī-l-Fikr al-cArabī al-Mucāṣir* (Cairo: Dār al-Thaqāfa al-Jadīda, 1986).

35. *al-Ādāb*, May 1974, "Khawāṭir ḥawl al-Takhalluf al-Fikrī fī-l-Mujtamaᶜ al-ᶜArabī," pp. 27–29. For a full English translation of this paper see Shereen Khairallah, trans., "Reflections on the Manifestations of Intellectual Backwardness in Arab society," *CEMAM Reports 1974*, pp. 25–35.

36. *al-Ādā*b, May 1974, "al-Dīn wa Azmat al-Taṭawwur al-Ḥaḍārī fī-l-Waṭan al-ᶜArabī," pp. 79–86.

37. Ibid., p. 83.

38. Ibid.

39. Ibid., pp. 84–85.

40. Ibid., p. 85.

41. Ibid., p. 86.

42. Ibid., p. 88.

43. Ibid., pp. 89–90.

44. "al-ᶜĀ'ila wa-l-Taṭawwur al-Ḥaḍārī fī-l-Mujtamaᶜ al-ᶜArabī," in *al-Maᶜrifa*, June 1974, pp. 142–162. See also Hishām Sharābī, "Ḥawl al-Idiyūlūjiyya al-Sā'ida fī-l-Mujtamaᶜ al-ᶜArabī: Usus al-Thaqāfa al-Iqṭāᶜiyya al-Burjuwāziyya," *Mawāqif*, No. 29 (Autumn 1974), pp. 65–77.

45. See the angry criticism of François Bāsīlī, "Iḥtifā'an bi-l-Mu'tamar al-Ḥaḍārī: Thalāth Naẓarāt Naqdiyya," in *al-Ādāb*, June 1974, pp. 71–73 where he takes the conferees to task, not only for excluding women and discussion of their problems and of sex in Arab mores, but also for the limitations they themselves placed—in their conference declaration—on freedom of thought and on discussions of religion in Arab society.

46. See Mahdī ᶜĀmil, *Azmat al-Ḥaḍāra al-ᶜArabiyya Am Azmat al-Burjuwāziyyāt al-ᶜArabiyya?* (Beirut: Dār al-Fārābī, July 1974), p. 7.

47. Ibid., pp. 155–183.

48. Ibid., pp. 183–187.

49. Ibid., pp. 187–206.

50. Ibid., p. 232.

51. (Berkeley: University of California Press, 1976) translated by Diarmid Cammell from the French: Abdallah Laroui, *La crise des intellectuels arabes: traditionalisme ou historicisme?* (Paris: Librairie François Maspero, 1974).

52. (Beirut: Dār al-Ḥaqīqa, 1973). There are later reprints.

53. Ibid., pp. 184–186. See also *The Crisis of the Arab Intellectual*, pp. 153–155.

54. Al-ᶜArwī, *al-ᶜArab wa-l-Fikr al-Tārīkhī*, p. 60.

55. See his series *Fajr al-Islām* (Cairo: Maṭbaᶜat al-Iᶜtimād, 1929) *Ḍūḥā al-Islām* 3 vols. (Cairo: Lajnat al-Ta'līf wa-l-Tarjama wa-l-Nashr, 1933–1936), *Ẓuhr al-Islām*, 4 vols. (Cairo: Lajnat al-Ta'līf wa-l-Tarjama wa-l-Nashr, 1945–1955), *Yawm al-Islām* (Cairo: Dār al-Maᶜārif, 1952).

56. See his *ᶜAlā Hāmish al-Sīra*, 3 vols. (Cairo: Dār al-Maᶜārif, 1933–1938), *al-Shaykhān* (Cairo: Dār al-Maᶜārif, 1960), *al-Fitna al-Kubrā*, 2 vols. (Cairo: Dār al-Maᶜārif, 1947–1953) and his many literary studies.

57. Especially his *ᶜAbqariyyāt: ᶜAbqariyyat Muḥammad* (Cairo: al-Maktaba al-Tijāriyya al-Kubrā, 1942), *ᶜAbqariyyat al-Ṣiddīq* (Cairo: Dār al-Maᶜārif, 1943), *ᶜAbqariyyat ᶜUmar* (Cairo: Maṭbaᶜat al-Istiqāma, 1943), *ᶜAbqariyyat al-Imām ᶜAlī* (Cairo: Maṭbaᶜat al-Maᶜārif wa-Maktabatuhā, 1943), *ᶜAbqariyyat Khālid* (Cairo: Dār Iḥyā' al-Kutub al-ᶜArabiyya, 1945), etc.

58. See his *Ḥayāt Muḥammad* (Cairo: Maṭbaᶜat Miṣr, 1935), *al-Ṣiddīq Abū Bakr* (Cairo: Maṭbaᶜat Miṣr, 1945), *al-Fārūq ᶜUmar*, 2 vols. (Cairo: Maṭbaᶜat Miṣr, 1945).

59. Adonis, *Dīwān al-Shiᶜr al-ᶜArabī*, 3 vols. (Beirut: al-Maktaba al-ᶜAṣriyya, 1964–1968).

60. Beirut: Dār al-ᶜAwda, 1974–1978.

61. Adonis, *al-Thābit wa-l-Mutaḥawwil*, vol. I, pp. 27–31.

62. Ibid., pp. 31–32.

63. Ibid., pp. 32–33.

64. Ibid., pp. 33–34.

65. Ibid., p. 34. In his Kuwait Conference paper, Adonis's formulation was slightly different when he said: " . . . the essence of man is not in being a conforming inheritor but rather in being a transforming creator." See note 35 above.

66. Ibid., p. 66.

67. Ibid., p. 66.

68. Ibid., p. 92. See, however, Adonis's position on the role of religion in the Iranian revolution in his article "Bayn al-Thabāt wa-l-Taḥawwul: Khawāṭir ḥawl al-Thawra al-Islāmiyya fī Irān," *Mawāqif*, No. 34 (Winter 1979), pp. 149–160.

69. See for example Jihād Fāḍil, "Ṣadmat al-Ḥadātha li-Adonis; Ṣadma li-Uṣūl al-Baḥth al-^{c}Ilmī wa-li-Rūḥ al-Ḥadātha," *al-Fikr al-^{c}Arabī*, vol. 1, no. 2 (July-August 1978), pp. 291–297. See also Muṭā^{c} Ṣafadī, "al-Mustashriq Adonis wa Ba^{c}th al-Shu^{c}ūbiyya al-Jadīda fī-l-Thaqāfa al-Mu^{c}āṣira," *Bayrūt al-Masā'*, Oct. 4, 1974.

70. (Beirut: Dār al-^{c}Awda, 1980).

71. Ibid., p. 225.

72. Ṭayyib Tīzīnī, *Mashrū^{c} Ru'ya Jadīda li-l-Fikr al-^{c}Arabī min "al-^{c}Aṣr al-Jāhilī" ḥattā al-Marḥala al-Mu^{c}āṣira*, vol. 1, *Min al-Turāth ilā al-Thawra: Ḥawl Naẓariyya Muqtaraḥa fī Qaḍiyyat al-Turāth al-^{c}Arabī* (Beirut: Dār Ibn Khaldūn, 1978, 2nd Printing), 1976 1st Printing; vol. 2 *al-Fikr al-^{c}Arabī fī Bawākīrih wa Āfāqih al-Ūlā* (Damascus: Dār Dimashq, 1982).

73. Tīzīnī, *Mashrū^{c} Ru'ya Jadīda*, vol. 1, p. 6.

74. Ibid., Part I, pp. 23–218.

75. Ibid., pp. 233–234.

76. Ibid., pp. 229–232.

77. Ibid., pp. 242–243.

78. Ibid., p. 239.

79. Ibid., p. 239 n. 1, and p. 241.

80. Ibid., p. 245.

81. Ibid., p. 263.

82. Ibid., pp. 267–280.

83. Ibid., p. 271.

84. Ibid., 288–306.

85. See Ṭayyib Tīzīnī, "al-Yasār al-^{c}Arabī wa-l-Turāth al-^{c}Arabī," in *al-Turāth wa-l-^{c}Amal al-Siyāsī* (Rabat: al-Majlis al-Qawmī li-l-Thaqāfa al-^{c}Arabiyya, Muntadā al-Fikr wa-l-Ḥiwār, 1984), pp. 125–170. The book contains the proceedings of a conference held in Rabat, Morocco between Nov. 25 and 27, 1982.

86. See for example Bū ^{c}Alī Yāsīn, "Min al-Turāth ilā al-Thawra: Ma^{c} Ṭayyib Tīzīnī," in *Mawāqif*, No. 34 (Winter 1979), pp. 73–107 reprinted in *al-Marksiyya wa-l-Turāth al-^{c}Arabī al-Islāmī* (Beirut: Dār al-Ḥadātha, 1982, 2nd Printing) pp. 5–60; see also Tawfīq Sallūm's articles in *al-Ṭarīq*(1979), reprinted in ibid. as "al-Māddiyya wa Tajalliyātuhā fi-l-^{c}Aṣr al-Wasīṭ," pp. 242–288.

87. See Riḍwān al-Sayyid, "Ṭayyib Tīzīnī bayn Jādhibiyyat al-Manhaj wa Mazāliq al-Taṭbīq," in *al-Marksiyya wa-l-Turāth al-^{c}Arabī al-Islamī*, pp. 155–165, and other articles in the book, esp. Yāsīn's and Sallūm's.

88. Ṭayyib Tīzīnī published an earlier work on medieval Arab thought in which he applied Marxist theory. Originally a doctoral dissertation in German, its Arabic title is *Mashrū^{c} Ru'ya Jadīda li-l-Fikr al-^{c}Arabī fī-l-^{c}Aṣr al-Wasīṭ* (Damascus: Dār Dimashq, 1971).

89. Ḥusayn Muruwwa, *al-Naza^{c}āt al-Māddiyya fī-l-Falsafa al-^{c}Arabiyya al-Islāmiyya*, 2 vols. (Beirut: Dār al-Fārābī, 1978–1979).

90. Ibid., vol. 1, pp. 5–171.

91. Ibid., pp. 17–24.

92. Ibid., p. 26.

93. Ibid., p. 28.

94. Ibid., pp. 29–30.

95. Ibid., pp. 629–887.

96. Ibid., p. 838.

97. Ibid., pp. 839–840 and 847–848.

98. Ibid., pp. 853–867.

99. Ibid., p. 854.

100. See for example Nāyif Ballūz, "Waqfa ma^{c}a kitāb: al-Naza^{c}āt al-Māddiyya fī-l-Falsafa al-^{c}Arabiyya al-Islāmiyya," in *al-Mārksiyya wa-l-Turāth al-^{c}Arabī al-Islāmī*, pp. 167–209 and Tawfīq Sallūm in ibid., pp. 242–288.

101. See for example ibid., Faraj Allāh Dīb Ṣāliḥ, "Ḥawl al-Naza^{c}āt al-Māddiyya fī-l-Falsafa al-^{c}Arabiyya al-Islāmiyya," pp. 210–241.

102. For a succinct exposé of Ḥusayn Muruwwa's position vis-à-vis the Arab heritage of religion and philosophy, see his article "al-

Mawqif min al-Turāth fī-l-Dīn wa-l-Falsafa," *al-Ādāb*, special number on Arab cultural revolution, May 1970, pp. 8–10 and 131–140.

103. Ḥasan Ḥanafī, *al-Turāth wa-l-Tajdīd: Mawqifunā min al-Turāth al-Qadīm* (Beirut: Dār al-Tanwīr, 1981).

104. Ibid., pp. 157–158, note 127. For a list of his Arabic, English and French publications see ibid., p. 160. For a general study on him see Marc Chartier, "La rencontre Orient-Occident dans la pensée de trois philosophes égyptiens contemporains: Ḥasan Ḥanafī, Fu'ād Zakariyyā, Zakī Nagīb Maḥmūd," *Oriente Moderno*, vol. 53, nos. 7–8 (July-August 1973), pp. 603–642, esp. 603–619.

105. Ḥanafī, *al-Turāth wa-l-Tajdīd*, p. 11.

106. Ibid., pp. 12–13.

107. Ibid., p. 13.

108. Ibid., pp. 16–17.

109. Ibid., pp. 23–29.

110. Ibid., p. 129.

111. Ibid., pp. 130–131.

112. Ibid., pp. 139–140.

113. Ibid., pp. 140–141.

114. Ibid., pp. 131–139.

115. For a detailed study, see Ḥasan Ḥanafī's *Les Méthodes d'exégèse: Essai sur la Science des Fondements de la Compréhension, ᶜIlm Uṣūl al-Fiqh* (Cairo: Conseil Supérieur des Arts, des Lettres et des Sciences Sociales, 1965). See also his *Dirāsāt Islāmiyya* (Beirut: Dār al-Tanwīr, 1982), pp. 11–82.

116. Ḥanafī, *al-Turāth wa-l-Tajdīd*, pp. 146–152.

117. Ibid., pp. 152–153. See also his *La Phénoménologie de l'exégèse: Essai d'une herméneutique existentielle à partir du Nouveau Testament* (Cairo, 1981) and his *L'Exégèse de la phénoménologie, l'état actuel de la méthode phénoménologique et son application au phénomène religieux* (Cairo, 1980). See also his *Qaḍāyā Muᶜāṣira*, vol. 2, *Fī-l-Fikr al-Gharbī al-Muᶜāṣir* (Cairo, 1977).

118. Ḥasan Ḥanafī edited a journal called *al-Yasār al-Islāmī* (The Islamic Left) of which only one issue appeared in Cairo in 1981.

It professed to be a continuation of *al-ᶜUrwa al-Wuthqā* of Jamāl al-Dīn al-Afghānī and Muḥammad ᶜAbduh, and of *al-Manār* of Rashīd Riḍā. It had three articles by Ḥasan Ḥanafī, one by Muḥammad ᶜAwda, and one article by ᶜAlī Sharīᶜatī translated into Arabic. Ḥasan Ḥanafī has also written on Camilo Torres (*Qaḍāyā Muᶜāṣira*, vol. 1, *Fī Fikrinā al-Muᶜāṣir* (Beirut, 1981), pp. 297–334) and studied Gustavo Gutiérrez among other Latin American writers of Liberation Theology.

119. (Beirut: Dār al-Ṭalīᶜa, 1980).

120. (Beirut: Dār al-Ṭalīᶜa, 1982).

121. Ibid., p. 182.

122. Ibid., p. 184.

123. Ibid., p. 187.

124. See ibid., particularly Chapter 1, Parts 1 and 2, pp. 17–57.

125. Ibid., pp. 188–189.

126. Ibid., pp. 190–191.

127. (Beirut: Dār al-Ṭalīᶜa, 1984).

128. (Beirut: Markaz Dirāsāt al-Waḥda al-ᶜArabiyya, 1986).

129. Al-Jābirī, *Naqd al-ᶜAql al-ᶜArabī*, vol. 1, pp. 56–71.

130. Ibid., pp. 80 et seq.

131. Ibid., pp. 100 et seq.

132. Ibid., pp. 111 et seq.

133. Ibid., pp. 186–219.

134. Ibid., pp. 220–252.

135. Ibid., pp. 253–294.

136. Ibid., pp. 285 and 290.

137. Ibid., pp. 295–331.

138. Ibid., pp. 333–334.

139. Ibid., pp. 339–343.

140. Ibid., pp. 343–347.

141. Ibid., pp. 337–338.

142. al-Jābirī, *Naqd al-^{c}Aql al-^{c}Arabī*, vol. 2, pp. 555–573.

143. Ibid., p. 568.

144. *Al-Turāth wa Taḥaddiyāt al-^{c}Aṣr fī-l-Waṭan al-^{c}Arabī (Al-Aṣāla wa-l-Mu^{c}āṣara)*, ed. al-Sayyid Yāsīn (Beirut: Markaz Dirāsāt al-Waḥda al-^{c}Arabiyya, 1985).

Chapter Three

1. On the life of Sayyid Quṭb see Tawfīq Barakāt, *Sayyid Quṭb* (Beirut, n.d.). For studies on him see ^{c}Alī Quṭb, *Sayyid Quṭb aw Thawrat al-Fikr al-Islāmī* (Cairo, 1977) and Mahdī Faḍl-Allāh, *Ma^{c}a Sayyid Quṭb fī Fikrih al-Siyāsī wa-l-Dīnī* (Beirut: Mu'assasat al-Risāla, 1978). For English studies on him see Yvonne Yazbeck Haddad, "Sayyid Quṭb: Ideologue of Islamic Revival," in *Voices of Resurgent Islam*, ed. John L. Esposito (New York-Oxford: Oxford University Press, 1983), pp. 67–98; and her article "The Qur'anic Justification for an Islamic Revolution: The View of Sayyid Quṭb," *Middle East Journal* 37 (Winter 1983), pp. 14–29. See also her book *Contemporary Islam and the Challenge of History* (Albany: State University of New York Press, 1982), pp. 89–96; and Kenneth Cragg, *The Pen and the Faith: Eight Modern Muslim Writers and the Qur'ān* (London: George Allen & Unwin, 1985), pp. 53–71. For a French study see Olivier Carré, *Mystique et Politique: lecture révolutionnaire du Coran par Sayyid Quṭb, Frère musulman radical* (Paris: Editions du Cerf - Presses de la Fondation Nationale des Sciences Politiques, 1984). See also Gilles Kepel, *Le prophète et pharoan. Les mouvements islamistes dans l'Egypte contemporaine* (Paris: Editions La Découverte, 1984).

2. Sayed Kotb, *Social Justice in Islam* trans. John B. Hardie (Washington, D.C.: American Council of Learned Societies, 1953).

3. Sayyid Qutb, *Milestones* (Cedar Rapids, Iowa: Unity Publishing Co., n.d.).

4. Sayyid Qutb, *In the Shade of the Qur'ān*, Vol. 30, trans. M. Adil Slahi and Ashur A. Shamis (London: MWH London Publishers, 1979, repr. 1981).

5. See a book by Muḥammad Quṭb, Sayyid Quṭb's brother, entitled *Jāhiliyyat al-Qarn al-^{c}Ishrīn* (Cairo: Maktabat Wahba, n.d.; repr. Cairo-Beirut: Dār al-Shurūq, 1980) elaborating on the idea of modern *jāhiliyya*.

6. Sayyid Quṭb, *Ma^{c}ālim fī-l-Ṭarīq* (Cairo: Maktabat Wahba, 1964), p. 224.

7. Ibid., p. 21.

8. Ibid., pp. 171–173.

9. Ibid., p. 173.

10. Ibid., p. 213.

11. Ibid., pp. 119–121.

12. Ibid.

13. Ibid., pp. 125–128.

14. Ibid., p. 31.

15. Sayyid Quṭb, *Ma^{c}rakat al-Islām wa-l-Ra'smāliyya*, 4th printing (Beirut: Dār al-Shurūq, 1975), p. 66.

16. Ibid., pp. 67–68.

17. Sayyid Quṭb, *Ma^{c}ālim*, p. 11.

18. Sayyid Quṭb, *Hādhā al-Dīn* (Cairo: Dār al-Qalam, 1962), p. 84.

19. Sayyid Quṭb, *al-^{c}Adāla al-Ijtimā^{c}iyya fī-l-Islām*, 4th printing (Cairo: Dār Iḥyā' al-Kutub al-^{c}Arabiyya, 1954), p. 94.

20. Ibid., pp. 96–99.

21. Ibid., p. 98.

22. Ibid., pp. 36–50.

23. Ibid., pp. 50–60.

24. Ibid., pp. 61–73.

25. Ibid., p. 73.

26. See Muḥammad al-Nuwayhī, *Naḥwa Thawra fī-l-Fikr al-Dīnī* (Beirut: Dār al-Ādāb, 1983), pp. 24–26.

27. Ibid., pp. 43–44.

28. Ibid., p. 95.

29. Ibid., p. 97.

30. Ibid., p. 100.

31. Ibid., p. 101.

32. Ibid., pp. 106–114.

33. Ibid., pp. 117–118.

34. Ibid., p. 119.

35. Ibid., pp. 119–122.

36. Ibid., pp. 122–125.

37. Ibid., pp. 123–124.

38. Ibid., pp. 125–126.

39. Ibid., pp. 128–129.

40. Ibid., pp. 132–133.

41. Ibid., pp. 133–135.

42. Ibid., p. 136.

43. Ibid., pp. 139–140.

44. Ibid., pp. 145–146.

45. Ibid., pp. 146–148.

46. Ibid., pp. 152–154.

47. Ibid., pp. 154–161.

48. Ḥasan Ṣa^{c}b, *al-Islām Tujāh Taḥaddiyāt al-Ḥayā al-^{c}Aṣriyya* (Beirut: Dār al-Ādāb, 1965), pp. 45–46.

49. Ibid., pp. 13–20 and pp. 27–29.

50. Ibid., p. 37.

51. Ibid., p. 38.

52. Ibid., pp. 41–42.

53. Ibid., pp. 43–44.

54. Ibid., p. 46.

55. Ibid., p. 51.

56. Ḥasan Ṣa^{c}b, *Taḥdīth al-^{c}Aql al-^{c}Arabī Dirāsāt ḥawl al-Thawra al-Thaqāfiyya al-Lāzima li-l-Taqaddum al-^{c}Arabī fī-l-^{c}Aṣr al-Ḥadīth*, 2nd printing (Beirut: Dār al-^{c}Ilm li-l-Malāyīn, 1972).

57. Ibid., p. 3.

58. Ibid., p. 34.

59. Ibid., pp. 7–38 and pp. 39–82.

60. Ibid., pp. 116–136.

61. Ibid., pp. 137–164.

62. Ibid., pp. 165–207.

63. Ibid., pp. 208–223.

64. Ibid., pp. 83–115.

65. Ibid., pp. 86–88.

66. Ibid., pp. 89–91.

67. Ibid., p. 101.

68. Ibid., p. 111.

69. Ibid., pp. 112–113.

70. Ibid., pp. 104–105 and pp. 110–112.

71. Muḥammad ᶜAmāra, *al-Islām wa-l-Sulṭa al-Dīniyya*, 2nd printing (Beirut: al-Mu'assasa al-ᶜArabiyya li-l-Dirāsāt wa-l-Nashr, 1980).

72. Ibid., p. 11.

73. Ibid., pp. 45ff.

74. Ibid., p. 13.

75. Ibid.

76. Ibid., p. 14.

77. Ibid., p. 14 and pp. 101ff.

78. Ibid., pp. 15–16.

79. Ibid., pp. 16–17.

80. Ibid., pp. 17–19.

81. Ibid., pp. 101–102.

82. Ibid., p. 102.

83. Ibid., p. 103.

84. Ibid.

85. Ibid., pp. 106–109.

86. Ibid., pp. 20ff.

87. Ibid., pp. 26–35.

88. Ibid., pp. 37–39.

89. Ibid., p. 36.

90. Ibid., p. 82.

91. Ibid., pp. 90–91.

92. Ibid., pp. 91–92.

93. Ibid., p. 132.

94. Muḥammad ᶜAmāra, *al-Islām wa-l-Waḥda al-Qawmiyya*, 2nd printing (Beirut: al-Mu'assasa al-ᶜArabiyya li-l-Dirāsāt wa-l-Nashr, July 1979). This book was first printed in Cairo in March 1979 under the title *al-Islām wa-l-Waḥda al-Waṭaniyya*. References will be to the 2nd printing.

95. Ibid., p. 5.

96. Ibid., pp. 50–86.

97. In Arabic, see Muḥammad Arkūn *al-Fikr al-ᶜArabī*, trans. ᶜĀdil al-ᶜAwwā (Beirut: Manshūrāt ᶜUwaydāt, 1983); idem, *al-Fikr al-Islāmī: Qirā'a ᶜIlmiyya*, trans. Hāshim Ṣāliḥ (Beirut: Markaz al-Inmā' al-Qawmī, 1987); idem, with Louis Gardet, *al-Islām: al-Ams wa-l-Ghad*, trans. ᶜAlī al-Muqallid (Beirut: Dār al-Tanwīr, 1983), Arkūn's parts of the book, pp. 93–214; idem, *Tārīkhiyyat al-Fikr al-ᶜArabī al-Islāmī*, trans. Hāshim Ṣāliḥ (Beirut: Markaz al-Inmā' al-Qawmī, 1986). For a list of Muḥammad Arkūn's relevant articles, including several in Arabic, see ibid., pp. 47–48.

98. See Abdallah Laroui, *The Crisis of the Arab Intellectual: Traditionalism or Historicism?*, trans. Diarmid Cammell (Berkeley: University of California Press, 1976).

99. Muḥammad Arkūn, "al-Islām, al-Tārīkhiyya wa-l-Taqaddum," *Mawāqif*, 40 (Winter 1981), pp. 6–39. See also the introduction to his *Tārīkhiyyat al-Fikr al-ᶜArabī al-Islāmī*, esp. pp. 24–29.

100. See interview with Arkūn, "al-Turāth wa-l-Mawqif al-Naqdī al-Tasā'ulī, *Mawāqif* 40 (Winter 1981), pp. 40–57.

101. See Muḥammad Arkūn in *al-Islām: al-Ams wa-l-Ghad*, p. 112; in French: Mohammed Arkoun et Louis Gardet, *L'Islam: Hier-Demain* (Paris: Editions Buchet/Chastel, 1978), p. 136.

102. Ibid.

103. Ibid., in Arabic, pp. 213–214; in French, p. 246.

104. Muḥammad Arkūn, *Tārīkhiyyat al-Fikr al-ᶜArabī al-Islāmī*, p. 10. See also Muḥammad Arkūn, "Naḥwa Taqyīm wa Istilhām Jadīdayn li-l-Fikr al-Islāmī," *al-Fikr al-ᶜArabī al-Muᶜāṣir*, No. 29 (Dec. 1983/Jan. 1984), pp. 39–45.

105. Mohammed Arkoun, *La Pensée arabe*, 2nd printing (Paris: Presses Universitaires de France, 1979), Chapters II and III. See also Arabic translation by ᶜĀdil al-ᶜAwwā, *al-Fikr al-ᶜArabī* (Beirut: Manshūrat ᶜUwaydāt, 1983), Chapters II and III.

106. Mohammed Arkoun, *Lectures du Coran* (Paris: Maisonneuve et Larose, 1982), p. xiii.

107. Ibid., pp. xiii–xiv. See also Muḥammad Arkūn, "al-Turāth: Muḥtawāh wa Huwiyyatuh, Ījābiyyātuh wa Salbiyyātuh," in *al-Turāth wa Taḥaddiyāt al-ᶜAṣr*, ed. Sayyid Yāsīn (Beirut: Markaz Dirāsāt al-Waḥda al-ᶜArabiyya, 1985), pp. 166–167.

108. Ibid., p. 167.

109. Ibid.

110. Ibid. See also Arkūn, *Tārīkhiyyat al-Fikr al-ᶜArabī al-Islāmī*, p. 188.

111. Arkoun, *Lectures du Coran*, p. xii.

112. See, for example, Arkūn, *Tārīkhiyyat al-Fikr al-ᶜArabī al-Islāmī*, p. 132.

113. Ibid.

114. Ibid., p. 10.

115. Ibid.

116. Al-Sayyid Yāsīn, ed., *al-Turāth wa Taḥaddiyāt al-ᶜAṣr fī-l-Waṭan al-ᶜArabī*, pp. 155–168.

117. Ibid., pp. 205–212.

118. Ibid. See also Arkūn, *Tārīkhiyyat al-Fikr al-ᶜArabī al-Islāmī*, pp. 34 and Arkoun, *La Pensée arabe*, pp. 107–108.

119. Arkūn, in *al-Turāth wa Taḥaddiyāt al-ᶜAṣr*, p. 211.

120. See for example John Wansbrough's remarks in his review of Arkoun's *Lectures du Coran*, in *Bulletin of the Oriental and African Studies* XLVII, 2 (1984), p. 413 where Arkoun's programs of integrating traditional Islamic and Orientalist scholarship with the prin-

cipal intellectual currents of the twentieth century is said to be "one unfortunately not yet realized to any practical extent."

121. See Mohammed Arkoun, *Contribution à l'étude de l'humanisme arabe au IVe/Xe siècle: Miskawayh, philosophe et historien* (Paris: J. Vrin, 1970); idem, "L'Humanisme arabe au IVe/Xe siècle, d'après le Kitāb al-Hawāmil wa l-šawāmil," *Studia Islamica*, XIV (1961), pp. 73–108 and XV (1961), pp, 63–89); idem, *Essais sur la pensée islamique* (Paris: Maisonneuve et Larose, 1973).

Chapter Four

1. See, for example, Hisham Sharabi, *Government and Politics of the Middle East in the Twentieth Century* (Westport, CT: Greenwood Press, 1987); idem, *Nationalism and Revolution in the Arab World* (Princeton: Princeton University Press, 1966); idem, *Palestine and Israel: The Lethal Dilemma* (New York: Pegasus, 1969); idem, *Palestine Guerrillas: Their Credibility and Effectiveness* (Washington, D.C.: Georgetown University, Center for Strategic and International Studies, 1970).

2. Hisham Sharabi, *Arab Intellectuals and the West: the Formative Years, 1875–1914* (Baltimore: Johns Hopkins Press, 1970); Hishām Sharābī, *al-Muthaqqafūn al-ᶜArab wa-l-Gharb: ᶜAṣr al-Nahḍa, 1875–1914* (Beirut: Dār al-Nahār, 1978).

3. Hishām Sharābī, *Muqaddimāt li-Dirāsat al-Mujtamaᶜ al-ᶜArabī* (Jerusalem: Manshūrāt Ṣalāḥ al-Dīn, 1975).

4. Ibid. See also Hishām Sharābī, "Al-ᶜĀ'ila wa-l-Taṭawwur al-Ḥaḍārī fī-l-Mujtamaᶜ al-ᶜArabī: Usus al-Thaqāfa al-Iqṭāᶜ-iyya al-Burjuwāziyya." *Mawāqif* No. 29 (Autumn 1974), pp. 65–77.

5. See Hishām Sharābī, "al-Niẓām al-Abawī wa-l-Tabaᶜiyya wa Mustaqbal al-Mujtamaᶜ al-ᶜArabī," in *al-ᶜAqd al-ᶜArabī al-Qādim: al-Mustaqbalāt al-Badīla*, ed. Hishām Sharābī (Beirut: Markaz Dirāsāt al-Waḥda al-ᶜArabiyya, 1986), pp. 259–267; and idem, "Cultural Critics of Contemporary Arab Society," *Arab Studies Quarterly* Vol. 9, No. 1 (1987), pp. 1–19. See also his book *Neopatriarchy: A Theory of Distorted Change in Arab Society* (New York-Oxford: Oxford University Press, 1988).

6. See Sharābī, "al-Niẓām al-Abawī," in *al-ᶜAqd al-ᶜArabī al-Qādim*, pp. 260–262; and Sharabi, "Cultural Critics," *Arab Studies Quarterly* Vol. 9, No. 1 (1987), pp. 2–3.

7. See "family, patriarchal" in *A Modern Dictionary of Sociology* by George A. Theodorson and Achilles G. Theodorson (New York: Barnes & Noble Books, 1979), p. 149.

8. Sharabi, "Cultural Critics," *Arab Studies Quarterly* Vol. 9, No. 1 (1987), p. 2.

9. Sharābī, "al-Niẓām al-Abawī," in *al-^{c}Aqd al-^{c}Arabī al-Qādim*, p. 262.

10. Ibid.

11. Ibid., p. 261.

12. Hisham Sharabi, "Cultural Critics," *Arab Studies Quarterly* Vol. 9, No. 1 (1987), p. 4.

13. Ibid., p. 14.

14. See Anouar Abdel-Malek, *La pensée politique arabe contemporaine* (Paris: Le Seuil, 1970, 1975, 1980) and idem, *Contemporary Arab Political Thought* (London: Zed Books Ltd., 1983); see also Anwar ^{c}Abd al-Malik, *Dirāsāt fī-l-Thaqāfa al-Waṭaniyya* (Beirut: Dār al-Ṭalī^{c}a, 1967) and idem, *al-Fikr al-^{c}Arabī fī Ma^{c}rakat al-Nahḍa* (Beirut: Dār al-Ādāb, 1974, 1978).

15. See Anouar Abdel-Malek, *Egypte, Société militaire* (Paris: Le Seuil, 1962), and idem, *Egypt: Military Society* (New York: Random House, 1968); idem, *Idéologie et renaissance nationale: L'Egypte moderne* (Paris: Anthropos, 1969, 1975). See also Anwar ^{c}Abd al-Malik, *al-Jaysh wa-l-Ḥaraka al-Waṭaniyya* (Beirut: Dār Ibn Khaldūn, 1974) and idem, *al-Mujtama^{c} al-Miṣrī wa-l-Jaysh 1952–1970* (Beirut: Dār al-Ṭalī^{c}a, 1974); and idem, *Nahḍat Miṣr* (Cairo: al-Hay'a al-Miṣriyya al-^{c}Āmma li-l-Kitāb, 1983).

16. See Anouar Abdel-Malek, *Sociologie de l'impérialisme* (Paris: Anthropos, 1971); idem, *La Dialectique sociale* (Paris: Le Seuil, 1971); idem, *Spécificité et théorie sociale* (Paris: Anthropos, 1977); idem, *Social Dialectics I: Civilizations and Social Theory* (London: Macmillan Press/Albany, N.Y.: SUNY Press, 1981) and *Social Dialectics II: Nations and Revolutions* (London: Macmillan Press/Albany, N.Y.: SUNY Press, 1981); see also Anwar ^{c}Abd al-Malik, *Rīḥ al-Sharq* (Cairo: Dār al-Mustaqbal al-^{c}Arabī, 1983).

17. See Anouar Abdel-Malek, *The Project on Socio-Cultural Development Alternatives in a Changing World: Report on the Formative Stage* (Tokyo: United Nations University Press, 1980) and books on related subjects which he edited with others, such as *Intellec-*

tual Creativity in Endogenous Culture (Tokyo: United Nations University Press, 1978) and *Science and Technology in the Transformation of the World* (Tokyo: United Nations University Press, 1978) and *Science and Technology in the Transformation of the World* (Tokyo: United Nations University Press, 1979).

18. See Anwar ᶜAbd al-Malik, *Rīḥ al-Sharq*, pp. 47–48.

19. Ibid., pp. 20–21.

20. Ibid., p. 250.

21. See Anwar ᶜAbd al-Malik, "Fā'iḍ al-Qīma al-Tārīkhī, *Dirāsāt ᶜArabiyya* Vol. 15, No. 5 (March 1979), pp. 3–12; reprinted in his *Rīḥ al-Sharq*, pp. 34–41.

22. Ibid., p. 37.

23. Ibid., pp. 38–39.

24. Although ᶜAbd al-Malik occasionally uses the expression "Third World" because, as he explains, it is widely used and understood, he thinks it is a Eurocentric concept perpetuating present undesirable attitudes and conditions. He prefers to use more neutral terms like the Three Continents. See Anwar ᶜAbd al-Malik, *Rīḥ al-Sharq*, pp. 221–224.

25. See Anouar Abdel-Malek, *La Dialectique sociale* (Paris: Le Seuil, 1972) and Anwar ᶜAbd al-Malik, *Rīḥ al-Sharq*, p. 20, pp. 189–191.

26. Ibid., pp. 224–225.

27. Ibid., p. 22.

28. Ibid.

29. Ibid., pp. 118–119.

30. See Anwar ᶜAbd al-Malik, "al-Khuṣūṣiyya wa-l-Aṣāla," in *Al-Ādāb*, May 1974, pp. 41–43.

31. See ᶜAbd al-Malik, *Rīḥ al-Sharq*, p. 96.

32. Ibid., reprinted from ᶜAbd al-Malik, "al-Islām al-Siyāsī," *Qaḍāyā ᶜArabiyya* Vol. 6, No. 5 (September 1979), pp. 175–184.

33. Anwar ᶜAbd al-Malik, "al-Islām al-Siyāsī," in *Rīḥ al-Sharq*, pp. 85–98.

34. Anwar ᶜAbd al-Malik, "al-Islām wa-l-ᶜUrūba," in *Rīḥ al-Sharq*, pp. 99–105.

35. Compare the inconsistencies found, for example, in his *Rīḥ al-Sharq*, pp. 20–21, p. 22, pp. 53–54, and pp. 224–225.

36. See Jalāl Amīn, *Mabādi' al-Taḥlīl al-Iqtiṣādī* (Cairo: Maktabat Sayyid Wahba, 1967), and *al-Iqtiṣād al-Qawmī: Muqaddima li-Dirāsat al-Naẓariyya al-Naqdiyya* (Cairo: Maktabat Sayyid Wahba, 1968).

37. See Jalāl Amīn, *Muqaddima ilā al-Ishtirākiyya* (Cairo: Maktabat Sayyid Wahba, 1966), and *al-Mārksiyya: ᶜArḍ wa Taḥlīl wa Naqd* (Cairo: Maktabat Sayyid Wahba, 1970).

38. See Galal A. Amin, *Food Supply and Economic Development, with Special Reference to Egypt* (London: Frank Cass, 1966); idem, *Urbanisation and Economic Development in the Arab World* (Beirut: Beirut Arab University, 1972); idem, *The Modernization of Poverty: A Study in the Political Economy of Growth in Nine Arab Countries 1945–1970* (Leiden: E. J. Brill, 1974, 1981), translated into Japanese in 1976; and Jalāl Amīn, *al-Mashriq al-ᶜArabī wa-l-Gharb*, 3rd printing (Beirut: Markaz Dirāsāt al-Waḥda al-ᶜArabiyya, 1981).

39. See Jalāl Amīn, *Miḥnat al-Iqtiṣād wa-l-Thaqāfa fī Miṣr* (Cairo: al-Markaz al-ᶜArabī li-l-Baḥth wa-l-Nashr, 1982); idem, *Tanmiya am Tabaᶜiyya Iqtiṣādiyya wa Thaqāfiyya?* (Cairo: Maṭbūᶜāt al-Qāhira, 1983).

40. See Galal A. Amin, "Dependent Development," *Alternatives* Vol. 2 (1976), pp. 379–403, of which a popularized and adapted Arabic version is entitled "Tanmiya am Tabaᶜiyya Iqtiṣādiyya wa Thaqāfiyya?" in Jalāl Amīn, *Tanmiya am Tabaᶜiyya Iqtiṣādiyya wa Thaqāfiyya: Khurāfāt Shāʾiᶜa ᶜan al-Takhalluf wa-l-Tanmiya wa ᶜan al-Rakhā' wa-l-Rafāhiya* (Cairo: Maṭbūᶜāt al-Qāhira, 1983), pp. 11–45. For the text of the U.N. General Assembly resolution adopted in the sixth special session, at the 2229th plenary meeting, May 1, 1974, see *Alternatives* Vol. 1 (1975), pp. 283–287.

41. See Galal A. Amin, "Dependent Development," *Alternatives* 2 (1976), esp. pp. 380–394.

42. Ibid., pp. 394–402, reproduced in part in Talal Asad and Roger Owen (eds.), *Sociology of "Developing Societies": The Middle East* (New York: Monthly Review Press, 1983), pp. 54–60. See also Jalāl Amīn, *Tanmiya am Tabaᶜiyya Iqtiṣādiyya wa Thaqāfiyya*, pp. 35–45.

43. Jalāl Amīn, "Man Yaᶜtamid Iqtiṣādiyyan ᶜalā Man?" in his *Tanmiya am Tabaᶜiyya Iqtiṣādiyya wa Thaqāfiyya?*, pp. 74–82.

44. Ibid., p. 77.

45. Galal A. Amin, "Dependent Development," *Alternatives* 2 (1976), p. 399.

46. Jalāl Amīn, "al-Ghazw al-Ḥaḍārī: Nataᶜāmal maᶜah am Naṣudduh?" in his *Tanmiya am Tabaᶜiyya Iqtiṣādiyya wa Thaqāfiyya*, pp. 114–121.

47. Ibid., p. 116.

48. Ibid., p. 118.

49. Ibid., p. 119.

50. Ibid., p. 120.

51. Ibid., pp. 125–126.

52. Ibid.

53. Jalāl Amīn, *al-Mashriq al-ᶜArabī wa-l-Gharb*, p. 158.

54. See Samir Amin, *The Arab Economy Today*, trans. Michael Pallis and intro. Aidan Foster-Carter (London: Zed Press, 1982), pp. 105–124; but note that, apart from one early book in Arabic, neither the Arabic translations of his works have been cited nor the other translations in more than twenty languages.

55. Samir Amin's first book originally written in Arabic is *Muḥāḍarāt fī Iḥṣā'iyyāt al-Tawāzun al-ᶜĀmm: Dirāsa Iḥṣā'iyya ᶜan al-Tayyārāt al-Māliyya wa-l-Naqdiyya fī-l-Iqtiṣād al-Miṣrī ᶜĀm 1957* (Cairo: Maᶜhad al-Dirāsāt al-ᶜArabiyya al-ᶜĀliya, 1959). Among his books in Arabic translation are the following: *al-Umma al-ᶜArabiyya: al-Qawmiyya wa Ṣirāᶜ al-Ṭabaqāt*, trans. Kāmil Qayṣar Dāghir, (Beirut: Dār Ibn Rashīd li-l-Ṭibāᶜa wa-l-Nashr, 1978); *al-Taṭawwur al-Lāmutakāfi': Dirāsāt fī-l-Tashkīlāt al-Ijtimāᶜiyya li-l-Ra'smāliyya al-Muḥīṭa* (Beirut: Dār al-Ṭalīᶜa, 1980); *al-Ṭabaqa wa-l-Umma fī-l-Tārīkh wa fī-l-Marḥala al-Imbiryāliyya*, trans. Henriette ᶜAbbūdī (Beirut: Dār al-Ṭalīᶜa, 1980); *al-Maghrib al-ᶜArabī al-Ḥadīth*, trans. Kāmil Qayṣar Dāghir (Beirut: Dār al-Ḥadātha, 1980).

56. Samir Amin, *L'Accumulation à l'échelle mondiale: Critique de la théorie du sous-développement* (Dakar and Paris: IFAN-Anthropos, 1970) translated into English as *Accumulation on a World Scale: A Critique of the Theory of Underdevelopment*, 2 vols. (New York: Monthly Review Press, 1974), also available in Arabic, Greek, Italian, Japanese, Serbo-Croat, Spanish and Swedish translations.

57. Samir Amin, *Le Développement inégal* (Paris: Editions de Minuit, 1973) translated into English as *Unequal Develompent* (New York: Monthly Review Press, 1976), also available in Arabic, German, Greek, Italian, Portuguese and Spanish translations.

58. As cited by Aidan Foster-Carter in Samir Amin, *The Arab Economy Today*, trans. Michael Pallis, p. 35.

59. Samir Amin, *L'Egypte nasserienne* (Paris: Editions de Minuit, 1964).

60. Samir Amin, *L'Economie du Maghreb* (Paris: Editions de Minuit, 1966). His book *Le Maghreb moderne* (Paris: Editions de Minuit, 1970) was translated into English as *The Maghreb in the Modern World* (Harmondsworth: Penguin, 1970).

61. Samir Amin, *La Nation arabe: Nationalisme et luttes de classes* (Paris: Editions de Minuit, 1976) translated into English as *The Arab Nation: Nationalism and Class Struggles* (London: Zed Press, 1978) and in Arabic as *Al-Umma al-^{c}Arabiyya: Al-Qawmiyya wa Ṣirā^{c} al-Ṭabaqāt* (Beirut: Dār Ibn Rashīd, 1978).

62. See Samir Amin, *The Arab Economy Today*, pp. 41–51.

63. See in particular Samir Amin, *The Arab Nation: Nationalism and Class Struggles*, pp. 7–9 et passim.

64. Ibid., pp. 109–111.

65. Ibid., pp. 112–113.

66. Ibid., p. 105.

67. Ibid., pp. 111–114.

68. Ibid., p. 113.

69. Samir Amin, *The Arab Economy Today*, pp. 80–81.

70. For some of his sociological writings see Abdelkebir Khatibi, *Bilan de la sociologie au Maroc* (Rabat: Publications de l'Association pour la recherche en sciences humaines, 1967); idem, *Etudes sociologiques sur le Maroc* (Rabat: Société d'études économiques, sociales, et statistiques, 1971). For some of his literary writings see his autobiography *La mémoire tatouée* (Paris: Denoël, 1971), his novel *Le livre du sang* (Paris: Gallimard, 1979), and his poems *Le lutteur de classe à la manière taoïste* (Paris: Sindbad, 1977) and *Dédicace à l'année qui vient* (Montpellier: Fata Morgana, 1986). See also his account of novel writing in the Maghrib *Le roman Maghrébin* (Paris: Maspero, 1968; 2nd ed., Rabat: SMER, 1979) which is available in Arabic in a transla-

tion by Muḥammad Barrāda, *Fī-l-Kitāba wa-l-Tajriba* (Beirut: Dār al-ᶜAwda, 1980), and his book written in cooperation with Mohammad Benjelloun Touimi and Mohammed Kably entitled *Ecrivains marocains du Protectorat à 1965: Choix, traduction de l'arabe et présentation* (Paris: Sindbad, 1974). A play of his, *La mort des artistes*, was presented in Paris in 1964 and he has written other unpublished plays.

71. See for example Abdelkebir Khatibi, *La blessure du nom propre* (Paris: Denoël, 1974), also available in Arabic in a translation by Mohammed Bennis (Muḥammad Binnīs), *al-Ism al-ᶜArabī al-Jarīḥ* (Beirut: Dār al-ᶜAwda, 1980).

72. Abdelkebir Khatibi, *Vomito blanco: le sionisme et la conscience malheureuse* (Paris: Union générale d'éditions, 1974), available in Arabic in a translation by ᶜAbd al-Salām Bin-ᶜAbd al-ᶜĀlī, "Al-Ṣahyūniyya wa-l-Yasār al-Gharbī," in *al-Naqd al-Muzdawij* (Beirut: Dār al-ᶜAwda, 1980),pp. 37–150.

73. Abdelkebir Khatibi, *Maghreb pluriel* (Rabat: Société marocaine des éditeurs réunis, 1982).

74. See ᶜAbd al-Kabīr al-Khaṭībī, *al-Naqd al-Muzdawij*, esp. pp. 155–165. See also his article "Double Criticism: The Decolonization of Arab Sociology," in Halim Barakat, ed., *Contemporary North Africa: Issues of Development and Integration* (London and Sydney: Croom Helm, 1985), pp. 9–19.

75. Ibid., p. 12.

76. Ibid.

77. Ibid., p. 13.

78. ᶜAbd al-Kabīr al-Khaṭībī, *al-Naqd al-Muzdawij*, p. 163.

79. Ibid., p. 164.

80. Ibid.

81. Khatibi, "Double Criticism: The Decolonization of Arab Sociology," p. 14.

82. ᶜAbd al-Kabīr al-Khaṭībī, *al-Naqd al-Muzdawij*, pp. 31–32.

83. Mohammed Bennis, "The Plurality of the One," in Halim Barakat, ed., *Contemporary North Africa*, pp. 250–251.

84. Al-Khaṭībī is as much fascinated by the aesthetic as by the metaphysical character of Arabic calligraphy. See also Abdelkebir Khatibi and Mohammed Sijelmassi, *The Splendour of Islamic Calligraphy*, translated from French by James Hughes (New York: Rizzolli, 1977).

Chapter Five

1. See for example Alice Shukrī Diyāb, *Fihris Alf Maqāl ^{c}an al-Mar'a al-^{c}Arabiyya khilāl mi'at ^{c}Ām* (Cambridge, MA: Harvard College Library, 1979). See also Ayad Al-Qazzaz, *Women in the Middle East and North Africa: An Annotated Bibliography* (Austin: University of Texas Press, 1977) and S. R. Meghdessian, *The Status of the Arab Woman: A Selected Bibliography* (Westport, CT: Greenwood Press, 1980).

2. See for example Elizabeth W. Fernea and Basima Q. Bezirgan, eds., *Middle Eastern Muslim Women Speak* (Austin: University of Texas Press, 1977) and Elizabeth W. Fernea, ed., *Women and the Family in the Middle East: New Voices of Change* (Austin: University of Texas Press, 1985).

3. ^{c}Abd al-Tawwāb ^{c}Abd al-Ḥayy, *^{c}Aṣīr Ḥayātī* (Cairo: al-Hay'a al-Miṣriyya al-^{c}Āmma li-l-Kitāb, 1966), p. 123.

4. For a partial list of her publications, see Issa J. Boullata, "Modern Qur'ān Exegesis: A Study of Bint al-Shāṭi''s Method," *Muslim World* Vol. 64, No. 2 (April 1974), pp. 102–103.

5. See her books: *Umm al-Nabī* (Cairo: Dār al-Hilāl, 1961?); *Nisā' al-Nabī* (Cairo: Dār al-Hilāl. 1961?); *Banāt al-Nabī* (Cairo: Dār al-Hilāl, 1963); *Sukayna bint al-Ḥusayn* (Cairo: Dār al-Hilāl, 1965?); *Baṭalat Karbalā'* (Cairo: Dār al-Hilāl, 1965?).

6. See ^{c}Ā'isha ^{c}Abd al-Raḥmān, *al-Mafhūm al-Islāmī li-Taḥrīr al-Mar'a* (Cairo: Maṭba^{c}at Mukhaymir, 1967).

7. Ibid., pp. 10–15.

8. C. Kooij, "Bint al-Shāṭi': A Suitable Case for Biography?" in Ibrahim A. El-Sheikh, C. Aart van de Koppel and Rudolph Peters, *The Challenge of the Middle East* (Amsterdam: University of Amsterdam, Institute for Modern Near Eastern Studies, 1982), p. 71.

9. See Zaynab al-Ghazālī, *Ayyām min Ḥayātī* (Cairo-Beirut: Dār al-Shurūq, n.d.), pp. 26–28.

10. Valerie J. Hoffman, "An Islamic Activist: Zaynab al-Ghazali," in Elizabeth W. Fernea, ed., *Women and the Family in the Middle East: New Voices of Change* (Austin: University of Texas Press, 1985), pp. 234–235.

11. Ibid., pp. 236–237.

12. Zaynab al-Ghazālī, *Ayyām min Ḥayātī*, pp. 36–38.

13. Sayyid Quṭb, *Maᶜālim fī-l-Ṭarīq* (Cairo: Maktabat Wahba, 1964).

14. Zaynab al-Ghazālī, *Ayyām min Hayātī*, pp. 39–41.

15. See an interview with her in Cairo by Assem Abdul Mohsen entitled "Muslim Brothers' Hajja Zeinab: East and West want to delay the return of Islam," in *The Middle East* No. 79 (May 1981), pp. 32–24.

16. Ibid., pp. 33–34.

17. See, for example, Nawal El Saadawi: *Woman at Point Zero*, trans. by Sherif Hetata (London: Zed Books, 1983); *God Dies by the Nile*, trans. by Sherif Hetata (London: Zed Books, 1985); *Two Women in One*, trans. by Osman Nusairi and Jana Gough (London: Al Saqi, 1985); *Death of an Ex-minister*, trans. by Shirley Eber (London: Methuen, 1987).

18. Nawāl al-Saᶜdāwī, *al-Mar'a wa-l-Jins: Awwal Naẓra ᶜIlmiyya Ṣarīḥa ilā Mashākil al-Mar'a wa-l-Jins fī-l-Mujtamaᶜ al-ᶜArabī*, 3rd printing (Beirut: al-Mu'assasa al-ᶜArabiyya li-l-Dirāsāt wa-l-Nashr, 1974), p. 167.

19. See, for example, Nawāl al-Saᶜdāwī *al-Mar'a wa-l-Jins 2: al-Unthā Hiya al-Aṣl* (Beirut: al-Mu'assasa al-ᶜArabiyya li-l-Dirāsāt wa-l-Nashr, 1974); *al-Rajul wa-l-Jins* (Beirut: al-Mu'assasa al-ᶜArabiyya li-l-Dirāsāt wa-l-Nashr, 1976); *al-Mar'a wa-l-Ṣirāᶜ al-Nafsī* (Beirut: al-Mu'assasa al-ᶜArabiyya li-l-Dirāsāt wa-l-Nashr, 1977).

20. Nawāl al-Saᶜdāwī, *al-Wajh al-ᶜĀrī li-l-Mar'a al-ᶜArabiyya* (Beirut: al-Mu'assasa al-ᶜArabiyya li-l-Dirāsāt wa-l-Nashr, 1977).

21. Nawal El Saadawi *The Hidden Face of Eve: Women in the Arab World*, translated and edited by Sherif Hetata (London: Zed Press, 1980), with a preface to the English edition by Nawal El Saadawi. An American edition of this book was published (Boston: Beacon Press, 1982) without the preface, but with a foreword by Irene L. Gendzier.

22. Irene L. Gendzier, "Foreword," in Nawal El Saadawi, *The Hidden Face of Eve* (Boston: Beacon Press, 1982), p. vii.

23. See Nawal El Saadawi, "Preface to the English Edition," in her *The Hidden Face of Eve*, p. iii. Note how she confuses historical data by considering ᶜUthmān (Osman) the fourth caliph of the Muslims in-

stead of the third, and places him in Damascus instead of Medina, and in the eighth century A.D. instead of the seventh!

24. Ibid., p. 4.

25. Ibid., p. 27.

26. Nawal El Saadawi, "Preface to the English Edition," *The Hidden Face of Eve*, p. viii.

27. Ibid.

28. Fatima Mernissi, *Beyond the Veil: Male-Female Dynamics in a Modern Muslim Society* (Cambridge, MA: Schenkman Publishing Company, 1975), Chapter 9.

29. Ibid. p. 89.

30. Fatima Mernissi, *Beyond the Veil*, p. xvi.

31. Ibid., Chapter 1.

32. Ibid., p. 4.

33. Ibid., pp. 11–12.

34. Ibid., p. 13.

35. Ibid., p. 16–17. See also Fāṭima al-Marnīsī, *al-Ḥubb fī Ḥadāratinā al-Islāmiyya* (Beirut: al-Dār al-ᶜĀlamiyya li-l-Ṭibāᶜa wa-l-Nashr, 1984), in which she collects classical proof texts on love in Islamic civilization.

36. Fatima Mernissi, *Beyond the Veil*, pp. 51–67.

37. Ibid., p. 106.

38. Ibid., p. ix et passim.

39. Ibid., p. 109. An Arabic translation of *Beyond the Veil* appeared entitled *al-Sulūk al-Jinsī fī Mujtamaᶜ Islāmī Ra'smālī Tabaᶜī*, trans. Uzwīl Fāṭima al-Zahrā' (Beirut: Dār al-Ḥadātha, 1982). A new English edition of *Beyond the Veil* (Bloomington: Indiana University Press, 1987) has a new introduction in which Mernissi argues that the current conservative wave in the Muslim world is a defense against the profound changes in male-female relations, gender roles and perceptions of sexual identity.

40. For an anthology of Arab women's poetry in English translation, see Kamal Boullata, ed., *Women of the Fertile Crescent: Modern Poetry by Arab Women* (Washington, D.C.: Three Continents Press, 1978).

41. See Hilary Kilpatrick, "Women and Literature in the Arab East," in Mineke Schlipper, ed., *Unheard Words: Women and Literature in Africa, the Arab World, Asia, the Caribbean and Latin America* (London and New York: Allison and Busby, 1985) pp. 72–90; see also Evelyne Accad, "Women's Voices from the Maghreb," in *Mundus Arabicus* Vol. 2 (1982): *Arabic Literature in North Africa*, (Cambridge, MA: Dar Mahjar, 1982) pp. 18–34.

42. See Hanan Awwad, *Arab Causes in the Fiction of Ghādah al-Sammān, 1961–1975* (Sherbrooke, Quebec, Canada: Editions Naaman, 1983); and Ghālī Shukrī, *Ghāda al-Sammān bilā Ajniḥa* (Beirut: Dār al-Ṭalīᶜa, 1977).

Chapter Six

1. See Michel Foucault, *Power/Knowledge: Selected Interviews and Other Writings 1972–1977*, ed. Colin Gordon, trans. Colin Gordon, Leo Marshall, John Mepham and Kate Soper (New York: Pantheon Books, 1980).

2. See for example Diane MacDonell, *Theories of Discourse: An Introduction* (Oxford: Basil Blackwell, 1986); and Gillian Brown and George Yule, *Discourse Analysis* (Cambridge: Cambridge University Press, 1983).

3. See for example Louis Althusser, *Essays on Ideology* (London: New Left Books, 1971); Ernesto Laclau, *Politics and Ideology in Marxist Theory: Capitalism, Fascism, Populism* (London: New Left Books, 1977); Michel Pêcheux, *Language, Semantics and Ideology* (New York: St. Martin's Press, 1982); John B. Thompson, *Studies in the Theory of Ideology* (Cambridge: Polity Press, 1984); and Pierre Bourdieu, *Ce que parler veut dire: l'économie des échanges linguistiques* (Paris: Fayard, 1981).

4. Thompson, *Studies in the Theory of Ideology*, pp. 130–131.

5. Pêcheux, *Language, Semantics and Ideology*, p. 111.

6. Ibid., pp. 153–154.

7. Ibid., p. 156.

8. Ibid., pp. 158–159.

9. Ernesto Laclau, *Politics and Ideology in Marxist Theory*, pp. 103–107.

10. Ibid., pp. 115–116.

11. Ibid., p. 175.

12. Ibid., p. 161.

13. See Max Weber, *Economy and Society: An Outline of Interpretive Sociology*, ed. Guenther Roth and Claus Wittich (Berkeley: University of California Press, 1978), esp. Chapters 1 and 3 of Volume 1.

14. See John B. Thompson, *Studies in the Theory of Ideology*, p. 131. Among the many ways in which ideology operates, he cites three as central: legitimation, dissimulation and reification.

15. Adeed Dawisha and I. William Zartman, eds., *Beyond Coercion: The Durability of the Arab State* (London-New York-Sydney: Croom Helm, 1988), pp. 282–283.

16. See Ghassān Imām, "Ma'ziq al-Ṣiḥāfa al-ᶜArabiyya," *An-Nāqid* Vol. 1, No. 2 (August 1988), pp. 22–24.

17. For example, see Nizār Qabbānī, *al-Aᶜmāl al-Siyāsiyya*, (Beirut: Manshūrāt Nizār Qabbānī, 1974); ᶜAbd al-Raḥmān Munīf, *Sharq al-Mutawassiṭ* (Beirut: al-Mu'assasa al-ᶜArabiyya li-l-Dirāsāt wa-l-Nashr, 1979); Adonis (ᶜAlī Aḥmad Saᶜīd), *Fātiḥa li-Nihāyāt al-Qarn: Bayānāt min Ajl Thaqāfa ᶜArabiyya Jadīda* (Beirut, 1980); ᶜAlī al-Dīn Hilāl et al., *al-Dīmuqrāṭiyya wa Ḥuqūq al-Insān fī-l-Waṭan al-ᶜArabī* (Beirut: Markaz Dirāsāt al-Waḥda al-ᶜArabiyya, 1983).

18. Nizār Qabbānī, "Naḥnu l-Muwaqqiᶜīn bi-Ḥawāfirinā Adnāhu," in *al-Mustaqbal* Vol. 6, No. 301 (Saturday, November 27, 1982), pp. 8–9.

19. See the Association of Arab-American University Graduates' *Newsletter* Vol. 17, No. 2 (April, May, June 1984), pp. 12–13; and *MERIP Reports*, January 1984, p. 23.

20. Saad Eddin Ibrahim, "The Future of Human Rights in the Arab World," in Hisham Sharabi, ed. *The Next Arab Decade: Alternative Futures* (Boulder: Westview Press/ London: Mansell Publishing Limited, 1988), pp. 38–44.

21. See the excellent studies in Adeed Dawisha and I. William Zartman, eds., *Beyond Coercion: The Durability of the Arab State*. See also Michael C. Hudson, *Arab Politics: The Search for Legitimacy* (New Haven and London: Yale University Press, 1977).

22. Lynn Simarski, "The Fabric Cracks: Urban Crises in the Arab World," in *The Middle East* No. 159 (January 1988), pp. 5–9.

23. Ibid., p. 7.

24. Ibid.

25. Ibid., p. 6.

26. Ḥalīm Barakāt, *al-Mujtama^{c} al-^{c}Arabī al-Mu^{c}āṣir: Baḥth Istiṭlā^{c}ī Ijtimā^{c}ī* (Beirut: Markaz Dirāsāt al-Waḥda al-^{c}Arabiyya, 1984), pp. 25–26.

27. Ibid.

28. See Ali E. Hillal Dessouki, ed., *Islamic Resurgence in the Arab World* (New York: Praeger, 1982).

29. Fu'ād Zakariyyā, "Al-Petro-Islām," in his *al-Ḥaqīqa wa-l-Wahm fī al-Ḥaraka al-Islāmiyya al-Mu^{c}āṣira* 2nd printing (Cairo: Dār al-Fikr li-l-Dirāsāt wa-l-Nashr wa-l-Tawzī^{c}, 1986), pp. 21–26. For a study of the influence of oil wealth on Islamic resurgence, see Daniel Pipes, "Oil Wealth and Islamic Resurgence," in Ali E. Hillal Dessouki, ed., *Islamic Resurgence in the Arab World*, pp. 35–53.

30. See Fu'ād Zakariyyā, *al-Ṣaḥwa al-Islāmiyya fī Mīzān al-^{c}Aql*, 2nd printing (Cairo: Dār al-Fikr al-Mu^{c}āṣir, 1987).

31. Fu'ād Zakariyyā, *al-Ḥaqīqa wa-l-Wahm*, pp. 119–125.

32. Ibid., pp. 11–12; see also his *al-Ṣaḥwa al-Islāmiyya*, pp. 31–32.

33. Fu'ād Zakariyyā, *al-Ḥaqīqa wa-l-Wahm*, pp. 5–10.

34. Ibid., pp. 157–180; see also his *al-Ṣaḥwa al-Islāmiyya*, pp. 30–31.

35. Ibid., pp. 18–20.

36. Ibid., pp. 20–21.

37. Ibid., p. 16.

38. See Faraj Fūda, *al-Ḥaqīqa al-Ghā'iba*, 2nd printing (Cairo: Dār al-Fikr li-l-Dirāsāt wa-l-Nashr wa-l-Tawzī^{c}, 1988), p. 12.

39. Ibid., pp. 15–32.

40. Ibid., p. 139.

41. Ibid., p. 11.

42. Ibid., pp. 53–56.

43. Ibid., pp. 58–62.

44. Ibid., pp. 42–46, 22–26, et passim.

45. Ibid., pp. 26–27.

46. Ibid., pp. 75–92.

47. Ibid., pp. 95–136.

48. Faraj Fūda, *Qabl al-Suqūṭ* (Cairo: the author, 1985), p. 23; see also Faraj Fūda, et al., *al-Ṭā'iffiyya: Ilā Ayn?* (Cairo: Dār al-Miṣrī al-Jadīd li-l-Nashr, 1987), pp. 11–58; and Faraj Fūda, *Ḥiwār ḥawl al-ᶜAlmāniyya* (Cairo: Dār al-Maḥrūsa li-l-Nashr, 1987).

49. This is a 54-page manifesto by a member of the group that assassinated President Anwar Sādāt in October of 1981. It became public during the trial of Sādāt's assassins and was published in December of 1981 by the Cairo newspaper *al-Aḥrār*, reprinted, and published again in Cairo in 1983 by the Egyptian Ministry of Awqāf. For a translation and a study of it, see Johannes J. G. Jansen, *The Neglected Duty: The Creed of Sadat's Assassins and Islamic Resurgence in the Middle East* (New York: Macmillan, 1986).

50. He is the leader of the group called Jamāᶜat al-Takfīr wa-l-Hijra which assassinated the Egyptian Minister of Awqāf, Shaykh Muḥammad Ḥusayn al-Dhahabī, in July of 1977. His tract consists of 85 pages. For an analysis of it, see Maḥmūd Amīn al-ᶜĀlim, *al-Waᶜy wa-l-Waᶜy al-Zā'if fī-l-Fikr al-ᶜArabī al-Muᶜāṣir* (Cairo: Dār al-Thaqāfa al-Jadīda, 1986), pp. 259–267.

51. See for example Faraj Fūda, *Qabl al-Suqūṭ*, pp. 159–167 where he discerns three trends in Egypt: (1) the traditional Islamic trend of the Muslim Brothers who, despite violent elements in the past, are now willing to play the political game: this trend is relatively the weakest; (2) the revolutionary Islamic trend of the radical groups that branched out of the Muslim Brothers and advocate violence against a society and regime they reject totally and consider to be *jāhilī*: it is the most dangerous though not the most influential trend; and (3) the wealth-based Islamic trend led by some Egyptians who made their fortunes in Saudi Arabia, joined by some of those who made theirs during Sādāt's economic open-door policy in Egypt, and who now control the Islamic banks, corporations and publishing houses and have begun to control the minds of the poor masses and preoccupy them with religious issues in order to distract them from the real issues of poverty, in fear of their revolt and in an attempt to preserve their own wealth and dominance: this trend is the strongest and insidiously the most effective.

52. The use of linguistic and non-linguistic methods in applying discourse analysis to the study of contemporary Arab discourses, Islamic and otherwise, and relating them to ideology can produce new insights and explore new dimensions of Arab thought. Two doctoral candidates with whose research supervision I am involved at McGill University in Montreal are writing their Ph.D. dissertations using such methods: Salwa Ismail (Department of Political Science) and John Calvert (Institute of Islamic Studies).

53. Ḥalīm Barakāt, *al-Mujtama^c al-^cArabī al-Mu^cāṣir: Baḥth Istiṭlā^cī Ijtimā^cī* (Beirut: Markaz Dirāsāt al-Waḥda al-^cArabiyya, 1984) An English version of this important book is being prepared by its author.

54. Ḥalīm Barakāt, *al-Mujtama^c al-^cArabī al-Mu^cāṣir*, p. 462.

55. Adeed Dawisha and I. Williams Zartman, eds., *Beyond Coercion: The Durability of the Arab State* (London-New York-Sydney: Croom Helm, 1988).

56. Ḥalīm Barakāt, *al-Mujtama^c al-^cArabī al-Mu^cāṣir*, pp. 462–463.

57. For the transcript of two anonymous cassettes secretly distributed in Saudi Arabia, probably by anti-regime forces, and containing a vicious attack on the idea of modernity as an anti-Islamic vision of life and the world, see "Ḥarb al-Kāsīt," in the London Arabic monthly *An-Nāqid* Vol. 1, No. 1 (July 1988), pp. 31–46, in which the most prominent contemporary Arab intellectuals advocating modern ideas and modes of thought and life are mentioned by name and severely maligned as enemies of Islam. For a philosophical and sociological critique of modernity in the capitalist West, see Peter L. Berger, "Toward a Critique of Modernity," in his *Facing up to Modernity: Excursions in Society, Politics, and Religion* (New York: Basic Books, Inc., Publishers, 1977), pp. 70–80, where he soberly discusses five dilemmas which, he believes, modernity has imposed on human life, namely, abstraction, futurity, individuation, liberation and secularization.

58. Hisham Sharabi, *Neopatriarchy: A Theory of Distorted Change in Arab Society* (New York-Oxford: Oxford University Press, 1988), p. 155.

Bibliography

^{c}Abd al-Ḥayy, ^{c}Abd al-Tawwāb. *^{c}Aṣīr Ḥayātī*. Cairo: al-Hay'a al-Miṣriyya al-^{c}Āmma li-l-Kitāb, 1966.

^{c}Abd al-Malik, Anwar. *Dirāsāt fī-l-Thaqāfa al-Waṭaniyya*. Beirut: Dār al-Ṭalī^{c}a, 1967.

——. "Fā'iḍ al-Qīma al-Tārīkhī," *Dirāsāt ^{c}Arabiyya*, Vol. 15, No. 5 (March 1979), pp. 3–12.

——. *al-Fikr al-^{c}Arabī fī Ma^{c}rakat al-Nahḍa*. Beirut: Dār al-Ādāb, 1974.

——. "al-Islām al-Siyāsī," *Qaḍāyā ^{c}Arabiyya*, Vol. 6, No. 5 (September 1979), pp. 175–184.

——. *al-Jaysh wa-l-Ḥaraka al-Waṭaniyya*. Beirut: Dār Ibn Khaldūn, 1974.

——. "al-Khuṣūṣiyya wa-l-Aṣāla," *al-Ādāb*, May 1974, pp. 41–43.

——. *al-Mujtama^{c} al-Miṣrī wa-l-Jaysh, 1952–1970*. Beirut: Dār al-Ṭalī^{c}a, 1974.

——. *Nahḍat Miṣr*. Cairo: al-Hay'a al-Miṣriyya al-^{c}Āmma li-l-Kitāb, 1983.

——. *Rīḥ al-Sharq*. Cairo: Dār al-Mustaqbal al-^{c}Arabī, 1983.

Abdel-Malek, Anouar (ed.). *Contemporary Arab Political Thought*, London: Zed Books Ltd., 1983.

Abdel-Malek, Anouar. *La Dialectique sociale*. Paris: Le Seuil, 1971.

——. *Egypt: Military Society*. New York: Random House, 1968.

——. *Egypte, Société militaire*. Paris: Le Seuil, 1962.

——. *Idéologie et renaissance nationale: L'Egypte moderne*. Paris: Anthropos, 1969.

—— et al. *Intellectual Creativity in Endogenous Culture*. Tokyo: United Nations University Press, 1978.

Abdel-Malek, Anouar (ed.). *La pensée politique arabe contemporaine*. Paris: Le Seuil, 1970.

Abdel-Malek, Anouar. *The Project on Socio-Cultural Development Alternatives in a Changing World: Report on the Formative Stage*. Tokyo: United Nations University Press, 1980.

—— et al. *Science and Technology in the Transformation of the World*. Tokyo: United Nations University Press, 1979.

Abdel-Malek, Anouar. *Social Dialectics I: Civilization and Social Theory*. London: Macmillan Press/Albany, N.Y.: State University of New York Press, 1981.

——. *Social Dialectics II: Nations and Revolutions*. London: Macmillan Press/Albany, N.Y.: State University of New York Press, 1981.

——. *Sociologie de l'impérialisme*. Paris: Anthropos, 1971.

——. *Spécificité et théorie sociale*. Paris: Anthropos, 1977.

ᶜAbd al-Raḥmān, ᶜĀ'isha. *Banāt al-Nabī*. Cairo: Dār al-Hilāl, 1963.

——. *Baṭalat Karbalā'*. Cairo: Dār al-Hilāl, [1965?].

——. *al-Mafhūm al-Islāmī li-Taḥrīr al-Mar'a*. Cairo: Maṭbaᶜat Mukhaymir, 1967.

——. *Nisā' al-Nabī*. Cairo: Dār al-Hilāl, [1961?].

——. *Sukayna bint al-Ḥusayn*. Cairo: Dār al-Hilāl, [1965?].

——. *Umm al-Nabī*. Cairo: Dār al-Hilāl, [1961?].

Abdul Mohsen, Assem. "Muslim Brothers' Hajja Zeinab: East and West want to delay the return of Islam," *The Middle East*, No. 79 (May 1981), pp. 32–34.

Abdulrazak, Fawzi et al. *Arabic Literature in North Africa: Critical Essays and Annotated Bibliography. Mundus Arabicus*, Vol. 2 (1982). Cambridge, MA: Dar Mahjar, 1982.

Accad, Evelyne, "Women's Voices from the Maghreb: 1945 to the present," *Mundus Arabicus*, Vol. 2 (1982), pp. 18–34.

Adonis [pseudonym of ᶜAlī Aḥmad Saᶜīd]. "Bayn al-Thabāt wa-l-Taḥawwul: Khawāṭir ḥawl al-Thawra al-Islāmiyya fī Irān," *Mawāqif*, No. 34 (Winter 1979), pp. 149–160.

——. *Dīwān al-Shi*ᶜ*r al-*ᶜ*Arabī*, 3 vols. Beirut: al-Maktaba al-ᶜAṣriyya, 1964–1968.

——. *Fātiḥa li-Nihāyāt al-Qarn: Bayānāt min Ajl Thaqāfa* ᶜ*Arabiyya Jadīda*. Beirut: Dār al-ᶜAwda, 1980.

——. "Khawāṭir ḥawl Maẓāhir al-Takhalluf al-Fikrī fī-l-Mujtamaᶜ al-ᶜArabī," *al-Ādāb*, May 1974, pp. 27–29.

——. "Reflections on the Manifestations of Intellectual Backwardness in Arab Society," trans. by Shereen Khairallah, pp. 25–35 in *CEMAM Reports 1974*.

——. *al-Thābit wa-l-Mutaḥawwil: Baḥth fī-l-Ittibā*ᶜ *wa-l-Ibdā*ᶜ ᶜ*ind al-*ᶜ*Arab*, 3 vols. Beirut: Dār al-ᶜAwda, 1974–1978.

al-ᶜĀlim, Maḥmūd Amīn. "Taᶜlīq ᶜalā Baḥth 'al-Khuṣūṣiyya wa-l-Aṣāla,' li-l-Duktūr Anwar ᶜAbd al-Malik," *al-Ādāb*, May 1974, pp. 44–51.

——. *al-Wa*ᶜ*y wa-l-Wa*ᶜ*y al-Zā'if fī-l-Fikr al-*ᶜ*Arabī al-Mu*ᶜ*āṣir*. Cairo: Dār al-Thaqāfa al-Jadīda, 1986.

Althusser, Louis. *Essays on Ideology*. London: New Left Books, 1971.

ᶜAmāra, Muḥammad. *al-Islām wa-l-Sulṭa al-Dīniyya*. 2nd printing. Beirut: al-Mu'assasa al-ᶜArabiyya li-l-Dirāsāt wa-l-Nashr, 1980.

——. *al-Islām wa-l-Waḥda al-Qawmiyya*. 2nd printing. Beirut: al-Mu'assasa al-ᶜArabiyya li-l-Dirāsāt wa-l-Nashr, 1979.

ᶜĀmil, Mahdī [pseudonym of Ḥasan Ḥamdān]. *Azmat al-Ḥaḍāra al-*ᶜ*Arabiyya am Azmat al-Burjuwāziyyāt al-*ᶜ*Arabiyya?* Beirut: Dār al-Fārābī, 1974.

Amīn, Aḥmad. *Ḍuḥā al-Islām*, 3 vols. Cairo: Lajnat al-Ta'līf wa-l-Tarjama wa-l-Nashr, 1933–1936.

——. *Fajr al-Islām*. Cairo: Maṭbaᶜat al-Iᶜtimād, 1929.

——. *Yawm al-Islām*. Cairo: Dār al-Maᶜārif, 1952.

——. *Ẓuhr al-Islām*, 4 vols. Cairo: Lajnat al-Ta'līf wa-l-Tarjama wa-l-Nashr, 1945–1955.

Amin, Galal A. "Dependent Development," *Alternatives*, Vol. 2 (1976), pp. 379–403.

——. *Food Supply and Economic Development, with Special Reference to Egypt*. London: Frank Cass, 1966.

——. *The Modernization of Poverty: A Study of the Political Economy of Growth in Nine Arab Countries, 1945–1970.* Leiden: E. J. Brill, 1981.

——. *Urbanisation and Economic Development in the Arab World.* Beirut: Beirut Arab University, 1972.

Amīn, Jalāl. *al-Iqtiṣād al-Qawmī: Muqaddima li-Dirāsat al-Naẓariyya al-Naqdiyya.* Cairo: Maktabat Sayyid Wahba, 1968.

——. *Mabādi' al-Taḥlīl al-Iqtiṣādī.* Cairo: Maktabat Sayyid Wahba, 1967.

——. *al-Mārksiyya: ᶜArḍ wa Taḥlīl wa Naqd* . Cairo: Maktabat Sayyid Wahba, 1970.

——. *al-Mashriq al-ᶜArabī wa-l-Gharb*, 3rd printing. Beirut: Markaz Dirāsāt al-Waḥda al-ᶜArabiyya, 1981.

——. *Miḥnat al-Iqtiṣād wa-l-Thaqāfa fī Miṣr.* Cairo: al-Markaz al-ᶜArabī li-l-Baḥth wa-l-Nashr, 1982.

——. *Muqaddima ilā al-Ishtirākiyya.* Cairo: Maktabat Sayyid Wahba, 1966.

——. *Tanmiya am Tabaᶜiyya Iqtiṣādiyya wa Thaqāfiyya?* Cairo: Maṭbūᶜāt al-Qāhira, 1983.

Amin, Samir. *L'Accumulation à l'échelle mondiale: Critique de la théorie du sous-développement.* Dakar and Paris: IFAN-Anthropos, 1970.

——. *Accumulation on a World Scale: A Critique of the Theory of Underdevelopment*, 2 vols. New York: Monthly Review Press, 1974.

——. *The Arab Economy*, trans. by Michael Pallis and intro. by Aidan Foster-Carter. London: Zed Press, 1982.

——. *The Arab Nation: Nationalism and Class Struggles.* London: Zed Press, 1978.

——. *Le Développement inégal.* Paris: Editions de Minuit, 1973.

——. *L'Economie du Maghreb.* Paris: Editions de Minuit, 1966.

——. *L'Egypte nasserienne.* Paris: Editions de Minuit, 1964.

——. *The Maghreb in the Modern World.* Harmondsworth: Penguin, 1970.

——. *Le Maghreb moderne.* Paris: Editions de Minuit, 1970.

Amīn, Samīr. *al-Maghrib al-^{c}Arabī al-Ḥadīth*, trans. by Kāmil Qayṣar Dāghir. Beirut: Dār al-Ḥadātha, 1980.

——. *Muḥāḍarāt fī Iḥṣā'iyyāt al-Tawāzun al-^{c}Āmm: Dirāsa Iḥṣā'iyya ^{c}an al-Tayyārāt al-Māliyya wa-l-Naqdiyya fī al-Iqtiṣād al-Miṣrī ^{c}Ām 1957.* Cairo: Ma^{c}had al-Dirāsāt al-^{c}Arabiyya al-^{c}Āliya, 1959.

Amin, Samir. *La Nation arabe: Nationalisme et luttes de classes.* Paris: Editions de Minuit, 1976.

Amīn, Samīr. *al-Ṭabaqa wa-l-Umma fī-l-Tārīkh wa fī-l-Marḥala al-Imbiryāliyya*, trans. by Henriette ^{c}Abbūdī. Beirut: Dār al-Ṭalī^{c}a, 1980.

——. *al-Taṭawwur al-Lāmutakāfi': Dirāsāt fī-l-Tashkīlāt al-Ijtimā^{c}iyya li-l-Ra'smāliyya al-Muḥīṭa.* Beirut: Dār al-Ṭalī^{c}a, 1980.

——. *al-Umma al-^{c}Arabiyya: al-Qawmiyya wa Ṣirā^c al-Ṭabaqāt*, trans. by Kāmil Qayṣar Dāghir. Beirut: Dār Ibn Rashīd li-l-Ṭibā^{c}a wa-l-Nashr, 1978.

Amin, Samir. *Unequal Development.* New York: Monthly Review Press, 1976.

al-^{c}Aqqād, ^{c}Abbās Maḥmūd. *^{c}Abqariyyat al-Imām ^{c}Alī.* Cairo: Maṭba^{c}at al-Ma^{c}ārif wa Maktabatuhā, 1943.

——. *^{c}Abqariyyat Khālid.* Cairo: Dār Iḥyā' al-Kutub al-^{c}Arabiyya, 1945.

——. *^{c}Abqariyyat Muḥammad.* Cairo: al-Maktaba al-Tijāriyya al-Kubrā, 1942.

——. *^{c}Abqariyyat al-Ṣiddīq.* Cairo: Dār al-Ma^{c}ārif, 1943.

——. *^{c}Abqariyyat ^{c}Umar.* Cairo: Maṭba^{c}at al-Istiqāma, 1943.

Arab League Educational, Cultural, and Scientific Organization (ALECSO). *Mu'tamar al-Aṣāla wa-l-Tajdīd fī al-Thaqāfa al-^{c}Arabiyya al-Mu^{c}āṣira.* Cairo: Directorate of Culture, 1973.

Arkoun, Mohammed. *Contribution à l'étude de l'humanisme arabe au IVe/Xe siècle: Miskawayh, philosophe et historien.* Paris: J. Vrin, 1970.

——. *Essais sur la pensée islamique.* Paris: Maisonneuve et Larose, 1973.

——. "L'Humanisme arabe au IVe/Xe siècle, d'après le Kitāb al-Hawāmil wa l-šawāmil," *Studia Islamica*, Vol. 14 (1961), pp. 73–108 and Vol. 15 (1961), pp. 63–89.

——. et Louis Gardet. *L'Islam: Hier-Demain*. Paris: Editions Buchet/Chastel, 1978.

Arkoun, Mohammed. *Lectures du Coran*. Paris: Maisonneuve et Larose, 1982.

——. *La Pensée arabe*. 2nd printing. Paris: Presses Universitaires de France, 1979.

Arkūn, Muḥammad. *al-Fikr al-^{c}Arabī*, trans. by ^{c}Ādil al-^{c}Awwā. Beirut: Manshūrāt ^{c}Uwaydāt, 1983.

—— wa Louis Gardet. *al-Islām: al-Ams wa-l-Ghad*, trans. by ^{c}Alī al-Muqallid. Beirut: Dār al-Tanwīr, 1983.

Arkūn, Muḥammad. "al-Islām, al-Tārīkhiyya wa-l-Taqaddum," trans. by Hāshim Ṣāliḥ. *Mawāqif*, No. 40 (Winter 1981), pp. 6–39.

——. "Naḥwa Taqyīm wa Istilhām Jadīdayn li-l-Fikr al-Islāmī," *al-Fikr al-^{c}Arabī al-Mu^{c}āṣir*, No. 29 (December 1983/January 1984), pp. 39–45.

——. *al-Fikr al-Islāmī: Qirā'a ^{c}Ilmiyya*, trans. Hāshim Ṣāliḥ. Beirut: Markaz al-Inmā' al-Qawmī, 1987.

——. *Tārīkhiyyat al-Fikr al-^{c}Arabī al-Islāmī*,. trans. by Hāshim Ṣaliḥ. Beirut: Markaz al-Inmā' al-Qawmī, 1986.

——. "al-Turāth: Muḥtawāh wa Huwiyyatuh, Ījābiyyātuh wa Salbiyyātuh," in Yāsīn, ed., *al-Turāth wa Taḥaddiyāt al-^{c}Aṣr*, pp. 155–167.

——. "al-Turāth wa-l-Mawqif al-Naqdī al-Tasā'ulī," *Mawāqif*, No. 40 (Winter 1981), pp. 40–57.

al-^{c}Arwī, ^{c}Abd Allāh. *al-^{c}Arab wa-l-Fikr al-Tārīkhī*. Beirut: Dār al-Ḥaqīqa, 1973.

Asad, Talal and Roger Owen (eds.). *Sociology of "Developing Societies": The Middle East*. New York: Monthly Review Press, 1983.

Association of Arab-American University Graduates (AAUG). "The Arab Organization for Human Rights," *Newsletter*, Vol. 17, No. 2, (April, May, June 1984), pp. 12–13.

Awwad, Hanan. *Arab Causes in the Fiction of Ghādah al-Sammān, 1961–1975*. Sherbrooke, Quebec, Canada: Editions Naaman, 1983.

^{c}Ayyād, Shukrī. "Mafhūm al-Aṣāla wa-l-Tajdīd wa-l-Thaqāfa al-^{c}Arabiyya al-Mu^{c}āṣira," *al-Ādāb*, November 1971, pp. 2–5.

Ballūz, Nāyif. "Waqfa ma^{c}a Kitāb: *al-Naza^{c}āt al-Māddiyya fī-l-Falsafa al-^{c}Arabiyya al-Islāmiyya*," pp. 167–209 in Yāsīn et al., *al-Marksiyya*.

Barakat, Halim (ed.). *Contemporary North Africa: Issues of Development and Integration*. London and Sydney: Croom Helm, 1985.

Barakāt, Ḥalīm. *al-Mujtama^c al-^{c}Arabī al-Mu^{c}āṣir: Baḥth Istiṭlā^{c}ī Ijtimā^{c}ī*. Beirut: Markaz Dirāsāt al-Waḥda al-^{c}Arabiyya, 1984.

Barakāt, Muḥammad Tawfīq. *Sayyid Quṭb: Khulāṣat Ḥayātih, Manhajuh fī-l-Ḥaraka, al-Naqd al-Muwajjah ilayh*. Beirut: Dār al-Da^{c}wa, [1973].

Bāsīlī, François. "Iḥtifā'an bi-l-Mu'tamar al-Ḥaḍārī: Thalāth Naẓarāt Naqdiyya," *al-Ādāb*, June 1974, pp. 71–73.

Bennis Mohammed. "The Plurality of the One," pp. 250–263 in Barakat, ed., *Contemporary North Africa*.

Berger, Peter L. *Facing up to Modernity: Excursions in Society, Politics, and Religion*. New York: Basic Books, Inc., Publishers, 1977.

——. "Toward a Critique of Modernity," pp. 70–80 in Berger, *Facing to Modernity*.

Bint al-Shāṭi'. See ^{c}Abd al-Raḥmān, ^{c}Ā'isha.

Boullata, Issa J. "Modern Qur'ān Exegesis: A Study of Bint al-Shāṭi''s Method," *Muslim World*, Vol. 64, No. 2 (April 1974), pp. 103–113.

Boullata, Kamal (ed.). *Women of the Fertile Crescent: Modern Poetry by Arab Women*. Washington, D.C.: Three Continents Press, 1978.

Bourdieu, Pierre. *Ce que parler veut dire: l'économie des échanges linguistiques*. Paris: Fayard, 1981.

Brown, Gillian and George Yule. *Discourse Analysis*. Cambridge: Cambridge University Press, 1983.

Carré, Olivier. *Mystique et Politique: lecture révolutionnaire du Coran par Sayyid Quṭb, Frère musulman radical*. Paris: Editions du Cerf - Presses de la Fondation Nationale des Sciences Politiques, 1984.

Center for the Study of the Modern Arab World, Saint Joseph's University, Beirut. *Vision and Revision in Arab Society 1974. CEMAM Reports 1974*. Beirut: Dar El-Mashreq, 1975.

CEMAM Reports 1974. See Center for the Study of the Modern Arab World [Centre pour l'étude du monde arabe moderne].

Chartier, Marc. "La rencontre Orient-Occident dans la pensée de trois philosophes égyptiens contemporains: Ḥasan Ḥanafī, Fu'ād Zakariyyā, Zakī Nagīb Maḥmūd," *Oriente Moderno*, Vol. 53, Nos. 7–8 (July-August 1973), pp. 603–642.

Cragg, Kenneth. *The Pen and the Faith: Eight Modern Muslim Writers and the Qur'ān*. London: George Allen & Unwin, 1985.

Dawisha, Adeed and I. William Zartman (eds.). *Beyond Coercion: The Durability of the Arab States*. London-New York-Sydney: Croom Helm, 1988.

Diyāb, Alice Shukrī. *Fihris Alf Maqāl ᶜan al-Mar'a al-ᶜArabiyya khilāl mi'at ᶜĀm*. Cambridge, MA: Harvard College Library, 1979.

Donohue, John J. "Crisis and Culture: The Kuwait Colloquium," pp. 1–4 in *CEMEM Reports 1974*.

Dessouki, Ali E. Hillal (ed.). *Islamic Resurgence in the Arab World*. New York: Praeger, 1982.

Esposito, John L. (ed.). *Voices of Resurgent Islam*. New York-Oxford: Oxford University Press, 1983.

Faraj, Muḥammad ᶜAbd al-Salām. *al-Farīḍa al-Ghā'iba*. Cairo: Wazārat al-Awqāf,1983.

Fernea, Elizabeth W. and Basima Q. Bezirgan (eds.). *Middle Eastern Muslim Women Speak*. Austin: University of Texas Press, 1977.

Fernea, Elizabeth W. (ed.). *Women and the Family in the Middle East: New Voices of Change*. Austin: University of Texas Press, 1985.

Foucault, Michel. *Power/Knowledge: Selected Interviews and Other Writings*, ed. Colin Gordon, trans. by Colin Gordon et al. New York: Pantheon Books, 1980.

Frye, Northrop. *Anatomy of Criticism*. Princeton: Princeton University Press, 1957. Paperback edition, 3rd printing, 1973.

Fūda, Faraj. *al-Ḥaqīa al-Ghā'iba*. 2nd printing. Cairo: Dār al-Fikr li-l-Dirāsāt wa-l-Nashr wa-l-Tawzī^c^, 1988.

——. *Ḥiwār ḥawl al-^c^Almāniyya*. Cairo: Dār al-Maḥrūsa li-l-Nashr, 1987.

——. *Qabl al-Suqūṭ*. Cairo: the author, 1985.

Gendzier, Irene L. "Foreword," pp. vii-xix in El Saadawi, *The Hidden Face of Eve*. Boston: Beacon Press, 1982.

al-Ghazālī, Zaynab. *Ayyām min Ḥayātī*. Cairo-Beirut: Dār al-Shurūq, n.d.

Haddad, Yvonne Yazbeck. *Contemporary Islam and the Challenge of History*. Albany: State University of New York Press, 1982.

——. "The Qur'anic Justification for an Islamic Revolution: The View of Sayyid Quṭb," *Middle East Journal*, Vol. 37, No. 1 (Winter 1983), pp. 14–29.

——. "Sayyid Quṭb: Ideologue of Islamic Revival," pp. 67–98 in Esposito, ed., *Voices of Resurgent Islam*.

Ḥamdān, Ḥasan. See ^c^Āmil, Mahdī.

Ḥanafī, Ḥasan. *Dirāsāt Islāmiyya*. Beirut: Dār al-Tanwīr, 1982.

——. *Les Méthodes d'exégèse: Essai sur la science de Fondements de la Compréhension, ^c^Ilm Uṣūl al-Fiqh*. Cairo: Conseil Supérieur des Arts, des Lettres et des Sciences Sociales, 1965.

——. *Qaḍāyā Mu^c^āṣira*. Vol. 1, *Fī Fikrinā al-Mu^c^āṣir*. Beirut: Dār al-Tanwīr, 1981. 2nd printing, Beirut: Dār al-Tanwīr, 1983.

——. *Qaḍāyā Mu^c^āṣira*. Vol. 2, *Fī-l-Fikr al-Gharbī al-Mu^c^āṣir*. Cairo: Dār al-Fikr al-^c^Arabī, 1977.

——. *al-Turāth wa-l-Tajdīd: Mawqifunā min al-Turāth al-Qadīm*. Beirut: Dār al-Tanwīr, 1981.

—— (ed). *al-Yasār al-Islāmī*. Vol. 1, No. 1 (1981).

Haykal, Muḥammad Ḥusayn. *al-Fārūq ^c^Umar*, 2 vols. Cairo: Maṭba^c^at Miṣr, 1945.

——. *Ḥayāt Muḥammad*. Cairo: Maṭbaᶜat Miṣr, 1935.

——. *al-Ṣiddīq Abū Bakr*. Cairo: Maṭbaᶜat Miṣr, 1945.

Hilāl, ᶜAlī al-Dīn et al. *al-Dīmuqrāṭiyya wa Ḥuqūq al-Insān fī-l-Waṭan al-ᶜArabī*. Beirut: Markaz Dirāsāt al-Waḥda al-ᶜArabiyya, 1983.

Hoffman, Valerie J. "An Islamic Activist: Zaynab al-Ghazālī," pp. 233–254 in Fernea, ed., *Women and the Family*.

Hudson, Michael C. *Arab Politics: The Search for Legitimacy*. New Haven and London: Yale University Press, 1977.

Ḥusayn, Ṭāhā. *ᶜAlā Hāmish al-Sīra*, 3 vols. Cairo: Dār al-Maᶜārif, 1933–1938.

——. *al-Fitna al-Kubrā*, 2 vols. Cairo: Dār al-Maᶜārif, 1947–1953.

——. *al-Shaykhān*. Cairo: Dār al-Maᶜārif, 1960.

Ibrahim, Saad Eddin. "The Future of Human Rights in the Arab World," pp. 38–44 in Sharabi, ed., *The Next Arab Decade*.

Imām, Ghassān. "Ma'ziq al-Ṣiḥāfa al-ᶜArabiyya," *al-Nāqid*, Vol. 1, No. 2 (August 1988), pp. 22–24.

al-Jābirī, Muḥammad ᶜĀbid. *al-Khiṭāb al-ᶜArabī al-Muᶜāṣir: Dirāsa Taḥlīliyya Naqdiyya*. Beirut: Dār al-Ṭalīᶜa, 1982.

——. *Naḥnu wa-l-Turāth: Qirā'āt Muᶜāṣira fī Turāthinā al-Falsafī*. Beirut: Dār al-Ṭalīᶜa, 1980.

——. *Naqd al-ᶜAql al-ᶜArabī*. Vol. 1, *Takwīn al-ᶜAql al-ᶜArabī*. Beirut: Dār al-Ṭalīᶜa, 1984.

——. *Naqd al-ᶜAql al-ᶜArabī*. Vo. 2, *Bunyat al-ᶜAql al-ᶜArabī: Dirāsa Taḥlīliyya Naqdiyya li-Nuẓum al-Maᶜrifa fī-l-Thaqāfa al-ᶜArabiyya*. Beirut: Markaz Dirāsāt al-Waḥda al-ᶜArabiyya, 1986.

Jansen, Johannes, J. G. *The Neglected Duty: The Creed of Sadat's Assassins and Islamic Resurgence in the Middle East*. New York: Macmillan, 1986.

Kepel, Gilles. *Le prophète et pharaon. Les mouvements islamistes dans l'Egypte contemporaine*. Paris: Editions La Découverte, 1984.

al-Khaṭībī, ᶜAbd al-Kabīr. *Fī-l-Kitāba wa-l-Tajriba*, trans. by Muḥammad Barrāda. Beirut: Dār al-ᶜAwda, 1980.

——. *al-Ism al-ᶜArabī al-Jarīḥ*, trans. by Muḥammad Binnīs [Mohammed Bennis]. Beirut: Dār al-ᶜAwda, 1980.

——. *al-Naqd al-Muzdawij*. Beirut: Dār al-ᶜAwda, [1980].

——. *al-Ṣahyūniyya wa-l-Yasār al-Gharbī*, trans. by ᶜAbd al-Salām Bin ᶜAbd al-ᶜĀlī, pp. 37–150 in al-Khaṭībī, *al-Naqd al-Muzdawij*.

Khatibi, Abdelkebir. *Bilan de la sociologie au Maroc*. Rabat: Publications de l'Association pour la recherche en sciences humaines, 1967.

——. *La blessure du nom propre*. Paris: Denoël, 1974.

——. *Dédicace à l'annnée qui vient*. Montpellier: Fata Morgana, 1986.

——. "Double Criticism: The Decolonization of Arab Sociology," pp. 9–19 in Barakat, ed., *Contemporary North Africa*.

—— et al. *Ecrivains marocains du Protectorat à 1965: Choix, traduction de l'arabe et présentation*. Paris: Sinbad, 1974.

Khatibi, Abdelkebir. *Etudes sociologiques sur le Maroc*. Rabat: Société d'études économiques, sociales, et statistiques, 1971.

——. *Le Livre du sang*. Paris: Gallimard, 1979.

——. *Le lutteur de classe à la manière taoïste*. Paris: Sindbad, 1977.

——. *Maghreb pluriel*. Rabat: Société marocaine des éditeurs réunis, 1982.

——. *La mémoire tatouée*. Paris: Denoël, 1971.

——. *Le roman maghrébin*. Paris: Maspero, 1968. 2nd ed., Rabat: SMER, 1979.

—— and Mohammed Sijelmassi. *The Splendour of Islamic Calligraphy*, trans. by James Hughes. New York: Rizzolli, 1977.

Khatibi, Abdelkebir. *Vomito blanco: le sionisme et la conscience malheureuse*. Paris: Union générale d'éditions, 1974.

Kilpatrick, Hilary. "Women and Literature in the Arab East," in Schlipper, ed., *Unheard Words*, pp. 72–90.

Kooij, C. "Bint al-Shāṭi': A Suitable Case for Biography?" pp. 67–72 in El-Sheikh et al., eds., *The Challenge of the Middle East*.

Kotb, Sayid [Quṭb, Sayyid]. *Social Justice in Islam*, trans. by John B. Hardie, Washington, D.C.: American Council of Learned Societies, 1953.

Laclau, Ernesto. *Politics and Ideology in Marxist Theory: Capitalism, Fascism, Populism*. London: New Left Books, 1977.

Laroui, Abdallah. *La crise des intellectuels arabes: traditionalisme ou historicisme?* Paris: Librairie François Maspero, 1974.

——. *The Crisis of the Arab Intellectual: Traditionalism or Historicism?* trans. by Diarmid Cammell. Berkeley: University of California Press, 1976.

MacDonell, Diane. *Theories of Discourse: An Introduction*. Oxford: Basil Blackwell, 1986.

al-Majlis al-Qawmī li-l-Thaqāfa al-ᶜArabiyya, *al-Turāth wa-l-ᶜAmal al-Siyāsī*. Rabat: Muntadā al-Fikr wa-l-Ḥiwār, 1984.

al-Marnīsī, Fāṭima. *al-Ḥubb fī Ḥaḍāratinā al-Islāmiyya*. Beirut: al-Dār al-ᶜĀlamiyya li-l-Ṭibāᶜa wa-l-Nashr, 1984.

——. *al-Sulūk al-Jinsī fī Mujtamaᶜ Islāmī Ra'smālī Tabaᶜī*, trans. by Uzwīl Fāṭima al-Zahrā'. Beirut: Dār al-Ḥadātha, 1982.

Maḥmūd, Zakī Najīb. "al-Ḥadātha wa Qaḍiyyat al-Taqaddum wa-l-Takhalluf," *al-Ādāb*, May 1974, pp. 6–9.

——. "Mawqif al-Thaqāfa al-ᶜArabiyya al-Ḥadītha fī Muwājahat al-ᶜAṣr," *al-Ādāb*, November 1971, pp. 6–12.

al-Mazālī, Muḥammad. "al-Aṣāla wa-l-Tafattuḥ," *al-Ādāb*, November 1971, pp. 13–17.

Meghdessian, S. R. *The Status of the Arab Woman: A Selected Bibliography*. Westport, CT: Greenwood Press, 1980.

Mernissi, Fatima. *Beyond the Veil: Male-Female Dynamics in a Modern Muslim Society*. Cambridge: MA: Schenkman Publishing Company, 1975.

——. *Beyond the Veil: Male-Female Dynamics in a Modern Muslim Society*. 2nd edition, new intro. by author. Bloomington: Indiana University Press, 1987.

Merquior, J. G. *Foucault*. Berkeley-Los Angeles: University of California Press, 1985.

Middle East Research and Information Project. *MERIP Reports*. January 1984.

Munīf, ᶜAbd al-Raḥmān. *Sharq al-Mutawassiṭ*. Beirut: al-Mu'assasa al-ᶜArabiyya li-l-Dirāsāt wa-l-Nashr, 1979.

Muruwwa, Ḥusayn. "al-Mawqif min al-Turāth fī-l-Dīn wa-l-Falsafa," *al-Ādāb*, May 1970, pp. 8–10 and 131–140.

——. *al-Naza^c^āt al-Māddiyya fī-l-Falsafa al-^c^Arabiyya al-Islāmiyya*, 2 vols. Beirut: Dār al-Fārābī, 1978–1979.

Muṣṭafā, Shākir. "al-Ab^c^ād al-Tārīkhiyya li-Azmat al-Taṭawwur al-Ḥaḍārī al-^c^Arabī," *al-Ādāb*, May 1974, pp. 13–24 and 111–112.

——. (ed.). *Azmat al-Taṭawwur al-Ḥaḍārī fī-l-Waṭan al-^c^Arabī: Waqā'i^c^ Nadwat al-Kuwayt mā bayn 7–12 Nīsān (April), 1974*. Kuwait: Jam^c^iyyat al-Khirrījīn al-Kuwaytiyya wa Jāmi^c^at al-Kuwayt, 1975.

Nadwat al-Kuwayt, 6–12 Nīsān [April 1974]. "Azmat al-Taṭawwur al-Ḥaḍārī fī-l-Waṭan al-^c^Arabī: al-Bayān al-Khitāmī," *al-Ādāb*, May 1974, pp. 2–5.

Nadwat al-Kuwayt [The Kuwait Colloquium]. "Final Declaration of the Kuwait Colloquium on the Crisis of Cultural Development in the Arab Nation," trans. by John J. Donohue, pp. 5–15 in *CEMAM Reports 1974*.

al-Nāqid. "Ḥarb al-Kāsīt," *al-Nāqid*, Vol. 1, No. 1 (July 1988), pp. 31–46.

al-Nuwayhī, Muḥammad. "al-Dīn wa Azmat al-Taṭawwur al-Ḥaḍārī fī-l-Waṭan al-^c^Arabī," *al-Ādāb*, May 1974, pp. 79–86.

——. *Naḥwa Thawra fī-l-Fikr al-Dīnī*. Beirut: Dār al-Ādāb, 1983.

Pêcheux, Michel. *Language, Semantics and Ideology*. New York: St. Martin's Press, 1982.

Pipes, Daniel. "Oil Wealth and Islamic Resurgence," pp. 35–53 in Dessouki, ed., *Islamic Resurgence*.

Qabbānī, Nizār. *al-A^c^māl al-Siyāsiyya*. Beirut: Manshūrāt Nizār Qabbānī, 1974.

——. "Naḥnu l-Muwaqqi^c^īn bi-Ḥawāfirinā adnāhu," *al-Mustaqbal*, Vol. 6, No. 301 (Saturday, November 27, 1982), pp. 8–9.

Al-Qazzaz, Ayad. *Women in the Middle East and North Africa: An Annotated Bibliography*. Austin: University of Texas Press, 1977.

Quṭb, Muḥammad. *Jāhilliyat al-Qarn al-^c^Ishrīn*. Cairo: Maktabat Wahba, n.d. Reprint. Cairo: Beirut: Dār al-Shurūq, 1980.

Quṭb, Muḥammad ^c^Alī. *Sayyid Quṭb aw Thawrat al-Fikr al-Islāmī*. [Beirut: ?] 1967.

Quṭb, Sayyid. *al-^c^Adāla al-Ijtimā^c^iyya fī-l-Islām*. 4th printing. Cairo: Dār Iḥyā' al-Kutub al-^c^Arabiyya, 1954.

——. *Hādhā al-Dīn*. Cairo: Dār al-Qalam, 1962.

——. *In the Shade of the Qur'ān*, Vol. 30, trans. by M. Adil Slahi and Ashur A. Shamis. London: MWH London Publishers, 1979, reprint. 1981.

——. *Ma^cālim fī-l-Ṭarīq*. Cairo: Maktabat Wahba, 1964.

——. *Ma^crakat al-Islām wa-l-Ra'smāliyya*. 4th printing. Beirut: Dār al-Shurūq, 1975.

——. *Milestones*. Cedar Rapids, Iowa: Unity Publishing Co., n.d.

El Saadawi, Nawal. *Death of an Ex-minister*, trans. by Shirley Eber. Methuen, 1987.

——. *God Dies by the Nile*, trans. by Sherif Hetata. London: Zed Books, 1985.

——. *The Hidden Face of Eve: Women in the Arab World*, trans. by Sherif Hetata, preface by author. London: Zed Press, 1980.

——. *The Hidden Face of Eve: Women in the Arab World*, trans. by Sherif Hetata, foreword by Irene L. Gendzier. Boston: Beacon Press, 1982.

——. "Preface to the English Edition," in El Saadawi, *The Hidden Face of Eve* (London: Zed Press, 1980), pp. i–xvi.

——. *Two Women in One*, trans. by Osman Nusairi and Jana Gough. London: Al Saqi, 1985.

——. *Woman at Point Zero*, trans. by Sherif Hetata. London: Zed Books, 1983.

Ṣa^cb, Ḥasan. *al-Islām tujāh Taḥaddiyāt al-Ḥayā al-^cAṣriyya*. Beirut: Dār al-Ādāb, 1965.

——. *Taḥdīth al-^cAql al-^cArabī: Dirāsāt ḥawl al-Thawra al-Thaqāfiyya al-Lāzima li-l-Taqaddum al-^cArabī fī-l-^cAṣr al-Ḥadīth*. 2nd printing. Beirut: Dār al-^cIlm li-l-Malāyīn, 1972.

al-Sa^cdāwī, Nawāl. *al-Mar'a wa-l-Jins: Awwal Naẓra ^cIlmiyya Ṣarīḥa ilā Mashākil al-Mar'a wa-l-Jins fī-l-Mujtama^c al-^cArabī*. 3rd printing. Beirut: al-Mu'assasa al-^cArabiyya li-l-Dirāsāt wa-l-Nashr, 1974.

——. *al-Mar'a wa-l-Jins 2: al-Unthā hiya al-Aṣl*. Beirut: al-Mu'assasa al-^cArabiyya li-l-Dirāsāt wa-l-Nashr, 1974.

——. *al-Mar'a wa-l-Ṣirā^c al-Nafsī*. Beirut: al-Mu'assasa al-^cArabiyya li-l-Dirāsāt wa-l-Nashr, 1977.

——. *al-Rajul wa-l-Jins*. Beirut: al-Mu'assasa al-ᶜArabiyya li-l-Dirāsāt wa-l-Nashr, 1976.

——. *al-Wajh al-ᶜĀrī li-l-Mar'a al-ᶜArabiyya*. Beirut: al-Mu'assasa al-ᶜArabiyya li-l-Dirāsāt wa-l-Nashr, 1977.

Ṣafadī, Muṭāᶜ. "al-Mustashriq Adonis wa Baᶜth al-Shuᶜūbiyya al-Jadīda fī-l-Thaqāfa al-Muᶜāṣira," *Bayrūt al-Masā'*, October 4, 1974.

Saᶜid, ᶜAlī Aḥmad. See Adonis [Adūnīs].

Ṣāliḥ, Faraj Allāh Dīb. "Ḥawl al-Nazaᶜāt al-Māddiyya fī-l-Falsafa al-ᶜArabiyya al-Islāmiyya," pp. 210–241 in Yāsīn et al., *al-Marksiyya.*

Sallūm, Tawfīq. "al-Māddiyya wa Tajalliyātuhā fī-l-ᶜAṣr al-Wasīṭ," pp. 242–288 in Yāsīn et al., *al-Marksiyya.*

al-Sayyid, Riḍwān. "Ṭayyib Tīzīnī bayn Jādhibiyyat al-Manhaj wa Mazāliq al-Taṭbīq," pp. 155–165 in Yāsīn et al., *al-Marksiyya.*

Schlipper, Mineke (ed.). *Unheard Words: Women and Literature in Africa, the Arab World, Asia, The Caribbean and Latin America*. London and New York: Allison and Busby, 1985.

Sharābī, Hishām. "al-ᶜĀ'ila wa-l-Taṭawwur al-Ḥaḍārī fī-l-Mujtamaᶜ al-ᶜArabī," *al-Maᶜrifa*, June 1974, pp. 142–162.

——. (ed.). *al-ᶜAqd al-ᶜArabī al-Qādim: al-Mustaqbalāt al-Badīla.* Beirut: Markaz Dirāsāt al-Waḥda al-ᶜArabiyya, 1986.

Sharabi, Hisham. *Arab Intellectuals and the West: The Formative Years, 1875–1914*. Baltimore: Johns Hopkins Press, 1970.

——. "Cultural Critics of Contemporary Arab Society," *Arab Studies Quarterly*, Vol. 9, No. 1 (1987), pp. 1–19.

——. *Government and Politics of the Middle East in the Twentieth Century*. Westport, CT: Greenwood Press, 1987.

Sharābī, Hishām. "Ḥawl al-Īdiyūlūjiyya al-Sā'ida fī-l-Mujtamaᶜ al-ᶜArabī: Usus al Thaqāfa al-Iqṭāᶜiyya al-Burjuwāziyya," *Mawāqif*, No. 29 (Autumn 1974), pp. 65–77.

——. *Muqaddimāt li-Dirāsat al-Mujtamaᶜ al-ᶜArabī.* Jerusalem: Manshūrāt Ṣalāḥ al-Dīn, 1975.

——. *al-Muthaqqafūn al-ᶜArab wa-l-Gharb: ᶜAṣr al-Nahḍa, 1875–1914*. 2nd printing. Beirut: Dār al-Nahār, 1978.

Sharabi, Hisham. *Nationalism and Revolution in the Arab World.* Princeton: Princeton University Press, 1966.

——. *Neopatriarchy: A Theory of Distorted Change in Arab Society.* New York-Oxford: Oxford University Press, 1988).

——. (ed.). *The Next Arab Decade: Alternative Futures.* Boulder: Westview Press/London: Mansell Publishing Limited, 1988.

Sharābī, Hishām. "al-Niẓām al-Abawī wa-l-Taba^{c}iyya wa Mustaqbal al-Mujtama^{c} al-^{c}Arabī," pp. 259–267 in Sharābī, ed., *al-^{c}Aqd al-^{c}Arabī al-Qādim.*

Sharabi, Hisham. *Palestine and Israel: The Lethal Dilemma.* New York: Pegasus, 1969.

——. *Palestine Guerrillas: Their Credibility and Effectiveness.* Washington, D.C.: Georgetown University, Center for Strategic & International Studies, 1970.

El-Sheikh, Ibrahim A. et al. (eds.). *The Challenge of the Middle East: Middle Eastern Studies at the University of Amsterdam.* Amsterdam: University of Amsterdam, Institute of Modern Near Eastern Studies, 1982.

Shukrī, Ghālī. *Ghāda al-Sammān bilā Ajniḥa.* Beirut: Dār al-Ṭalī^{c}a, 1977.

Simarsky, Lynn. "The Fabric Cracks: Urban Crises in the Arab World," *The Middle East*, No. 159 (January 1988), pp. 5–9.

Stork, Joe. "The Hammamat Declaration," *MERIP Reports*, January 1984, p. 23.

Theodorson, George A. and Achilles G. Theodorson. *A Modern Dictionary of Sociology.* New York: Barnes & Noble Books, 1979.

Thompson, John B. *Studies in the Theory of Ideology.* Cambridge: Polity Press, 1984.

Tīzīnī, Ṭayyib. *Mashrū^{c} Ru'ya Jadīda li-l-Fikr al-^{c}Arabī fi-l-^{c}Aṣr al-Wasīṭ.* Damascus: Dār Dimashq, 1971.

——. *Mashrū^{c} Ru'ya Jadīda li-l-Fikr al-^{c}Arabī min "al-^{c}Aṣr al-Jāhilī" ḥattā al-Marḥala al-Mu^{c}āṣira*, Vol. 1, *Min al-Turāth ilā al-Thawra: Ḥawl Naẓariyya Muqtaraḥa fī Qaḍiyyat al-Turāth al-^{c}Arabī.* 2nd printing. Beirut: Dār Ibn Khaldūn, 1978.

——. *Mashrūᶜ Ru'ya Jadīda li-l-Fikr al-ᶜArabī min "al-ᶜAṣr al-Jāhilī" ḥattā al-Marḥala al-Muᶜāṣira*, Vol. 2, *al-Fikr al-ᶜArabī fī Bawākīrih wa Āfāqih al-Ūlā*. Damascus: Dār Dimashq, 1982.

——. "Mulāḥaẓāt hawl Mafhūm al-Ḥaḍāra ladā Zakī Najīb Maḥmūd," *al-Ādāb*, June 1974, pp. 13–15.

——. "al-Yasār al-ᶜArabī wa-l-Turāth al-ᶜArabī," pp. 125–170 in al-Majlis al-Qawmī, *al-Turāth*.

Wansbrough, John. Review of: Mohammed Arkoun, *Lectures du Coran* (Paris: Maisonneuve et Larose, 1982), in *Bulletin of Oriental and African Studies*, Vol. 47, No. 2 (1984), p. 413.

Weber, Max. *Economy and Society: An Outline of Interpretive Sociology*, ed. Guenther Roth and Claus Wittich. Berkeley: University of California Press, 1978.

Yāsīn, Bū ᶜAlī et al. *al-Marksiyya wa-l-Turāth al-ᶜArabī al-Islāmī*. 2nd printing. Beirut: Dār al-Ḥadātha, 1982.

Yāsīn, Bū ᶜAlī. "Min al-Turāth ilā al-Thawra: Maᶜa Ṭayyib Tīzīnī," *Mawāqif*, No. 34 (Winter 1979), pp. 73–107.

Yāsīn, al-Sayyid (ed.). *al-Turāth wa Taḥaddiyāt al-ᶜAṣr fī-l-Waṭan al-ᶜArabī*. Beirut: Markaz Dirāsāt al-Waḥda al-ᶜArabiyya, 1985.

Zakariyyā, Fu'ād. *al-Ḥaqīqa wa-l-Wahm fī-l-Ḥaraka al-Islāmiyya al-Muᶜāṣira*. 2nd printing. Cairo: Dār al-Fikr li-l-Dirāsāt wa-l-Nashr wa-l-Tawzīᶜ, 1986.

——. "al-Petro-Islām," pp. 21–26 in Zakariyyā, *al-Ḥaqīqa wa-l-Wahm*.

——. *Al-Ṣaḥwa al-Islāmiyya fī Mīzān al-ᶜAql*. 2nd printing. Cairo: Dār al-Fikr al-Muᶜāṣir, 1987.

——. "al-Takhalluf al-Fikrī wa Abᶜāduh al-Ḥaḍāriyya," *al-Ādāb*, May 1974, pp. 30–37.

Index